FASHION FORWARD

fb

FASHION

FORWARD

CHELSEA ROUSSO

The Art Institute of Fort Lauderdale

FAIRCHILD BOOKS, INC. New York

Executive Director & General Manager: Michael Schluter
Executive Editor: Olga T. Kontzias
Senior Associate Acquiring Editor: Jaclyn Bergeron
Assistant Acquisitions Editor: Amanda Breccia
Development Editor: Jon Preimesberger
Assistant Art Director: Sarah Silberg
Production Director: Ginger Hillman
Production Editor: Linda Feldman
Ancillaries Editor: Amy Butler
Associate Director of Sales: Melanie Sankel
Copy Editor: Edwin Chapman
Cover Design: Carly Grafstein
Cover Art: Craig McDean / Art + Commerce
Text Design: Chris Welch and Vanessa Han
Page Layout: Tom Helleberg
Photo Research: Sarah Silberg
Illustrations: Vanessa Han

Library of Congress Catalog Card Number: 2010941992

ISBN: 1-56367-924-7

GST R 133004424

Printed in Canada

TP14

Contents

Extended Contents

2 BRIEF HISTORY OF CONTEMPORARY FASHION 37

3 FASHION MOVEMENT 99

4 SOCIAL AND CULTURAL INFLUENCES 119

5 MARKET AND SALES RESEARCH FOR FORECASTING 143

PART II DEVELOPING AND PRESENTING A FASHION FORECAST 162

6 THEME 165

10 CREATING AND PRESENTING A FORECAST 255

Preface

Fashion Forward: A Guide to Fashion Forecasting is a book dedicated to providing an overview of fashion forecasting and offers a detailed guide for creating a fashion forecast. *Fashion Forward* explains the theory of fashion forecasting and presents instructions for learning how to develop a fashion forecast. The book looks at important elements of forecasting from both objective and subjective approaches. In addition, the book includes examples of fashion forecasts from students and professionals as a visual guide to the process and as inspiration for forecasts to come.

This textbook is organized in two main parts. Part One provides an introduction, theories, and concepts relevant to fashion forecasting. Part Two is a "how-to guide" that focuses on developing and presenting a forecast. In both portions of the book, interviews, images, and illustrations enhance the text.

The first portion of the book covers the concepts and theories needed to successfully forecast fashion. The introduction provides an overview of forecasting. Each of the following chapters in the section explain the principles of fashion's evolution, the cyclical nature of fashion, the role that culture plays in forecasting, and the relationship between marketing and forecasting.

In Chapter 1, fashion forecasting is introduced and terminology is defined. Who, what, where, when, why, and how forecasting is accomplished provides readers with an overview of the complexity of the topic. The chapter also introduces several of today's prominent fashion forecasting services. Fashion forecasting is identified as a tool that is used by both professionals and students to enhance success in the complex contemporary fashion industry or any style-related business.

Chapter 2 begins by defining "zeitgeist"—the spirit of the times that is rudimental in forecasting. The majority of the chapter examines historical fashion eras beginning in the mid-1800s. For each era, key historical, political, social, and cultural events that shaped the time are discussed, predominant fashions of the time are described, and how fashion moved forward is explained.

Chapter 3 identifies important aspects of fashion movement, from recognizing fashion cycles to understanding theories of fashion adoption. An important concept to comprehend is the pace at which fashion moves through society. The chapter ends by stressing how precise timing in forecasting is imperative for any successful fashion business.

Chapter 4 explains long-term forecasting by identifying extended social and cultural shifts that alter society. The chapter introduces the concept of consumer segmentation, how to identify a target audience, and the sociological and psychological influences of lifestyle in today's fashion. From global politics to environmental forces, the chapter challenges the reader to consider all major societal influences on new trends. Finally, the chapter explains how long-term insights inform the fashion forecaster.

Chapter 5 explores the relationship between marketing, sales, and forecasting. The chapter introduces retail trade organizations and agencies that conduct research on retailing, details modern methods of market research, and highlights the importance of the Internet, viral marketing, and social media in forecasting.

Part Two of the book explains the elements of a forecast as well as offers a step-by-step guide to follow to develop forecasts. Four chapters focus on specific portions of a forecast: theme, color, textiles and material, and the look. The final chapter describes how to create and present a fashion forecast. Throughout the book there are many images that provide visual illustration of the ideas and concepts. The images are taken from actual forecasts, both professional and student work.

Chapter 6 focuses on theme development by illustrating how inspiration for theme creation is found and ideas are developed. Important steps in this process include researching, editing, interpreting, analyzing, and predicting the theme concept to explain why the idea is relevant to future fashion and trends. The chapter concludes with theme, mood, and story development.

Chapter 7 outlines color forecasting. From color theory to the progression of color, the chapter emphasizes the importance of color in forecasting. It is essential for forecasters to consider the psychology of color and color preferences. Steps are provided for the development of a color palette and a color story including color names, numbers, and details about the selections.

Chapter 8 identifies the integral components of a forecast: textiles, materials, trims, and findings. The chapter details the stages of textile production, ideas about textile innovations, and the importance of understanding fabrications and their acceptability and evolution. Steps are included to source textiles, accurately describe the selections, and add them to the forecast.

Chapter 9 explores the look of objects and apparel and discusses design elements and principles including the importance of design innovation. Steps are provided in how to formulate ideas about the look, develop the story, and predict the evolution.

Chapter 10 is dedicated to creating and presenting a well-crafted forecast. Details about preparing a visually exciting presentation, a well-written script, and planning a successful presentation are outlined.

Each chapter contains key terms and definitions of fashion vocabulary. At the end of each chapter are activities that give the reader an opportunity to apply the theories and develop skills needed to forecast successfully. The activities focus on the processes used in forecasting, encouraging experimentation with the conceptual ideas.

Included in this book are the voices from inside the fashion business, professionals, who are skilled at forecasting, telling their own stories. Interviews with fashion professionals describing their viewpoints about fashion forecasting add industry insiders' real-life experiences to the book. These stories include great fashion finds, important trend developments, changes that are influencing the industry, and the professionals' understanding of forecasting.

They include:

- Itay Arad—CEO and cofounder of Fashion Snoops
- Lilly Berelovich—Owner, President, and Chief Creative Officer of Fashion Snoops
- Frank Bober—CEO of Stylesight
- Kai Chow—Creative Director, Doneger Creative Services
- Lori Holliday Banks—Director of Research and Analytics, Tobe Report, a division of The Doneger Group
- Frank Iovino—President of Miroglio Textiles USA
- Scott Markert—Sales Manager for London Times
- Pat Tunsky—Creative Director, Doneger Creative Services
- David Wolfe—Creative Director, Doneger Creative Services
- Adam Yankauskas—Design Director at Maggy London

As a New York designer and design director, I honed my skills as I spent many years predicting forward fashion. My forecasting process involves keeping a pulse on fashion trends, being intellectually curious about why changes occur, and spotting newness in the world around me by scanning art, politics, culture, technology, media, marketing, and more for the latest developments. After gathering and analyzing repetitive looks and styles from all around the globe, I develop forecasting presentations, prepare engaging and carefully crafted narratives, and deliver the information to audiences in visually exciting formats using innovative textiles, cohesive color palettes, modern silhouette photos and illustrations, and stylish layouts. Now, I also teach what I know to fashion design and merchandising college students, preparing them for exciting, challenging, and truly fantastic careers in fashion.

Acknowledgments

I am grateful to many people and organizations that helped me with this book. The industry professionals who are icons in the fashion industry were so generous with their time, information, and encouragement. I am thankful to the forecasting firms that supported this project with access to their insight and information. The students who created projects for the book provided me with great hope for the fashion industry's future, and I am appreciative for all of the dedicated work that they submitted. I am grateful to all of those who helped and encouraged me to write this book, although there are too many to name. However, I would like to personally thank several people who provided loving encouragement and support for this project. Rick Benjamin, from Goddard College, gave me the courage to begin. Thanks go to my colleagues, especially Andre West, fashion department chairperson at The Art Institute of Fort Lauderdale, for giving me the opportunity to share my passion and experience with students. I thank the staff at Fairchild Publications, including Sarah Silberg, for her work on photo researching and art; Jon Preimesberger, for his editorial expertise; and finally a special thank you to Jaclyn Bergeron, Senior Associate Acquisitions Editor, for her graciousness throughout the project. Thanks to Luzmaria Palacios, a former student, who eagerly worked beside me through all stages of the book development. I am grateful for my dearest friends, Brenda Waters, Douglas Esselmann, Gretchen Heinsen, Desiree Daly, and Kathy Iwanowski, for always listening. I especially want to thank my mother, Lucy Slezycki, for her artistic vision and everlasting love. Finally, thanks to the two most precious gifts in my life, my children, Clay and Derek Rousso.

—Chelsea Rousso

About the Forecasters

Itay Arad—CEO and cofounder of Fashion Snoops

With background in Internet technologies and online marketing, Itay is the cofounder and business force behind Fashion Snoops. As a technological innovator, his initial role was to make possible the delivery of trend forecasting information to fashion professionals around the globe. Itay used his engineering skills to launch innovative online applications that assist the product development process and allow users to assemble their own trend collections and communicate them to their peers. As the CEO of Fashion Snoops, Itay's main goal is to spearhead the company's global business development and expansion plans.

Lilly Berelovich—Owner, President, and Chief Creative Officer of Fashion Snoops

Lilly started her career spending more than ten years in the fashion industry as a children's wear and junior designer in New York and Montreal. In 2001, frustrated with the limited access that designers had to accurate and timely trend information, she launched Fashionsnoops.com. Today, Lilly is the creative force behind the company. She applies the service to her work as a consultant for companies needing branding, positioning design, and merchandising for labels in New York and around the globe. Lilly is also a renowned consultant for clients in the licensing world, creating licensing deals and providing trend direction.

Frank Bober—CEO of Stylesight

A native New Yorker, Frank began his career in the 1960s as a menswear designer with a collection under his name. He held senior executive positions at Arthur Richards and Polo before starting his own company, CMT Enterprises, in 1979, which pioneered a then-new private label concept of apparel design and product development for many of America's top retail companies. Answering a long-ignored call from the industry for a faster and more effective approach to the process of product inspiration and development, Frank founded Stylesight in 2003. At Stylesight, he has been a technological pioneer, developing software solutions to the trend forecasting, product development, merchandising, and design cycle.

Kai Chow—Creative Director, Doneger Creative Services

Kai leads a team of designers and analysts to provide clients with color, lifestyle, fabric, and print forecasts as well as retail, runway, trade show, and streetwear reports. From 1983 to 2006, he was the creative force behind Here & There, a fashion-forecasting firm acquired by The Doneger Group. Kai's prior experience includes designing apparel and accessories in Paris, London, and Hong Kong for an international roster of clients.

Lori Holliday Banks—Director of Research and Analytics, Tobe Report, a division of The Doneger Group

Lori has more than thirty years of retail and consulting experience in the fashion industry. She joined the Tobe Report in 1980 as a fashion editor. During this time she has advised merchants, fashion directors, and top management, helping them identify consumer growth opportunities. Lori's business acumen, her reality-based, in-depth knowledge of the better apparel business, and her keen eye are widely recognized throughout the apparel industry.

Frank Iovino—President of Miroglio Textiles USA

Frank began his career in the textile industry forty years ago as a salesperson for a heat transfer supplier. In 1982, he joined Miroglio Textiles, a leading Italian textile manufacturer, to spearhead the heat transfer division of the company. As a result of his division's success, Frank became president of the entire American division of Miroglio Textiles, where he grew U.S. operations from $6 million to $50 million. Recently he has also begun selling Miroglio's Italian collection in the United States while designing and styling a collection in Italy and the United States to be produced in China.

Scott Markert—Sales Manager for London Times

Scott is the sales manager for London Times, a division of Maggy London, a long-established better dress firm. The collections are sold to department stores, specialty stores, and chain stores both domestically and globally. Scott is recognized as a leading sales professional in the fashion industry.

Pat Tunsky—Creative Director, Doneger Creative Services

Pat, a highly respected color and trend authority, joined The Doneger Group in 1997 after its merger with Color Projections, the consulting firm she founded in 1972. She is responsible for developing seasonal color, fabric, and merchandising direction. Pat's prior experience includes positions as vice president/fashion director at Grey Advertising, and fashion director of Monsanto Textiles.

David Wolfe—Creative Director, Doneger Creative Services

David is one of the fashion industry's most quoted authorities, with international credentials as a fashion, color, and trend forecaster. His expertise and entertaining personality keep him in demand as a public speaker and lecturer. Prior to joining The Doneger Group in 1990, David spent ten years at The Fashion Service, a trend-forecasting service he founded and managed. He was previously creative director at I.M. International, one of the world's first fashion forecasting and consulting firms.

Adam Yankauskas—Design Director at Maggy London

Adam is the creative director for Maggy London, a leading better dress firm. He is responsible for leading a team of fashion and textiles designers. In addition to creating seasonal collections, Adam works closely with retailers developing private label apparel. He is known for his keen fashion sense and ability to recognize consumers' changing tastes.

FASHION FORWARD

Stylesight's "RAW ENERGY" forecast was inspired by the correlation between the human body and the power of the universe. The dynamic theme is illustrated through intense hues of red and orange; images of complex textures; and fashion looks for apparel, accessories, and home furnishings.

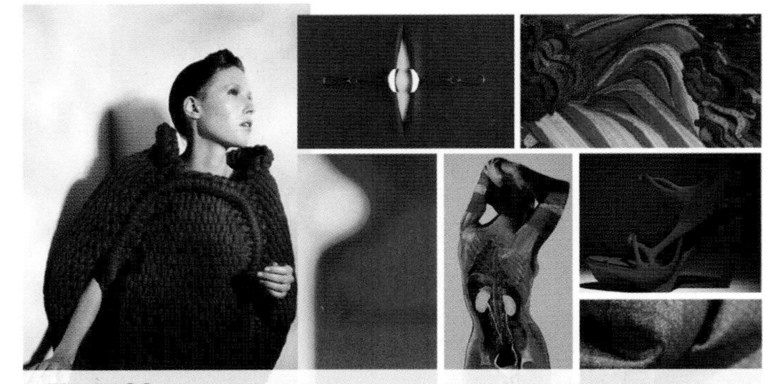

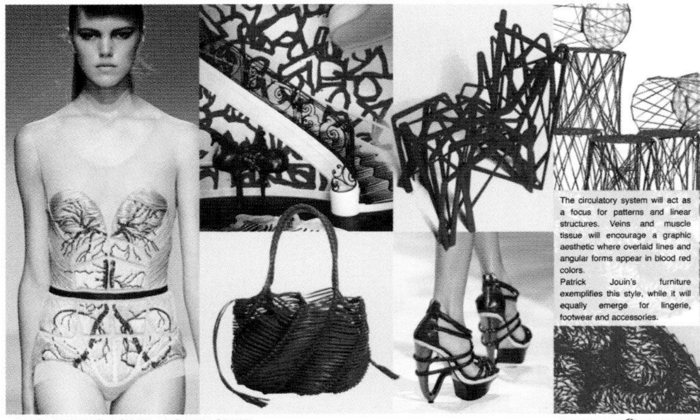

Part One

THE PRINCIPLES OF FASHION FORECASTING

IN THE FIRST HALF OF THE BOOK, five chapters examine the principles of fashion forecasting and provide the reader with an overview of contemporary history, fashion movement and cycles, social and cultural influences in fashion, and the role of the consumer and the market in predicting future fashion.

INTRODUCTION TO FASHION FORECASTING

1

Objectives

- Identify the who, what, why, where, and when of fashion forecasting.
- Introduce how fashion forecasting is done.
- Define fashion forecasting and key terms.
- Identify fashion forecasting services.

In 1965, skirt lengths rose several inches above the knee, and that style became known as the miniskirt. However, it was not until the late 1960s that short skirts were widely worn by women. The miniskirt reached beyond a youth-inspired fashion into a major international trend. During the mid-1970s, women returned to wearing longer skirt lengths such as the midi or maxi. Again in the 1980s and 1990s, short skirts were popular. How did this revival happen?

In the mid-1970s, pants and pantsuits were acceptable day wear for women almost anywhere. Just a decade before, however, women were not allowed admission into famous New York City restaurants wearing pants. Who paved the way for the widespread acceptance of women wearing pants outside the home, for business and leisure?

FIGURE 1.1 Fashion is forever changing—sometimes repeating itself throughout history, oftentimes merging cultures, and shifting people's attitudes: fashion that was once considered unacceptable or avant garde frequently evolves into mainstream.

In the 1990s, rebellious young people began to decorate their bodies with tattooing and body piercing. What happened to make this not only fashionable but suitable for the runways in high fashion?

In the mid-1990s, the new genre of music called hip-hop was introduced into the American entertainment scene. Along with this type of music came fashions like baseball caps worn backward, stylized sneakers worn untied, and oversized baggy pants. Fifteen years later, hip-hop–inspired fashions have been accepted into mainstream. Where did this movement originate?

What makes a product fashionable? What makes merchandise new and exciting or old and out of style? Who decides what will be "in fashion" in the next season? Where do these ideas and concepts come from?

These are some of the questions that fashion professionals ask themselves when trying to plan for the upcoming season. The key to answering these questions lies in the field of fashion forecasting, which will be explained throughout the chapters of the book.

WHAT IS FASHION FORECASTING?

Fashion forecasting is the practice of predicting upcoming trends based on past and present style-related information, the interpretation and analysis of the motivation behind a trend, and an explanation of why the prediction is likely to occur. By communicating the information to designers, retailers, product developers, manufacturers, and business professionals, they are able to produce products that consumers will want to purchase and profits can be made. Since fashion is constantly changing and evolving, forecasting has a pivotal role in the fashion process. Focus must be continually directed forward, always looking for what will be in the future. Forecasting future trends is a complex process that involves a fusion of skills, some that are objective and scientific and others that are more subjective and artistic. The ideal method of fashion forecasting should include a mixture of methodical and creative means. Sourcing and data collection, analysis of data, and interpretation of facts are scientific methods. Awareness, observation, intuition, and memory are considered more artistic approaches.

When developing a fashion forecast, one must understand the difference between a **trend report** and a fashion forecast. A trend report is an account describing in detail something that already exists or has happened. Trend reports are often written based on observations from runway collections, red carpet events, or street fashions. For instance, a recent trend

FOWARD THINKER

PAT TUNSKY, CREATIVE DIRECTOR, DONEGER CREATIVE SERVICES

Shifting Buying Habits of Consumers

The consumer's buying habits shift as the forces of forecasting move fashion forward. The consumer's attitudes about buying are always changing. For instance, customers in the past would purchase head-to-toe looks to make up an outfit. Today, customers buy items to add to their existing wardrobe. In spring of 2010, seven to eight tops were selling to every bottom that was sold in women's wear.

report confirmed the appearance of bows as a new detail on dresses for ladies, not only for children. Bows, large or small, appeared on the shoulders, backs and waistlines of fashionable dresses. The trend report showed images from the runways and the streets illustrating the commercial viability and consumer acceptance of the trend. A fashion forecast, on the other hand is the combination of both past trend reports with present information and insight into the future to create the prediction of upcoming trends. Most importantly, forecasts explain why new trends may occur.

Three questions that forecasters must undertake are: What has already happened in the past that influences fashion today? What is presently happening that will notably affect fashion in the near future? What is likely to occur in fashion in the distant future?

Through a variety of methods, fashion forecasting is the practice of looking for clues that help in predicting the mood, actions, and retail habits of consumers by focusing on their current wants and needs and then anticipating consumers' future wishes. Successful forecasting depends on up-to-date information and sensitivity to the ever-changing desires of fashion consumers.

Fashion forecasters, through their understanding of the fundamentals of fashion and the fashion industry, often predict the shape of things to come with considerable accuracy. To assess the scene, forecasters use a combination of savvy, gut instinct, up-to-date market information, and fashion knowledge developed from years of watching fashions come and go. Fashion forecasters or trend forecasters make predictions based on an array of observations, data, and fashion intuitions. Among the things that forecasters take into account are:

- Acquired knowledge of historical and contemporary fashion and ideas about future fashion.
- Observations of the movement and direction of change.
- Social and cultural shifts in society.
- Analysis of sales and consumer data.
- A broad understanding, honed by experience, of the inner workings of a trend.

TERMINOLOGY OF FASHION

To understand forecasting, the differentiation between fashion, style, taste, and trends must be clear.

Fashion can be defined as that which characterizes or distinguishes the habits, manners, and dress of a period or group. Fashion is what people choose to wear.

Style is a distinctive appearance and combination of unique features that creates a look that is acceptable at the time by a majority of a group. To be "in style" means to assemble an overall distinguishing look including apparel, accessories, hairstyle, and makeup.

Taste is the prevailing opinion of what is or is not appropriate for a particular occasion.

Trends are the first signal of change in general direction or movement. To identify a trend, forecasters recognize the similarities of information about style and details of a look and translate these details for potential consumers. Trends are not limited to fashion; they also affect the consumer's perception and choice of foods, movies, books, vacation destinations, and products. Trends of the moment are constantly changing as consumers reevaluate their ideas about style and taste.

Several years ago, urban American men began wearing their pants well below the natural waist, exposing a top portion of their boxer shorts. This low-slung style, known as "saggy pants," is an example of a trend that became the "style" of disaffected young males, and it challenged prevailing notions of "taste" as older generations, politicians, and school officials condemned saggy pants as a breakdown of the moral order. When musicians, celebrities, and people outside the urban community adopted this look, it evolved into mainstream fashion. Eventually, this urban trend was replaced by styles that include "skinny jeans" and high-waist pants.

WHY FORECAST FASHION?

Like any business that caters to consumers' ever-changing tastes, the fashion business can be complex and full of uncertainties, dependent on the whims of the consumer. For fashion entrepreneurs, reliable trend direction can lead to early business successes. Understanding, knowing, and predicting the needs and desires of consumers help the designers, retailers, and manufacturers make well-informed decisions.

By knowing and understanding the consumer, fashion firms can deliver the right product or service into the market at the right time, the right place, in the right quantities priced for the right customer. For business success, all five elements (product, time, place, quantities, and

FIGURE 1.2 The secret to a successful fashion business is to have the five R's: right product, right customer, right price, right quantity, and right place.

customer) must come together. When a new look is first spotted by a forecaster, the look is often accepted by early trend followers prior to mass market acceptance. If a manufacturer whose clients are mass marketers ships the products too soon, the consumers may not be ready for the new look and will not buy the products. If the mass market consumer only had more time to become familiarized with the new look, they may be more eager to purchase. Or if the retailer purchases too small of a quantity of a look and does not have enough merchandise to sell to the consumer, sales will be lost and the retailer will not be maximizing their sales opportunities. On the other hand, if a retailer purchases too much quantity and the market is oversaturated in the look, the retailer will end up with unwanted merchandise and loss of revenue.

WHO FORECASTS FASHION?

Fashion forecasters are the individuals or teams that strive to identify upcoming trends and deliver the findings to the industries that provide products for the consumers. Designers and manufacturers often rely on the forecaster's information to guide them in the process of creating products that blend the trend information with their own brand image or identity.

These **trend forecasters** are the prescient individuals who combine knowledge of fashion, history, consumer research, industry data, and intuition to guide product manufacturers and business professionals into the future. They help to maximize the opportunity for triumph in fashion businesses. Their vision helps designers and manufacturers ride the wave of barely perceived novelty to profit and mainstream recognition. In addition to fashion forecasters, a variety of industry professionals participate in trend forecasting as part of their jobs. Designers and creative directors have historically been involved in identifying and creating fashion trends but are not the only professionals who forecast. Business and retail executives, buyers, product developers, and merchandisers collect, interpret, analyze, and predict trends to increase their business's potential profit. Magazine and book editors, promotional directors, and advertising specialists create forecasts to help to maintain a competitive, commercial edge. Fashion design students forecast to create novel garments and collections that are relevant to current and future fashion. Fashion merchandising students learn to maximize marketing opportunities through understanding fashion forecasting. Many forecasters work in collaboration with other fashion specialists: teams of **trend spotters**, researchers, consultants, and fashion forecasting services.

FOWARD THINKER

DAVID WOLFE, CREATIVE DIRECTOR, DONEGER CREATIVE SERVICES

Money Empire—Change from Creative to Financial

The new industry of fashion is one of building a money empire. The business direction of fashion is the modern direction; therefore, accurate forecasting relies on retail ties to inform about financial matters. Heads of big business and financial investors are now interested in forecasting, since many of their portfolios contain companies from the apparel sector. My clients from the past were usually the creative ones: designers, illustrators, and apparel manufacturers. But now the clients are from the business sector: merchandisers, retailers, and the money people.

Fashion forecasters must be intelligent, talented, and able to think "outside the box." They need to be able to identify newness when it arrives and to have a heightened sense of inquisitiveness about all things.

Forecasters do not just focus on apparel, of course. Among other things, there are forecasters who specialize in electronics, interior design, housewares, automobile design, and even packaging.

Some forecasting specialists foresee fabric or color direction. Major fiber producers, like Cotton Incorporated, employ staff forecasters whose focus is specific to their company's needs. At Cotton Incorporated, product trend analysis services are a key factor in maintaining cotton's position as the leading fiber producer in the world of fashion. Frequent presentations and dialogue with leading designers and sourcing specialists highlight the company's trend research and supplier information, helping to keep cotton in the minds of those who decide what will be offered to consumers in future seasons.

FOWARD THINKER

PAT TUNSKY, CREATIVE DIRECTOR, DONEGER CREATIVE SERVICES

Forecasting for Diversified Products

For the past several years, I have been consulting for a large overseas company on apparel in the bridge-, better-, and popular-priced markets. I help them by giving direction that spans several different product categories.

FIGURE 1.3 Trend forecasters help Cotton Incorporated maintain its dominant position as a fiber producer.

FIGURE 1.4 The color standards developed by Pantone, Inc., are used as standardized reference tools by fashion professionals.

At Pantone, Inc., the most widely used and recognized color standards system in the world, color forecasts are developed. Each season, Pantone surveys the designers of New York Fashion Week to collect feedback on prominent collection colors, color inspiration, and color philosophy. This information is used to create the *Pantone Fashion Color Report*, which serves as a reference tool throughout the year for fashion enthusiasts, reporters, and retailers.

The **trendsetters** play a critical role in the fashion process. Identifying trendsetting groups while observing their style and taste selections gives forecasters important clues about upcoming ideas. From celebrities to contemporary artists and fashion leaders, the styles of these "fashionistas" are observed and imitated. In film, music, and celebrity circles, trendsetters emerge offering looks for ordinary people to

FIGURE 1.5A Celebrities are followed and observed for new cutting-edge trends: Jennifer Lopez causes a stir in a Roberto Cavalli animal print dress.

FIGURE 1.5B Kim Kardashian attends the CFDA fashion awards.

FIGURE 1.5C Lauren Conrad takes the spotlight at a runway show.

FIGURE 1.5D Robert Pattinson arrives at the 81st Annual Academy Awards.

imitate. For example, when Kim Kardashian, Robert Pattinson, Jennifer Lopez, and Lauren Conrad step into the spotlight, their styles are emulated by many. Industry gurus exert a powerful influence too. They include Anna Wintour, editor and chief at *Vogue*; Marc Jacobs, the head designer for his own line as well as the prestigious French designer line, Louis Vuitton; Michael Kors, judge on Lifetime's *Project Runway*, and Tyra Banks from *America's Next Top Model*. Like fashion itself, the trendsetter is continuously changing, and society's focus on "fashionable people" evolves.

FIGURE 1.6
First ladies Michelle Obama and Carla Bruni-Sarkozy emerged in 2009 as leading fashionistas in international political circles.

Fashion trends can also begin in the political arena. In the 1960s, First Lady Jackie Kennedy was a fashion trendsetter wearing her famous pillbox hats, dark sunglasses, and neatly tailored suits. In 2009, First Lady Michelle Obama emerged as a fresh fashion icon and trendsetter from the political world as did French First Lady Carla Bruni-Sarkozy.

LILLY BERELOVICH, OWNER, PRESIDENT, AND CHIEF CREATIVE OFFICER OF FASHION SNOOPS

Trendsetters

The social groups that are being closely observed at this time are students and young unconfined minds who haven't been restricted by industry's requirements. I feel that there is great creativity coming from Danish design. I attribute this to freer, happier people. At this time, the bloggers are a group that is being observed but, like fashion itself, this too will change and a new style tribe will be the next to focus on.

WHERE DO FORECASTERS FIND THEIR INFORMATION?

Curiosity about events, both newsworthy and otherwise, makes for a more informed forecaster. With society's increasing infatuation with celebrities, forecasters track trends in entertainment, media, the Internet, and the arts. Forecasters keep their eyes on such population trends as family size and spending habits. They monitor innovations in science and technology. From a Friday night in an ethnic neighborhood to a high fashion gala, downtown vintage boutiques to Paris runways, the seeds for new fashions are found close to home and sometimes in exotic locales. Fashion can be found almost anywhere including at events and gathering places such as:

- Fashion shows
- Fabric fairs
- Red carpet events
- Club scene
- On the streets

Forecasters receive clues of new fashion directions from industry insiders as well. Fabric fairs such as Premiére Vision in France, Interstoff in Europe and Asia, and Material World in New York, or regional apparel trade shows such as Magic in Las Vegas or Moda in New York—all provide signposts for forecasters.

Often at the shows or fairs, displays fill a trend pavilion and offer the first look at the upcoming season, including new themes, colors, and fabrics. At these gatherings, buyers, designers, editors, and manufacturers congregate and can update forecasters on their business trends by sharing their insights and specific information related to their businesses. In turn, the forecaster can give the clients direction that is most appropriate for their brand, products, and consumers.

FIGURE 1.7A
Where fashion is found: a Christian Dior 2009 runway show.

FIGURE 1.7B
Searching through the displays of a Salon International de la Lingerie trade show.

FIGURE 1.7C
Street fashions catch the eye in Harajuku, Japan.

FIGURE 1.7D
Nightlife reveals the fashion of Will.i.am.

FIGURE 1.7E
Hilary Swank's star power adds to a Gucci gown on the red carpet.

In practice, forecasters, whether attending a fair or walking down the street, are always on the alert for fashion elements that catch their eyes. They become gatherers of bits and pieces of information that, collectively, add up to fashion developments. Lifestyle trends including vacation destinations, entertainment choices, and artistic interests can also act as clues to uncovering new developments and ideas.

On the streets, innovative youths experiment with new style ideas. On the runways, the top designers challenge the acceptable norms and re-create fashion with a sense of newness and imagination. Established and prominent design houses, as well as new and up-and-coming designers, forge ahead with fresh ideas that can be significant sources for forecasters. Emerging designers, seeking to establish a reputation in the industry, can also contribute trendsetting collections that anticipate new directions in fashion.

The fashion media have some of the industry's most perceptive observers reporting for them, offering forecasters useful, sometimes mold-breaking perspectives. *Women's Wear Daily*, the fashion newspaper for the industry, photographs and reports the events of the industry. Books and magazines including *Vogue, Harper's Bazaar, InStyle, Lucky*, and *Elle* capture fashionable trends. Many countries around the world promote their fashion industries and styles through their own regional publications. Forecasters research by observing trends from multiple cultures and use this information to shape their predictions.

The Internet gives forecasters a speedy method to survey fashion using social networking sites such as Facebook, MySpace, and Twitter. Blogs, which are types of Web sites, are another place to read about or participate in tracking fashion trends. Bloggers, or the people who partake in a blog, enter information, commentary, and descriptions of events or ideas. Many blogs provide photos and ideas about certain fashions; therefore, forecasters get insight and response by participating in the interactive format. *Web sites*: www.blogspot.com; www.tumblr.com; www.twitter.com.

FIGURE 1.8
Fashion magazines and publications show what's hot and what's not for the season as well as giving the inside scoop of what's to come.

From retail sites to social networking sites, the Internet is a valuable source for up-to-date fashion news. Information on fashion can be found on numerous locations. *Web sites*: www.style.com; www.dailycandy.com; www.fashioninformation.com; www.design-options.com; www.whowhatwear.com; www.coolhunting.com.

Fashion churns and thrives in major cities known for advanced trends, such as Paris, London, Milan, New York, Los Angeles, and Tokyo but also in emerging cities such as Mumbai, Shanghai, Rio de Janeiro, Dubai, and Moscow.

LILLY BERELOVICH, OWNER, PRESIDENT, AND CHIEF CREATIVE OFFICER OF FASHION SNOOPS

Global Researching and Blogs

The job of fashion forecasting has changed with the increase of global researchers who cover many facets of fashion; from runways to streets—events to blogs. Fashion services rely on the information of many researchers who are specific to segments of fashion. For instance, one researcher focuses on bloggers. She reads and contributes to blogs as well as immerses herself in the blogging community. She personally knows many current bloggers, knows where they are traveling, what events they are attending, understands their fashion sensibilities, and listens to their ideas.

Shopping in multiple cities and observing ever-changing style is necessary to stay informed. Fashion forecasters visit cities throughout the world not only to find new fashions but also to observe the variations from a prior trip. Looking for newness is like hunting for change. By researching continuously, forecasters and trend spotters observe change at emerging boutiques, high-end retailers, department stores, or mass market discounters. While this research can also be done on the Internet or through publications, the experience is heightened when the forecaster is in the environment where fashion is taking place.

Designers and manufacturers often travel to the headquarters of their clients or the flagship stores in the cities where their headquarters are located. The gathering of information can lead to the plans for the next season. The process never stops.

Even the past can be a resource for diligent forecasters. They can use museum collections, antique and vintage stores, and libraries to focus on details from historical eras of fashion. The Metropolitan Museum of Art in New York City houses an extensive historical fashion collection.

FIGURE 1.9 Events at the Metropolitan Museum of Art in New York City, such as this "Alexander McQueen: Savage Beauty" exhibition, can have a major influence on the fashion industry.

The museum periodically shows portions of the collection in exhibitions, which often become influential to the fashion professionals of the day. "Alexander McQueen: Savage Beauty" was presented in 2011. *Web site*: www.metmuseum.org.

The Museum at FIT (Fashion Institute of Technology) in New York City creates exhibitions that are educational and entertaining. They collect, conserve, and present fashions as historical presentations as well as inspire through creative interpretations. *Web site*: www.fitnyc.edu.

At the Cooper-Hewitt Museum in New York City, Sonia Delaunay's work was shown in an exhibit called "Color Moves: Art and Fashion by Sonia Delaunay." *Web site*: www.cooperhewitt.org.

The Victoria and Albert Museum in London presents fashion exhibits including contemporary fashion icons such as Yohji Yamamoto and Vivienne Westwood, as well as historical exhibitions presenting fashions from the nineteenth and twentieth centuries. *Web site*: www.vam.ac.uk.

The Tate Gallery in London periodically presents inspirational fashion exhibits or fine art exhibits that inspire fashion trends. *Web site*: www.tate.org.uk.

In Paris, the Bourdelle Museum presented a historical exhibit showcasing the work of Madame Grès.

The Montreal Museum of Fine Arts presented a retrospective celebrating the French couturier, Jean Paul Gaultier. *Web site*: www.mbam.cq.ca.

Throughout the world, fashion exhibitions are created and shared with society to show fashions of the past as well as inspire fashions of the future. Most fashion forecasters keep informed by attending shows at galleries and museums, reviewing the show's publications or periodicals, or experiencing the shows virtually by visiting the Web sites.

Last but not least, market research consultants are independent firms that study trends and supply advice and solutions about the future to forecasters or clients. Market research consultants conduct strategic studies to identify emerging movements to acquire relevant data for analysis. The consultants aim to explain how society is affected by cultural, social, political, economic, and environmental forces and how these forces can influence the future of fashion.

WHEN DO FORECASTERS FIND FASHION IDEAS?

Traditionally, the fashion industry rolls out new fashions in seasonal fashion events in major cities during the spring and fall. The couture and ready-to-wear runway shows in the major fashion capitals host the designers, the retailers, and the press. In recent years, however, designers have shifted slightly from these seasonal events by increasing the number of showings and hosting events in more cities around the globe. Now, designers may show their products in regional trade shows or in their own showrooms, often previewing a new collection each month.

With an increasing interest in fashions from the streets, there is no specific time when new styles will be available. Any major event in politics, music, theater, art, or sports can be the place to spot new trends.

Forecasters can take a short-term view or a long-term view. Predicting trends up to approximately two years in advance is considered short term. In **short-term forecasting**, themes or concepts are developed, color stories are created, textile and material selections are made, and the look or silhouettes of fashion are identified. Details or specific design features are highlighted. Most forecasters develop short-term forecasts so that their clients can immediately use the current information to influence the creating of new products.

In **long-term forecasting**, trends are predicted at least two years ahead but most often five to ten years in advance. This extended type of forecasting seeks to identify the cultural shifts that represent the mood of the era, the kind of ominous thinking or high spirits that can mark a historical period. Long-term forecasting is less about specific details and more about positioning one's business for long-term growth.

FOWARD THINKER

KAI CHOW, CREATIVE DIRECTOR, DONEGER CREATIVE SERVICES

Presenting a Forecast at Interstoff Asia

I am the creative director for the trend forum at Interstoff Asia, where I do deliver presentations to a large audience.

HOW IS FORECASTING DONE?

The five processes that are followed to develop a forecast are:

1. **Researching** is the process of exploring or investigating to collect information and imagery while looking for new, fresh, and innovative ideas and recognizing inspiration, trends, and signals.
2. **Editing** is the process of sorting and identifying patterns in the research, data, and images.
3. **Interpreting and Analyzing** are the processes of examining carefully to identify causes, key factors, and possible results while investigating what fuels upcoming trends and considering why and how the trend will manifest.
4. **Predicting** is the process of declaring or telling in advance potential outcomes by developing scenarios to foretell projected possibilities.
5. **Communicating** is the process of conveying information, thoughts, opinions, and predictions about the forecast through writings, visual boards, and verbal presentations.

Forecasters research and gather information, edit the data, interpret and analyze the materials, make predictions, and communicate the information as clearly and in as timely a manner as possible. Forecasters project social and cultural shifts, population trends, technological advances, demographic movements, developments in consumer behavior, and their possible implementation in the fashion spectrum.

Once forecasters have collected all of their information, they begin the task of interpreting and analyzing the data. They formulate ideas about new themes, stories, moods, colors, textiles and materials, and looks and silhouettes. Oftentimes a team of professionals work to gather and decode the collected information. Forecasts can be customized to fill the specific needs of the particular market for which they are intended.

FIGURE 1.10
In this menswear fashion forecast by Fabiana Negron, named Lycanthropy, the inspiration, title, mood, color palette, textiles, and boards illustrate the look.

In today's industry, different categories of fashion are all subjected to the forecaster's discerning scrutiny. These include, among others, women's wear, menswear, footwear, accessories, intimate apparel, children's wear, swimwear, interiors, knitwear, denim, active sports, and the youth market. Forecasters can also view these categories from multiple perspectives. Forecasters, for example, can focus on a particular portion of a forecast such as theme development, color forecasting, textile and materials forecasting, the look forecaster, or specific details. Popular fabrications including knits and denim have their own forecasting niche. Thus, within the forecasting services, there are specialties within specialties.

The forecast can be prepared in a variety of formats. In the past, all forecasters presented their information in sophisticated books and multimedia presentations that were created seasonally, including themes, colors, and silhouette predictions. Fashion moved at a slower pace and the new trends often were an evolution of themes from prior seasons. Eventually, forecasters began to predict trends aimed at women's wear, menswear, and children's wear. Over time, wider audiences and more varied clienteles developed, in-

cluding home furnishings manufacturers, package designers, automakers, and investors. In recent years, the Internet has afforded many forecasters the opportunity to present their information in a detailed and timely manner.

New methods of saving and sharing the forecast have allowed for prompt global access. Forecasting Web sites not only have information about a current forecast, they often have a database that allows access to specific information. Design details, fashion shows, shopping locations, travel and culinary trends, and in-depth color, fabric, and style information can easily be found. The job of forecasters is to evaluate and sort the information so that it can be delivered in a practical and understandable way.

Forecasts are often conveyed at specific events, including major trade shows, fabric fairs, and training seminars, as well as at meetings in clients' offices. A spokesperson for the forecasting service, or the forecasters themselves, present the information in polished, engaging format designed not only to convey information but to inspire the viewers. Forecasters must present their findings with a confident ability to convince the listeners that the forecast is accurate and feasible. Needless to say, strong public speaking skills and presentation savvy can persuade the audience.

EXAMPLE OF A FASHION FORECAST

A typical forecast includes:

- Theme—the ideas, stories, and moods of the forecast
- Color
- Textiles and materials
- Look

FORECASTING SERVICES

While there are individuals who keep tabs on the shape of things to come, forecasting firms have developed the business of predicting the future of trends. Each service has its own philosophy and delivers its information in its own way. From books detailing color, fabric, and style to integrated Web-based informative systems, the services develop user-friendly methods to communicate their findings.

KAI CHOW, CREATIVE DIRECTOR, DONEGER CREATIVE SERVICES

The Format of a Typical Forecast

The forecasts are created by season—spring and fall. Within each season, all forecasts include four stories—a portion with a youth-inspired tone and a portion which is edgier and more contemporary. The seasonal projection boards are assembled with mood pictures, color stories, and fabrications. In addition, silhouette illustrations are included. This information is then prepared for publication, which is released in portions beginning with concept, color, fabrics, then workshop (silhouette) books. In addition, the information is available to the clients on the Web site. The process of creating a seasonal forecast starts at least 18 months prior to its release date.

FRANK BOBER, CEO OF STYLESIGHT

Parallel Business Plan and Dream

I created a service that offers magnificent amounts of information appealing not only to the artistic community but also to the business leaders. I believe that the idea of a parallel track that includes both a sound business plan and a dream makes most sense.

Some of the most influential fashion forecasting services, a description of each service and how it functions, are listed below.

- **Carlin International** trend books are twice-a-year information guides that include major trends, color, fabric, and silhouettes. The firm's creative team of 30 international designers and researchers anticipate the trends of the future releasing information 18 to 24 months in advance of the season. *Web site*: www.carlin-groupe.com.
- **Doneger Creative Services** is the trend and forecasting division of The Doneger Group in New York, offering a broad range of products and services for the apparel, accessories, and lifestyle markets in the apparel, accessories, and beauty categories through printed publications, online content, and live presentations. The firm provides clients with in-depth fashion intelligence, color, and fabric direction, and up-to-the-minute retail, street, and runway analysis. In September 2006, the prestigious forecasting company **Here & There** joined the team. *Web site*: www.doneger.com.
- **Fashion Snoops** is an online forecasting service and consulting company that empowers leading companies around the world by providing them with inspiring content, irrefutable research, and strategic guidance. *Web site*: www.fashionsnoops.com.

- **Mudpie** is a leading commercial online fashion trend forecasting service. It offers fashion industry designers, buyers, and executives the global creative inspiration and consumer intelligence needed to succeed. A subscription to its Web site keeps clients informed of rapidly changing fashion and consumer trends and provides creative inspiration, market research, and a library of usable resources, 24 hours a day. *Web site*: www.mudpie.co.uk.
- **Peclers Paris** is a service that deciphers today's trends, envisions the future, and infuses meaning to products by bridging the gap between creativity and industry. The firm's tailored consulting services are designed to assist the clients in asserting their uniqueness and boosting their businesses. They track new impulses, analyze new options, and recommend new creative directions. *Web site*: www.peclersparis.com.
- **Promostyl** is a global trend forecasting agency with headquarters in Paris and a network of agents worldwide. Focusing on lifestyle trends, Promostyl offers across-the-board adaptations for any market needing color and silhouette direction with a balance of both creativity and commercial viability. For more than 40 years, Promostyl has worked with major companies in an array of different fields including apparel, beauty, automotive design, consumer products, and more. *Web site*: www.promostyl.com.
- **Stylesight** is an online trend and forecasting service based in New York that allow clients an immediate sense of what is happening globally. This firm specializes in trend analysis, forecasting, and reporting for merchandising and apparel manufacturing. *Web site*: www.stylesight.com.
- **Tobe Report** was founded by Tobe Coller Davis, as fashion's retail consultant, publishing a private report looking at the fashion industry, analyzing the market, and translating the findings to the retailers. The report became a guide to the merchants as an understandable tool that filters the

information for potential retail profits. Today, the report not only covers the fashion trends but also maintains a wider focus on the societal changes that influence the consumer. *Web site*: www.tobereport.com.

- **Trendstop** is an exciting online trend information service. It is dedicated to providing fast, focused, and accurate fashion forecasts and global trend information. As the trend forecasting tool for leading designers and stylists, as well as fashion, creative, and media professionals, it translates trends. Trendstop offers downloads of editable trend silhouettes for Illustrator and other design programs. *Web site*: www.trendstop.com.
- **Trend Union** specializes in trend forecasting, creating a collection of seasonal trend books and audiovisuals for the textile and fashion industries as well as the interior, retail, and design industries. Twice a year, Li Edelkoort creates a 20-minute audiovisual presentation that sets out in a clear and inspiring manner the trends that correspond to her general Trend Book. This presentation is shown to Trend Union's clients, with viewings in Paris, London, Stockholm, New York, Tokyo, Seoul, and Amsterdam. *Web site*: www.trendunion.com.
- **WGSN** is the online global service providing research, trend analysis, and news to the fashion, design, and style industries. Its team of creative and editorial staff travels extensively on behalf of subscribers and works with a network of experienced writers, photographers, researchers, analysts, and trend spotters in cities around the world, tracking the latest stores, designers, brands, trends, and business innovations. Clients have access to all the latest international style intelligence. The service is also used by many other related industries requiring research, analysis, and news, combined with extensive intelligence on emerging style trends. WGSN is based in London with offices in New York, Hong Kong, Seoul, Los Angeles, Melbourne, and Tokyo. *Web site*: www.wgsn.com.

CAREER OPPORTUNITIES

Because forecasting can relate to a myriad of fashion specialties, the possibilities for jobs in the field are numerous. Each area of fashion forecasting offers a broad range of career choices, and specific jobs in the field require a variety of skills. Creative directors, managing editors, trend analysts, researchers, graphic designers, web designers, marketers, illustrators, photographers, and videographers all contribute to the challenging task of peering into the fashion future. Reporting, writing, public speaking, and sales skills are all essential in making convincing presentations to clients.

Most forecasting jobs require at least a bachelor's degree. Industry employers often look first at applicants with fashion design, merchandising, or textiles degrees. Degrees in sociology, business, journalism, and art are also relevant to the tasks at hand. An internship with a forecasting team can offer a valuable entrée for the newcomer seeking to break into the field. Experience in fashion-related fields can also help a candidate gain entry to a forecasting interview. Involvement in event planning, trade shows, retail, buying, public relations, fashion show production, styling, management, publishing, and media can all be valuable assets for applicants seeking a position in forecasting.

DAVID WOLFE, CREATIVE DIRECTOR, DONEGER CREATIVE SERVICES

Who Is a Candidate for Forecasting?

I look for newcomers to the fashion forecasting profession who have high levels of intellectual curiosity. A candidate with limited fashion tunnel vision is not well equipped to understand how fashion today reflects our ever-changing environment.

KAI CHOW, CREATIVE DIRECTOR, DONEGER CREATIVE SERVICES

Advice for a Student of Forecasting

Understanding the technical side of fashion creations and understanding the way that things are made is essential. I believe that taking an internship in a factory is a great way to get the necessary experience.

Beyond the degree and the résumé entries, candidates for fashion forecasting positions must show that they are attuned to fashion cycles and understand the ways in which culture influences fashion. Forecasters must also understand the manufacturing process. It is difficult to forecast about the styles and details of a product if one does not understand how that product is designed, constructed, and made.

Of course, all of the effort required to land a prestigious fashion forecasting job can pay off in the end. The field is small and competitive, however, and salary is based on performance and experience.

A look at the résumés of the industry's most prominent creative directors, editors, fashion curators, and high-level fashion executives will probably show that most have extensive experience with forecasting and trends. Most professionals begin with some forecasting exposure and continue to hone their skills through experience while working in the industry.

Forecasting is not only about the ability to gaze into the future and miraculously identify next year's popular items. Forecasters must be able to promote themselves and their ideas. A forecaster who has a good track record in identifying trends develops noteworthy credentials and can help lead clients to great triumphs. With intelligence, curiosity, skill, and intuition, a successful forecaster learns to identify prominent trends and translate this information into profitable decisions.

SUMMARY

Fashion forecasters use a potent mix of experience, vision, and carefully targeted research to figure out what will appeal to the consumer's next desire. Forecasters look for clues at runway shows, the club scene, and red carpet events, as well as gather data on spending trends and demographic distinctions, keeping an eye on trendsetters and on adventurous street fashionistas.

Combined with the forecaster's instinctive understanding of fashion, all of the data and observational research can add up to an accurate glimpse of things to come. Forecasting fashion is more than a mere guessing game, but an exercise of analysis, creativity, and developed skill. Designers and manufacturers rely on the fashion forecaster's ability to predict new trends to turn out lines of successful products that profit from market developments. No wonder, then, that an entire industry relies so much on the predictions of the forecasting specialists. No wonder that the forecasting niche has become a thriving industry in its own right.

KEY TERMS

- Fashion forecasting
- Trend report
- Fashion
- Style
- Taste
- Trends
- Trend forecasters
- Trend spotters
- Trendsetters
- Short-term forecasting
- Long-term forecasting
- Researching
- Editing
- Interpreting and Analyzing
- Predicting
- Communicating

ACTIVITIES

1. Current Fashion Information and Essay

Collect one item for current fashion events discussion. This item must represent information that will help in formulating fashion forecast for an upcoming season. The item may be a clipping from *Women's Wear Daily*, or a newspaper or magazine that you believe is an indicator for predicting change that will relate to your forecast.

Write a short essay to accompany a copy of the item describing the item. Include the origin of information (designer's names, publication, etc.), relevance to fashion of the past or future, and reason why you believe that this is an important indicator for fashion of the future.

Be prepared to show the item to the class and discuss its importance to fashion forecasting.

2. Style.com Assignment

Create your own lookbook on the Web. Choose twenty photos from designers' collections that you see that are interesting to you. Save them in your lookbook. Add to the lookbook by creating folders for the photos and information. *Web site*: www.style.com.

3. Fashion Forecasting Services Research

Conduct research on fashion forecasting services. Identify any services that are available. Visit a library to check availability of forecasting information. Search the Web and begin navigating the sites.

BRIEF HISTORY OF CONTEMPORARY FASHION

2

Objectives

- Understand how fashion history is important to forecasting.
- Identify how the "spirit of the time" shapes fashion.
- Identify how political, social, and cultural events affect fashion.
- Identify predominant styles and designers of each era.
- Explain the effects of changing fashion.
- Track the evolution of fashion in history.

How does fashion history help forecasters to know where fashion will likely go next? How do political, social, and cultural events of an era help to shape future fashion? How do certain looks capture an era's spirit? How does the evolution of fashion happen?

One must have an understanding of history to be able to forecast fashion successfully. Fashion forecasters examine the past, assess the present, and then predict trends for the future. A successful fashion forecaster understands that the past is crucial to projecting the future direction of fashion. The expression "history repeats itself" is completely applicable in the context of fashion. Also, fashion forecasters must understand that fashion is an evolution not a revolution. Changes in fashionable standards progress over time as cultural attitudes change.

WHAT IS ZEITGEIST?

The "spirit of the times," or **zeitgeist,** refers to the current state of culture: the expression of the present. The mode of an era is determined by a complex mixture of historical, social, psychological, and aesthetic factors. During each era, creative artists and designers are inspired by current influences that they interpret into innovative ideas and products. It is not surprising that there are commonalities that influence an era. New aesthetics can often be found in various aspects of the contemporary era: art, architecture, interior design, beauty products, as well as apparel. For instance, fashionable trends frequently appear in multiple art forms simultaneously. During the 1920s, clothing, architecture, and fine arts all used similar shapes, materials, and color. Examples of sweeping lines, V-shapes, and symmetry appeared in Art Deco architecture such as the Chrysler Building in New York, the Bacardi Building in Havana, Cuba, and even in the Underground in London. Sleek materials such as chrome and mirrors produced crisp, reflective surfaces. Similar geometric motifs appeared in textiles, such as embossed velvet and silky jacquards that had a monochromatic color scheme of gunmetal gray, black, and silver accented with muted cobalt blue. Clothing designer Paul Poiret incorporated geometric lines in his designs that were based on rectangles embellished with shimmering cut beads. The geometric shapes went hand in hand with modernization in the decade known as Art Deco.

Like the styles of the 1920s, the 1960s showed a new interpretation of familiar ideas as the spirit of both eras was fueled by the desires of youth for change. Sometimes in fashion the "retro" influence came quite literally from a specific look, while other times the look has only subtle nostalgia for a past time. Once the zeitgeist of the era is understood, a fashion revival can be traced to its time of inception or its most recent reappearance. Usually the new versions of a revival have the essence of the earlier sense of style morphed into contemporary variations that infuse the current era's mood of the moment or zeitgeist.

ZEITGEIST AT WORK

Knowledge of both past and current political, social, and cultural trends is needed as a forecaster begins to examine events to understand directional shifts and the evolution of fashion. During each era, changes in attitudes and lifestyles move fashion forward. Sometimes an era begins or ends with a huge event, such as a financial crisis like the stock market crash of 1929 or a war. Other times, an era can be identified by a society's changing outlook that captures the spirit of the time, such as the hippie era of the 1960s, fueled by rebellion. Similar to the influence of the industrial revolution of the twentieth century, the technology revolution of the twenty-first century has helped shape the ideology of the current era. By examining the events of an era or decade, clues can be found as to why people chose to wear what they did. Whether the issues are about war or peace, breakthroughs in medicine and technology, developments in transportation and communication, or new genres of music and entertainment, the events bring on change. This change manifests in the fashions that society accepts and wears.

This chapter identifies eras in fashion and the key factors that shaped the creative impulses of the time. For each era, the chapter identifies the zeitgeist, describes the fashions of the time, and discusses the ideas that moved fashion forward. Starting in the 1860s, the eras are roughly divided by decade or by time periods that began or ended with dramatic changes due to major events.

DAVID WOLFE, CREATIVE DIRECTOR, DONEGER CREATIVE SERVICES

For Fashion to Be Part of History, It Must Be Worn by Society

When asked about the history of modern fashion, I saw the impact of great change when Kenzo entered the Parisian scene in the 1970s. His revolutionary approach challenged the established world of couture. The excitement, the colors, bold prints, and the references to global culture showed in the clothing and stores, and people bought and wore his apparel and accessories. Unlike the 1980s, when Comme des Garcons stormed Paris, and people didn't actually wear the dark, tattered, and deconstructed shrouds. Although this attack on beauty was provocative, it went from the retailers to the museums and wasn't worn by many. I think of the famous quote by Coco Chanel: "A fashion that does not reach the streets is not a fashion."

1860–1899: VICTORIAN FASHION AND CHARLES WORTH

identify the "spirit of the time"

Before the 1860s, several European countries dominated political and social ideals. Paris and London were considered the leading urban centers of society and commerce. Although the United States was viewed as a young nation, it continued to expand and develop a culture of its own.

In England, a conservative era was led by Queen Victoria, who ruled for nearly half of the nineteenth century. England experienced great prosperity as its trade and commerce flourished. Wealth was displayed openly as ornamentation and opulence appeared in fashion, art, and architecture. England's progress was envied by other nations.

After the turmoil of the French Revolution subsided, France regained leadership as the fashion capital of the world. In Paris, the modern era of clothing is often credited to have begun with the work and ideals

FIGURE 2.1A During the reign of Queen Victoria, it was fashionable to display opulence and wealth.

FIGURE 2.1B Dresses of the period displayed frilly ornamentation including bustles, with or without a train, bows, and an exaggerated silhouette.

FIGURE 2.1C The Civil War brought great societal change to the United States.

FIGURE 2.1D The California Gold Rush propelled movement into the West and also inspired America's western fashions.

of **Charles Fredrick Worth**, known as the "Father of Haute Couture." Worth received this title because his innovative approach to fashion differed from other dressmakers of his era. Worth created fashions for his prestigious clients using his own aesthetics instead of following his client's ideas. Worth opened the first **haute couture** (literally translated to mean "high sewing") fashion house in Paris in 1858, the House of Worth. He was the first to include a label with his name on each garment.

In the United States, the Civil War ended and slavery was abolished. The American public had to face new social attitudes about race and class. Nearing its first centennial as a nation, the country continued to expand with mass migration to both urban and rural areas. The Gold Rush in California helped to increase westward movement to the Pacific.

Realism and Impressionism were the major artistic movements, while music felt the fusion of cultural influences. In literature, writers revealed deep human feelings and imagination through myth, symbols, and dreams.

Important films that showcased the fashion of this era that were made later include *Gone with the Wind*, *Young Victoria*, *Butch Cassidy and the Sundance Kid*, and *Gangs of New York*.

fashion of the time

The increasing prosperity of the Victorian period was manifested in frilly and ornamented clothing for women. Heavily embellished clothing was used to display social status and respectability. Women's clothing restricted movement with the bustle, corsets, hoops, and multiple crinolines. Exaggerated silhouettes created hourglass curves by tightening the waist. Day dresses had high necklines, wide sleeves, and skirts extended to the floor. These conservative styles covered the body, allowing little skin to be seen and little freedom to be felt. For evening, necklines were lower, sleeves were shorter, and fingerless gloves made of lace were popular. Fancy hats replaced bonnets.

Men's clothing, which was not much different from the preceding decades, was formal and rigid and continued the conservative trend. Business suits were worn for day, tailcoats and formal overcoats for evening. Men accessorized with walking sticks, top hats or derbies, and pocket watches.

moving forward

Before the 1850s, most fashions were made in the home by women. When sewing machines were introduced into factories, mass production of clothes began. This modernization led to changes in the workforce, altered financial status, and changed communication and transportation. Women started to work outside the home.

FIGURE 2.2A The hoop skirt had a large metal foundation under the fabric to support the massive gown.

FIGURE 2.2B Fashionable gentlemen wore conservative coats and adorned themselves with overstated accessories including a top hat and walking stick.

FIGURE 2.2C Extravagant workmanship went into this Charles Worth gown of lustrous satin and delicate lace.

The invention of photography influenced fashion developments. *Vogue* magazine began publication, providing information and images that allowed widespread opportunities to follow fashion trends. New textile technology, including power looms and synthetic dyes, modernized textile development. Department stores were created, along with mail-order catalogues that provided access to manufactured clothes to people in both urban and rural areas.

As the Victorian Era came to a close in the late 1890s, new attitudes and changing values emerged. As prosperity spread, the wealthy society elites experienced the influx of the nouveau riche, and a new middle class. European dominance was drawing to a close as the U.S. economy grew and gained strength. Transformation and a sense of freedom was in the air.

1900–1919: EDWARDIAN PERIOD AND WORLD WAR I

identify the "spirit of the time"

The twentieth century began with the modern countries of the world celebrating the new era with special expositions, celebrations, and optimism. In England the decade was marked by the Edwardian Period, lasting from 1901 until 1910, when King Edward VII reigned. This was a time of great extravagance and opulence in England, which was the world's leading economic and military power. In France, this same era was known as *La Belle Époque* or "The Beautiful Age." Haute couture fashions featured costumes filled with opulence and luxury for the wealthy. The rich paraded their splendor in fine Parisian restaurants, visited spas, and enjoyed cabarets. In both European countries, the times were excessive and classical.

The population growth of the United States was augmented by immigration from all over the world. Before the 1900s, most U.S. immigrants were from northern Europe. After the 1900s, immigrants also began to arrive from southern Europe and Asia. A disparity between the established rich and the newly immigrated poor became recognizable. Racial justice, peace, and gender equality continued to be important issues for the country.

Great advancements were made in U.S. transportation. The Ford Motor Company began manufacturing a low-cost automobile, which many Americans could afford. The Wright brothers made the first flight, introducing the prospect of air travel.

Culturally, new art movements including Post-Impressionism, Fauvism, Cubism, and Expressionism introduced artists such as Paul Cézanne, Vincent Van Gogh, Henri Matisse, Paul Gauguin, and Pablo

FIGURE 2.3A
The extravagance of the Edwardian Period in England was celebrated through the first decade of the century.

FIGURE 2.3B
World War I caused great political and economic upheaval in Europe and the United States.

FIGURE 2.3C
The Model T Ford contributed to a revolution in transportation.

FIGURE 2.3D
Pablo Picasso was an influential artist of the period.

FIGURE 2.3E
Film comedy star Charlie Chaplin helped popularize silent movies.

Picasso. Theatrical performances, vaudeville, and motion pictures became important leisure activities. Mary Pickford, Theda Bara, and Charlie Chaplin became movie stars. Spectator sports, including baseball and horse racing, became part of high society life. *Harper's Bazaar* started to publish a monthly magazine, and newspapers added sections including sports and cartoon strips.

The peaceful times ended when World War I (1914–1918) began. Initially the war was a European conflict with Russia, Britain, and France aligned against Germany and Austria-Hungary. But the war spread worldwide and the United States entered hostilities in 1917. Acquiring new status as a military and economic power, the war greatly changed the role and image of the United States on the international stage. Because the war led to the absence in the country of millions of men who were called to serve, many American women were needed to fill vacant jobs in the workplace. After the war, while many women left their jobs to return home, others remained in the workforce, and the revolutionary idea of the American working woman became part of U.S. culture.

Important films that showcased the fashion of this era that were made either during the era or later include *Kid Auto Races at Venice*, *A Room with a View*, and *Titanic*.

fashion of the time

The century began with a formal but festive fashion attitude that favored a mature woman's shape that focused on a full bust and small waist. The predominating silhouette for women was the "S"-shaped style. Bodices were boned, putting pressure on the abdomen and creating a straight front while shifting the hips to the back. The long skirt was smooth over the hip and extended to cascade to the floor. The "Gibson Girl," created in illustrations by Charles Dana Gibson, was considered by many a perfect standard of feminine beauty of the time, emphasizing the full bust and long swirled skirt with a train. Clothing was highly ornamented with laces, ribbons, and decorative features allowing wearers to flaunt their riches. Parisian **Jacques Doucet** embodied the spirit of the times by connecting his fashion creations with the aesthetics of the Art Nouveau movement that continued through the early part of the twentieth century.

Paris was regarded as the starting ground for major fashion trends. In 1910 **Paul Poiret** radically change the silhouette by introducing the hobble skirt and empire silhouette, and women removed their corsets. Oriental costumes, Greek draping, turbans, harem pants, and kimonos were introduced, fusing Eastern and Western cultures. Styles were looser, fabric was lighter, and colors were brighter. Along with Poiret, **Mariano Fortuny** created innovative pleated gowns rich in fabrications and color. Doucet, Poiret, and Fortuny became known as fashion leaders in the world of haute couture.

FIGURE 2.4A The elongated silhouette of the Gibson Girl was considered by many a perfect standard of beauty.

FIGURE 2.4B Paul Poiret, an influential designer, freed women from corsets and changed the established rigid silhouette.

FIGURE 2.4C The beginning of World War I revolutionized fashion with the need for women in the workplace.

FIGURE 2.4D Heavily ornamented clothing was paraded to display status and wealth.

By 1915, skirts and dresses rose above the ankle and hit midcalf, due to the scarcity of materials caused by the war. Ornamentation was lost and the silhouette was simplified. Practicality and utility replaced the extravagance seen earlier. Women also began to widely participate in sports: cycling, gymnastics, tennis, and sunbathing. American designer **Amelia Bloomer** introduced pants for women decades earlier, but with the increasing need for garments that allowed for movement, pants for women were worn during this era.

During the war, fashion was of little interest. Many designers closed their businesses during the wartime period. Working women needed clothing that would better suit their new activities. Conservative tailor-mades (women's suits) were worn with blouses.

At the beginning of the era, men's clothing was rectangular with no emphasis on the waistline. Men wore morning coats, striped trousers, and top hats as formal wear. During the period, men's styles became more relaxed as men started to wear tweed jackets and striped blazers for casual wear. Shortened pants, called knickers, were adopted for activities such as bicycling, starting the trend of practicality in men's clothing. The trench coat was also introduced during the war years as a utilitarian style in basic colors, essentially the same coat that can still be seen in fashion today.

moving forward

While at war, nations worked on scientific and industrial advancements to help the war effort succeed. Once the war was over, these advancements were implemented in the manufacturing sector. The industrial revolution promoted change within the working classes. More machinery was used for textile and garment production, and that paved the way for ready-to-wear (RTW) clothing. Rayon became available for mass market, and the zipper was invented.

Haute couture elevated the designer into a role as a creative force dictating fashion and styling. The designer, much like the artist, was affected by the spirit of the time.

Motion pictures had a tremendous impact on fashion followers. The clothing styles worn by actors and actresses influenced not just moviegoers but the whole of society. The contemporary styles seen on the big screen were mimicked and copied by the public. At the end of World War I, it was apparent that society was changing. World political power was shifting, cultural attitudes were changing, and a modern type of woman emerged with new outlooks and actions.

1920–1929: ROARING TWENTIES AND THE FLAPPER

identify the "spirit of the time"

Following the end of World War I, the "Roaring Twenties" in the United States was characterized by a time of extravagance and fun. It was a time of great change, wealth, and accomplishments. Advances in transportation included Charles Lindbergh's first flight across the Atlantic Ocean and more affordable automobiles. Sigmund Freud's psychological theories revolutionized morals and values, especially in the young.

Women fought for equality and began to reject social norms, limited roles in society, and patterns of behavior. In 1920, the 19th amendment to the U.S. Constitution gave women the right to vote. The new woman was free, uninhibited, and pleasure-seeking. She enjoyed jazz music, new styles of dancing, and clothing. "**The flapper**" was a nickname given to young girls who smoked, drank, and danced the Charleston and the Foxtrot. Even though Prohibition, which had gone into effect in 1919, banned the distilling, brewing, and sale of alcoholic beverages, institutions like the speakeasy (a clandestine drinking, dancing, and dining club) replaced saloons.

FIGURE 2.5A
Jazz music was introduced to the world.

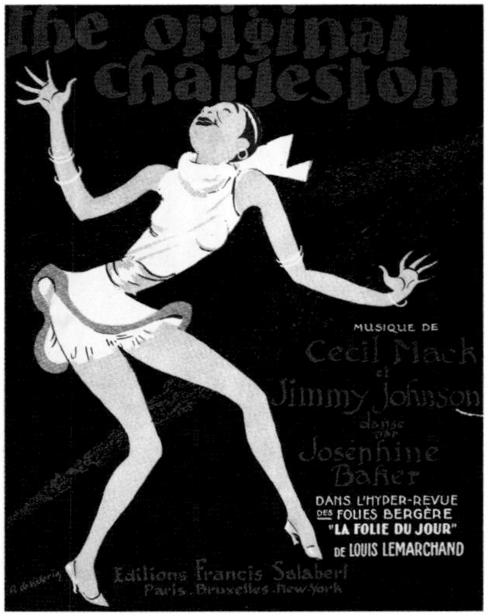

FIGURE 2.5B
The Art Deco style of architecture was exemplified by the Chrysler building.

FIGURE 2.5C
The Charleston was the dance rage of the era.

FIGURE 2.5D
Prohibition saw the dumping of alcohol on the streets but clandestine drinking in speakeasies came into prominence.

FIGURE 2.5E
Women secured the right to vote.

FIGURE 2.5F
Smoking was seen as a rebellious act as young women challenged traditional moral attitudes.

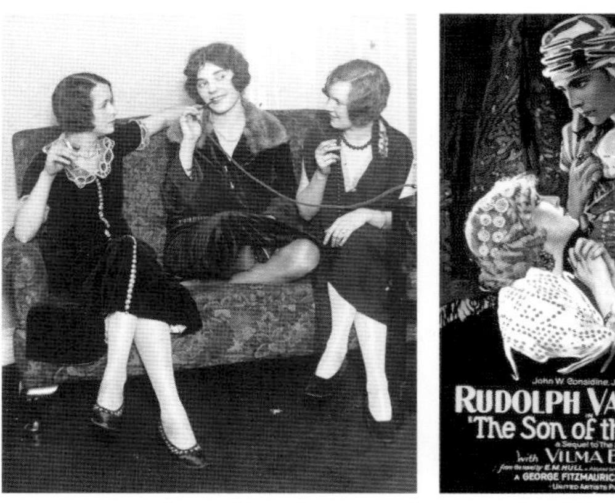

FIGURE 2.5G
Film icon Rudolph Valentino had bankable sex appeal.

In Europe, countries and governments restructured following the war amid revolutionary changes. In Russia, the monarchy of the czar had been overthrown in 1917, and a Communist government had been established. In Italy Benito Mussolini established a fascist dictatorship.

Artistic movements included Art Deco, which was characterized by geometric shapes. The artist Erté, called the "Father of Art Deco," became known for his stylized illustrations. Another art movement was surrealism, which was influenced by Freudian theory. Paintings by artists such as Salvador Dali were influenced by the subconscious imagination.

In entertainment, silent movies, which had long been part of everyday life, were replaced with the movie industry's newest innovation—films with sound. The movies brought visions of glamour and the pursuit of pleasure. The makeup, hairstyles, and clothes of actors and actresses were copied across the nation. Movie stars such as Joan Crawford personified the fast and daring styles of the flapper. Marlene Dietrich started wearing tuxedos with trousers to create a more masculine look for women. Rudolph Valentino was the idol of men and women with his smooth hair and sex appeal. Important films that showcased the fashion of this era that were made either during the era or later include *The Jazz Singer*, *Camille*, and *The Great Gatsby*.

After the first commercial radio broadcast in 1920, the new medium quickly spread across the country. Radios, mostly sold for home use, gave the public access to free music, entertainment, and sports. The music of the period was mostly jazz, from such famous artists as Duke Ellington, Louis Armstrong, and Bessie Smith. Radio allowed the public to follow baseball, football, boxing, tennis, and golf. Along with radio broadcasts came advertising. The cowboy figure was used to market Marlboro cigarettes and the "Marlboro Man" became an American icon.

fashion of the time

The era was characterized by sweeping changes and the disappearance of conventional behavior for women that manifested in the styles of the era. The flappers wore shapeless chemise dresses often ornamented with fringe and beads allowing for freedom of movement. Hemlines rose above the knee revealing legs covered by nude stockings. The flapper look included exceptionally short boyish haircuts called the bob and the shingle. Bright shades of rouge and red lipstick were preferred. Mask-like powder and thinly plucked eyebrows predominated. Beaded evening dresses made of chiffon, soft satins, velvets, and silk taffeta were almost costume-like. Accessory styles included drop earrings, long pearl or bead necklaces, bracelets, and a small close-fitting hat called the cloche.

Bias cut was used by **Madeleine Vionnet**, allowing for beautifully draped, close-fitting garments. **Coco Chanel** introduced jersey knits, allowing for increased movement for the modern woman. Chanel also introduced the "little black dress" that is still considered a classic today. **Jean Patou** introduced new sportswear that included pullover tops and separate skirts.

Men's fashions remained conventional during the 1920s. Men wore sack suits with vests, trousers, and jackets matching in color and fabric (linen or flannel). Single- and double-breasted suits with wide lapels and pronounced waists were used. The trousers were wide-legged, commonly known as "Oxford bags." Neckties, bow ties, and ascots made up the neckwear. Hair was sleek; pencil-thin mustaches were worn. Fedora hats, panama hats, and sports caps were common. With the increase of sports and activities, separates or sportswear was popularized, including sweaters, swimwear, and tennis clothes.

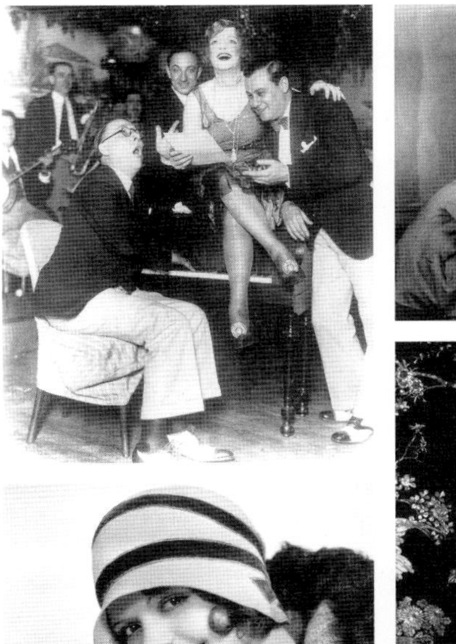

FIGURE 2.6A
Women referred to as "flappers" frequented speakeasies where they drank, smoked, and danced to the rhythm of jazz.

FIGURE 2.6B
The flappers stylishly exposed their legs by rolling down their silk stockings.

FIGURE 2.6C
The cloche was a bell-shaped fitted hat.

FIGURE 2.6D
Gabrielle "Coco" Chanel changed the way women dressed, introducing shorter skirt lengths and comfortable shapes made of jersey knits. The looks were accessorized with boyish hair styles and pearls.

moving forward

Although most of the design direction of the time came from Paris, French designers began to pay attention to U.S. consumers and merchants. In the United States, general merchandise chains and variety stores offered popular merchandise that replaced custom-made garments or the products previously made at home. U.S. retailers began to focus on the business of selling fashions. The beginning of chain stores brought consumer prices down and increased purchasing power. Ready-to-wear fashions became popular with seasonal collections. Garment production of copies, or knockoffs, of French designs became a long-standing practice of the American fashion industry, while deplored by the French couturier.

Toward the end of the decade, the prosperity of the time began to change. The joyous and festive attitude became somber as an international financial downturn began across the world. The excess of the era came to an abrupt end in 1929 with the stock market crash. In fashion forecasting, it is important to understand that nearly all trends end in excess. The 1920s clearly exemplifies this idea. The style of the age was born of radical change and extravagance that could not be maintained. Society often cannot keep up with the speed of change. Observing this type of pattern, forecasters can sense upcoming shifts in fashion.

1930–1945: GREAT DEPRESSION AND WORLD WAR II

identify the "spirit of the time"

Dominating the zeitgeist of the 1930s, the Great Depression was an economic catastrophe that affected people worldwide and led to significant economic, political, and social changes. Unemployment was widespread and crime, bankruptcy, suicide, and prostitution rates rose. Franklin Roosevelt, taking office as president in 1933, led the nation over the next decade to combat the economic crisis that permeated every part of society. During the 1930s, Roosevelt instituted bank reform, established new government agencies, and brought liberal social changes, such as Social Security.

At the end of the decade, the world faced another catastrophic event: World War II. Although the war began in Europe with an invasion of Poland by Nazi Germany led by Adolf Hitler, it eventually spread to include countries from all over the world. The United States entered the fighting in 1941 on two fronts: in Europe with England and the Allies against the Germans, and in the Pacific against the Japanese. The war, which lasted from 1939 'til 1945, quickly dominated the lives of people worldwide. In the United States, rubber tires, gas, and fuel were rationed,

FIGURE 2.7A
Rosie the Riveter represented strong women in the workforce who produced war supplies.

FIGURE 2.7B
The Great Depression left many people without jobs.

FIGURE 2.7C
World War II disrupted the fabric of society.

FIGURE 2.7D
Radio brought communication and entertainment into the home.

and the use of personal vehicles was restricted. The war came to an end in 1945 with the United States and the Allies victorious.

During the war, the Great Depression receded as the war led to the creation of millions of jobs. American factories started to supply the Allied countries with guns, ships, and tanks. About 2 million women took jobs formerly held by men in factories, while another 17 million worked in offices. Attendance at the movies increased during this period. People escaped, albeit briefly, from the realities of the Depression and war into a fantasy world of celluloid glamour and elegance. Lifestyles continued to be influenced by Hollywood movies. Stars of this period included Greta Garbo, Fred Astaire, Clark Gable, Bette Davis, Rita Hayworth, Katharine Hepburn, and child star Shirley Temple. Important films that showcased the fashion of this era that were made either during the era or later include *Bringing Up Baby*, *The Grapes of Wrath*, *Casablanca*, *The Fountainhead*, *It's a Wonderful Life*, *Death on the Nile*, *The Aviator*, *Atonement*, and *The Notebook*.

The popularity of radio broadcasts increased. Swing music created the Big Band Era. Sports became a big business, promoting athletes such as baseball stars Babe Ruth and Joe DiMaggio. In addition to musical broadcasts, there were comedy and drama shows. For example, Orson Welles broadcast *The War of the Worlds* in 1938. With the mass production of books and magazines, reading became a favorite pastime. Television broadcasts also were introduced to the public.

In transportation, cars allowed workers to live in the suburban areas and commute to the cities to jobs. The cars also gave the opportunity to families to spend leisure time in the country and visits to national parks increased. Amelia Earhart became the first woman to successfully fly across the Atlantic Ocean.

Technological and scientific advances included the development of synthetic fibers used to create fabrics. During wartime, the federal government rationed shoes and issued regulations to preserve materials. The government also controlled the amount of fabric that could be used to create clothing.

fashion of the time

During the Depression, daytime fashions for women were conservative suits, or ladylike dresses of simple floral or geometric prints often from recycled fabrics. The silhouette was slender and emphasized the natural waist. Skirt lengths were long for evening. Nylon stockings were popular. Colors for daywear reflected the somber mood of the time: black, navy, gray, brown, and green.

FIGURE 2.8A Fashions of the Great Depression for daytime were conservative ladylike styles.

FIGURE 2.8B Evening wear styles were extremely glamorous, modeled after the stars that appeared on the big screen such as Jean Harlow.

FIGURE 2.8C Pinup girls, with their strong sex appeal, were admired by men at war.

FIGURE 2.8D The movie *Casablanca*, featured beautiful, classic daytime fashions and extraordinary evening wear.

During the 1930s, men's clothing was narrower and fit closer to the body. Men often wore three-piece suits with wide-structured shoulders. The pants were wide and high-waisted. Fedora felt hats and overcoats were worn. Sweater vests often replaced the woven vest as sportswear was becoming increasingly accepted.

Women's fashions changed once the war began. Skirt lengths reached midcalf for daywear; the waist and bust were emphasized with belts. Shoulders were enhanced with the "padded look." Fabrics were in short supply and rationed. Rayon, acetate, and cotton were commonly used fabrics. The war isolated U.S. designers from the European influence, which opened the way for American designers. **Claire McCardell** designed with fabric rations in mind as she introduced separate blouses, skirts, and jackets. The simple and practical concept of sportswear was accepted. Platform shoes were introduced and hats were the essential accessory.

Fashions for men were influenced by military styling, including the pea coats and double-breasted sailor looks. Sportswear for men was a casual alternative, with jackets and pants made of different fabrics instead of the matching suit. Polo shirts made of knits with attached collars, Hawaiian shirts with tropical prints, and western shirts inspired by cowboys were worn.

Evening dresses of the 1930s and early 1940s were stylish and elegant. Emulating the glamorous styles of movie stars, the evening gown was full length and often backless. The designer **Adrian** dressed actress Joan Crawford for films. **Elsa Schiaparelli** was inspired by surrealist art and created avant-garde wearable art. Cheaper versions of embellishments, such as plastic sequins and metallic lamé gave women the expensive look for less. Women looked to the movies, big department stores, mail-order catalogs, and magazines to learn what was current and stylish. The pinup girls such as Betty Grable imitated the glamour of Hollywood and were popular among the soldiers.

moving forward

Following the worldwide Depression and World War II, the roles of men and women shifted and values changed. A new less formal lifestyle emerged and appeared in clothing, entertainment, and recreation.

As a result of the lack of communication and isolation from Europe during wartime, the American fashion industry came into its own, developing a different method of distributing fashion. The French haute couture designers were the creative innovators who sold their garments to private clients, but during the war, many were forced to close. Unlike the European system, the American designer worked mainly for ready-to-wear manufacturers developing seasonal collections that were offered to buyers from retail stores that then sold to the general public. Retail stores bought the merchandise so that, in turn, the customer could view and purchase it. This new system of shopping became a leisure activity as well as a way for clothing to be purchased, giving access to style and fashion trends to many. Department stores created a shopping experience for their customers by carrying great varieties of products, providing restaurants in the store, and holding events to enhance the shopping experience. Stores organized stock by expensive, moderate, and budget departments for clothing.

After more than a decade of restrictions and rations, at the conclusion of the war society was ready for change. British and American designers and manufacturers were prepared for mass production.

1946–1959: THE NEW LOOK AND FASHION CONFORMITY

identify the "spirit of the time"

After World War II ended, a new era began with global interaction between cultures. No longer was the influence from one particular country dominant. Instead, a fusion of politics and culture from many nations helped shape worldwide advancements. The Soviet Union, Eastern Europe, the Middle East, and Asia all influenced long-established European and American ways.

In Europe, the postwar era was filled with the need to rebuild economically, socially, and structurally following the devastation from the war. In England, Winston Churchill was prime minister and Queen Elizabeth began her reign. While France reestablished itself as the fashion capital of the world, the British and American fashion industries that developed significantly during the isolation of the war remained strong forces in fashion.

FIGURE 2.9A
Queen Elizabeth began her reign in England.

FIGURE 2.9B
New forms of entertainment included television.

FIGURE 2.9C
During the 1950s, families moved to the suburbs and enjoyed economic prosperity.

FIGURE 2.9D
The United States and Soviet Union began the race to space.

FIGURE 2.9E.
The first credit card was introduced.

FIGURE 2.9F
Elvis Presley helped to popularize rock and roll.

The United States, after the war, joined in the formation of the North Atlantic Treaty Organization (NATO), a pact for the mutual defense of North America and Europe. The years of U.S. isolation were over. In addition, the U.S. space agency, NASA, was formed and the race to space against the Soviet Union began. The space race was just one aspect of the Cold War between the United States and the Soviet Union. This was the period where these two World War II victors, with their differing ideologies, communism and democracy, competed to be the world's leading superpower. The Korean War, in the early 1950s, although it involved the United Nations, was also viewed as a proxy war between forces and allies of the two superpowers.

The U.S. economy and birth rate grew significantly during this period. New homes were built as families moved to the suburbs. The traditional roles of men and women resumed with men in the workplace and women in the home. Housekeeping and raising a family were considered ideal female roles. As more and more appliances and furnishings were purchased, the demand and manufacturing of household items increased. Family life prospered because of extra leisure time and a rise in income. Credit cards were introduced to the nation. The popularity of television overtook radio, and TV became the main form of entertainment at home. Racial segregation was ruled unconstitutional in the United States. In medicine and technology, the vaccine for polio was created and human DNA was discovered.

The birth of "rock-n-roll" music united American youth, creating icons such as Elvis Presley and Buddy Holly. The show *American Bandstand* became a television hit. Jackson Pollock and Willem de Kooning received official recognition for their work in abstract expressionism. Film star James Dean became a cultural icon for the rebellious youth. Important films and television shows that showcased the fashion of an era that were made either during the era or later include *Rear Window*, *Rebel Without a Cause*, *The Wild One*, *Funny Face*, *Grease*, *Back to the Future*, *I Love Lucy,* and *Happy Days.*

FIGURE 2.10A Christian Dior's new look brought a sense of classic femininity.

FIGURE 2.10C Women left the workplace and returned to the home, as portrayed in the show *I Love Lucy*.

FIGURE 2.10B With his leather jacket and jeans, actor James Dean was an icon of rebellion.

fashion of the time

In France, **Christian Dior** introduced the feminine "New Look"—full skirts and tight waists, in marked contrast to practical wartime styles. Hats and stilettos completed the looks. Chanel reopened her design shop and popularized the collarless tweed suit accessorized with pearls. In the United States, designers created their own looks, from formal evening wear by **Charles James** and **Arnold Scaasi** to comfortable sportswear by Claire McCardell and **Bonnie Cashin**. Women wore dresses even when working in the yard. Pants and jeans were against the accepted rules of fashion.

In the "soda fountain style," teenage fans of rock 'n' roll wore clothes to show off on the dance floor. Full knee-length skirts with tight elastic cinch belts were worn over layers of nylon-net petticoats. Poodle skirts sported checks or large polka dots. Ponytails, bobby socks, and flat shoes completed the outfit.

FIGURE 2.10D Teenagers attended sock hops, popularizing poodle skirts.

FIGURE 2.10E Actress Marilyn Monroe wore glamorous and sexy looks.

Men's fashion stayed more "Ivy League," with conservative suits and button-down shirts. The gray flannel suit was a staple, often worn with a fedora hat. For sports and leisure time, separates, including knit shirts, trousers, and sport jackets were worn. Toward the end of the 1950s, rebellious looks inspired additions to young men's fashion: leather jackets, jeans, T-shirts, and biker boots.

Advancements in fashion were driven by new products and manufacturing methods. The development of polyester and new artificial fibers and fabrics brought a new wash-and-wear ease. Velcro was introduced. Clothing was produced more rapidly, and garments were being produced globally.

moving forward

Culturally, this decade was one of significant change. The 1950s generation is known as the "The Baby Boomers." College became accessible to many. Young people began to question the conservative values of their parents, and the conventional mood left the young and disenfranchised isolated. Support for civil rights grew and protests for equality increased. It became apparent that going back to the way that things were before the war was not possible. The young people and the elders of society began to clash, fueling the momentum for the decade ahead.

1960–1969:
MOD AND THE YOUTH REVOLUTION

identify the "spirit of the time"

The era of the 1960s was one of change, revolution, and rebellion: culturally, socially, and politically. Space was explored, values and attitudes changed, and a new political direction was born. Environmental and energy issues became a concern. New attitudes about sexual freedom and drug experimentation created a generation gap that shaped the era.

In the United States, the nation elected a youthful John F. Kennedy as its 35th president, bringing hope for change. Unfortunately, Kennedy was assassinated three years into his term of office, and the war between North Vietnam and the United States escalated. This led to rebellion by American youth, as protests against the war erupted in the streets. The creation of the Peace Corps, however, allowed some American young people the chance to live and work in developing countries, advancing world peace and friendship. Space exploration continued, and *Apollo 11* landed on the moon. Becoming the first human to walk on the moon, Neil Armstrong inspired the world when he said, "One small step for a man, one giant leap for mankind."

ADAM YANKAUSKAS, DESIGN DIRECTOR AT MAGGY LONDON

The Importance of Fashion History and Vintage Collections

I get my ideas from vintage collections. Both for fabric ideas and silhouette styles, the vintage collections offer inspiration. Knowing fashion history is a must for any designer or merchandiser. So much of what is current comes from the past. When purchasing from the vintage collectors, often I buy because of the fabric; special patterns or prints are reinterpreted by the textile designers in new color combinations or layouts. A few seasons later, the silhouette of the vintage garment may be used in the collection.

FIGURE 2.11A The Beatles brought the English music invasion to America.

FIGURE 2.11B The young people of the era who opposed the conventional lifestyles became known as the hippie generation, promoting love and peace.

FIGURE 2.11C Division over the Vietnam War tore American society apart.

FIGURE 2.11D The United States succeeded in landing the first man on the moon.

FIGURE 2.11E Martin Luther King, Jr. led the civil rights movement.

Equality rose as a major issue for women and ethnic groups. The feminist movement surged during this period, and the introduction of the birth control pill gave a new sense of sexual freedom to women. Moving forward from the civil rights advances of the 1950s, the Reverend Dr. Martin Luther King Jr. and his "I Have a Dream" speech inspired the movement for greater racial equality in the 1960s. The civil rights movement lost much of its passion after the assassinations of King and civil rights supporter Senator Robert Kennedy; however, it still achieved major goals in this decade.

FIGURE 2.12A First Lady Jacqueline Kennedy (later Jackie Kennedy Onassis or "Jackie O") was known for her signature pill-box hat and her time-less sophistication.

FIGURE 2.12B A woman at a sit-in wears typical hippie attire: crystal jewelry, a headscarf, and exaggerated eye shadow.

FIGURE 2.12C Mini-dresses in wildly colored psychedelic prints were popular with the mods.

Socially and culturally, the turmoil of the era fueled originality in art and music. The Beatles led the English music invasion of the United States with "Beatlemania" while American musicians such as The Beach Boys, Janis Joplin, and Jimi Hendrix became popular. The followers of rock 'n' roll music became known as the hippie generation and rebelled against the norms of society. This youth culture opposed the conventional lifestyles and attitudes of their parents. The 1969 music festival, Woodstock, was the significant event for the youth of that era.

Pop artist Andy Warhol became known for paintings and prints of iconic American products such as the Campbell's Soup can, Coca-Cola, and celebrity portraits of 1950 pop icons Marilyn Monroe and Elvis Presley. Important films and television shows that showcased 1960's fashion that were made either during the era or later include *Breakfast at Tiffany's*, *West Side Story*, *Blow-Up*, *The Graduate*, *The Outsiders*, *The Dick Van Dyke Show*, and *The Doris Day Show*.

FIGURE 2.12D Twiggy, a famous British fashion model, was known for her thin, angular build and large dramatic eyes.

FIGURE 2.12E The hippies dressed unconventionally with tie-dyed apparel, long hair, love beads, and freestyle clothing.

fashion of the time

Fashion of this period was divided by its conformity and anti-establishment appeals. Clothing became a way to explore new values and find a sense of belonging to a group. The beginning of the era saw more conservative fashions than the later years. Men wore jackets, pants, and sport shirts, maintaining a clean-cut look. Women wore ladylike fitted dresses with hemlines below the knee. The style of First Lady Jackie Kennedy, with her classic suits and signature pillbox hats, was copied. Audrey Hepburn wore polished styles in the movie *Breakfast at Tiffany's*. Designers such as **Yves St. Laurent, Valentino, Anne Klein,** and **Bill Blass** were known for their updated but conventional styles.

The ready-to-wear market expanded and more fashion styles were available to the consumer. Manufacturers began to make garments in countries where costs were lower. In addition, the landscape of retail changed with the rise of trendy boutiques, Army-Navy stores, shopping malls, and a revived interest in vintage clothing.

The public wore synthetic fibers and used new fabric technologies. Clothing became wearable art through customization and op art prints.

Psychedelic prints, highlighter colors, and mismatched patterns became popular. Global influences filled the market, including Indian-style Nehru jackets and African caftans. No style was more defining of the era than the miniskirt; the shortest that the skirt length had ever gone, exposing the knee and upper thigh.

As the decade progressed, fashions became more radical, with styles that appealed to specific groups or **style tribes**. Style tribes are specialized groups of people that wear distinctive looks to demonstrate their association to the group. Young people, often adolescents, identified with their own groups, which were divided from mainstream culture and identified by the fashions they wore. The counterculture looks were based on lifestyle choices that ranged from music interests to leisure-time pursuits. New styles of dressing and trends often emerged as street styles instead of coming from the fashion runways.

The **Mod Style** became popular first through the Beatles and the influences from England. **Mary Quant** introduced the miniskirt, with accessories, tights, and knee-high boots to match. Men wore Edwardian styles, longer hair in a bowl-cut, and glasses. Women idealized Twiggy, the hot model of the time, with bouffant hairstyles or wigs, miniskirts, and go-go boots. Wild patterns and bright colors were popular.

The **Hippie Style** became a "free" style worn by both young men and women. Clothing was often loose and made of natural fibers in gypsy-like styles. Handmade detailing on clothing was seen, such as tie-dye, batik, and embroideries. The flower child outfit included bell-bottom jeans, sheer tunic tops worn without a bra, headbands, and love beads. Long hair styles and afro hairstyles for men and women were worn.

Space Age Style clothing became popular, with futuristic synthetic fabrics made into geometric silhouettes. Materials such as metal, paper, or plastic were linked or glued together. Metallic colors such as silver and gold supported the look. Designers such as **Paco Rabanne**, **Pierre Cardin,** and **André Courrèges** were known for their futuristic designs.

moving forward

The 1960s radically changed the direction of fashion of the future. Individuality and self-expression became of utmost importance. The fact that people were no longer following the styles of the elite of society and developing looks of their own changed the way fashion was later perceived and created. Even the couturiers of Europe began developing prêt-à-porter collections after observing the increases in the American ready-to-wear industry.

Fashion became nearly unisex during the 1960s, reflecting the changes in attitudes about gender traditions. Men and women were wearing similar types of clothing, including pants and jeans. Women appeared in suits and smoking jackets. For the decade to come, women worked diligently to find equality and rebelled against established ideas about feminine beauty.

Toward the end of the decade, the optimism felt earlier began to disappear as the economic climate deteriorated and social instability continued.

1970–1979: STREET FASHION AND THE "ME" GENERATION

identify the "spirit of the time"

The 1970s were plagued with social unrest. Several major events occurred in this period, including the antiwar demonstrations against the Vietnam War, the first Gay Pride march, and the beginning of the Earth Day movement. Women and minorities continued to strive for equal rights. Economic conditions and continuing inflation added to the chaos of the era. People attempted to escape reality and searched to find themselves. This period was known as "the Me Decade" because the dominant concerns of most people shifted from issues of social and political justice that were so important in the 1960s to a more self-centered focus on individual well-being. As Americans turned inward, they sought comfort through spiritual

FIGURE 2.13A Studio 54, in New York City, was the renowned disco frequented by partygoers and celebrities who danced the night away.

FIGURE 2.13B Antiwar demonstrations were held to protest the Vietnam War.

renewal, reading self-help books, or exercising. Many people stopped trying to perfect the world and instead tried perfecting themselves.

In the early 1970s, the Vietnam War was at its most intense, and antiwar protests escalated. The American political system was shaken with the Watergate scandal and the likely impeachment of President Richard Nixon. Nixon, who in 1974 became the first U.S. president to resign, became a symbol of the public's mistrust of politicians.

From the end of World War II until the end of the 1960s, the American economy had enjoyed one of the longest extended periods of growth, but an Arab embargo on oil in 1973 caused the price of gas to rise and rationing to occur. The U.S. economy in the mid-1970s reached its lowest point since the Depression.

The aging of the population changed the social structure. Baby boomers were leaving college and settling down with families of their own. Women advanced successfully in business, politics, education, science, the law, and even the home. New attitudes about marriage emerged and the divorce rates began to rise.

The gay movement took a huge step forward in the 1970s with the election of openly gay political figures to public office, such as Harvey Milk, who won a seat on the San Francisco Board of Supervisors. Federal and state legislatures also passed measures outlawing antigay

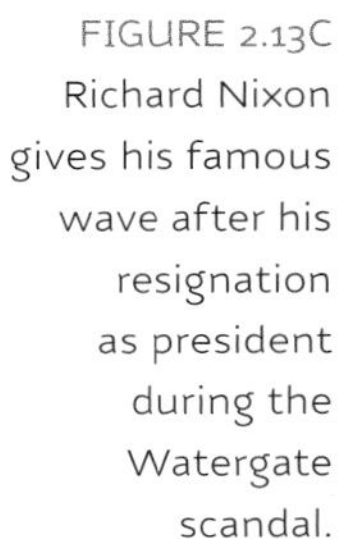

FIGURE 2.13C
Richard Nixon gives his famous wave after his resignation as president during the Watergate scandal.

FIGURE 2.13D
Star Wars became a worldwide phenomenon. It was based on a fictional universe that appealed to pop culture.

FIGURE 2.13E
The movie *Saturday Night Fever* featured John Travolta in a legendary white disco suit.

discrimination. Many celebrities "came out" during this decade, bringing gay culture into the limelight.

Popular culture continued to influence fashion, driven by the most popular form of entertainment, the television. By the 1970s, virtually every American family had color TV. Some families had two or more TVs. At the movies, *Saturday Night Fever* and *Star Wars* were huge hits. Other important films and television shows that showcased the fashion of the 1970s that were made either during the era or later include *Dazed and Confused*, *Shaft*, *Annie Hall*, *Almost Famous*, *The Brady Bunch*, *Charlie's Angels*, and *That '70s Show*.

Music went through changes in this decade as rock 'n' roll continued to evolve, producing new variations such as punk rock, new wave, and heavy metal. Funk also emerged as a uniquely African-American musical form, and soul elements of funk and rock created a dance craze named disco.

Advances in technology included the development of computers. The floppy disc was introduced as computers gained in popularity. The first retail bar code was used to manage inventory. In travel, jumbo jets revolutionized commercial flights, and it became more common for individuals in families to have their own cars.

In the fashion world, magazines took into account new values and lifestyles. Beverly Johnson made history as the first black model to appear on the cover of American *Vogue*. Brand and label awareness grew, and American designers were successfully accepted by the global consumer. More American products were manufactured overseas.

Polyester was widely used and was known for its bright colors and textures. Polyester clothes were appealing because they were easy to wash and did not need ironing. Polyester flooded the fashion market in such large quantities that it lost its fashionable edge. Stretch was added to fabrics with the introduction of spandex.

fashion of the time

The fashions of the 1970s were as unconventional as the era. It was a period where rules dictating which styles were in and which styles were out no longer mattered. Even skirt lengths varied between mini, maxi, and midi, with women also beginning to wear pants adding to the confusion.

Prior to the 1970s, pants were not generally seen on women, and certain top restaurants refused entrance to women wearing pants. Once pants became acceptable, new varieties of pants, including flowing, evening wear palazzo pants, pantsuits, and hot pants were seen. Hot pants were very short shorts that came in a variety of different colors and

FIGURE 2.14A
The hippie look evolved, fusing crafts and ethnicities into a look with afro hair and patchwork unisex garments.

FIGURE 2.14B
Designer jeans became the staple item of clothing for both men and women. Designer labels were introduced.

FIGURE 2.14C
Farrah Fawcett popularized the feathered hairstyle.

FIGURE 2.14D
The TV series *Charlie's Angels* was one of the early shows to have women in roles customarily reserved for men.

FIGURE 2.14E
London designer Vivienne Westwood became synonymous with extreme punk rock fashions.

fabrics. The concept of hot pants allowed women to wear something even shorter than the micro-miniskirt of the 1960s. Women for the first time felt as though they were able to wear any length bottoms, something that had not occurred before in fashion.

Men and women both started dressing more casually, and denim jeans became a staple in the modern wardrobe. Designers capitalized on the denim craze, creating "designer jeans" that openly showed the designer's label, and **Calvin Klein** became a household name. His company began to sign licenses for cosmetics and men's wear.

Varieties and options allowed for increasing individuality and strengthened the influence of style tribes. People who shared similar lifestyles and preferences continued to be categorized according to their look. Some fashion followers preferred classic, punk, hippie, or disco looks.

The **classic looks** included designs by **Ralph Lauren,** who marketed old-fashioned Anglo-American–style clothing, including polo shirts, tweeds, tartans, and boat shoes. The brand not only added comfort to one's leisure activities but also focused on lifestyle living. Other classic looks, such as working women's suits, borrowed styling from traditional menswear. For men, fitted blazers and leisure suits were a hit. Made of polyester, the leisure suit consisted of a matching flared pants and a less structured jacket with an open collar. Leisure suits came in colors that were not typical in menswear prior to the 1970s. For women, **Diane von Furstenberg** introduced the "wrap dress." Usually made out of jersey knit fabrics, this dress wrapped around the body and was held with a belt that tied around the waist. The dress was appealing to working women who needed stylish, professional clothing.

The **punk look** was extreme in the late 1970s and is traced to designer **Vivienne Westwood**. She became renowned for designing and styling the punk rockers, The Sex Pistols, in bondage pants and distressed shirts held together with only safety pins. Black leather, stud embellishments, and chains were part of the punk look. Safety pins became nose and ear jewelry, and spiked dog collars were worn around the neck. Mohawks, outrageous hair, and makeup finished the look.

The **hippie look** continued to be popular with an increased infusion of diverse cultural styles. **Kenzo** mixed wild patterns and bold color into garments, creating exciting ethnic looks. From peasant tops to Chinese quilted jackets to Indian cotton voile dresses, it seemed that every ethnic image set a trend, reviving craft skills from all over the world. Mood rings were also extremely popular, promising to be able to indicate the mood of the person wearing it by changing colors.

The **disco look** gained great popularity in the 1970s at the legendary Studio 54. **Halston** was one of the most quintessential designers of the decade. He dressed many celebrities and trendsetters of the time, designing chic and elegant apparel of all price ranges. He was known for introducing Ultrasuede, as well as creating the halter dress and simple body-conscious dresses often worn for dancing. Disco styles also included platform shoes with soles ranging from two to four inches, leotards, and androgynous looks that appealed to both men and women. Glitz, glamour, and shine appealed to the disco dancer. John Travolta's white suit from *Saturday Night Fever* is a perfect example of the disco look. Using drugs became glamorous and a norm at parties, clubs, and amongst celebrity and social gatherings.

moving forward

By the end of the 1970s, the war in Vietnam was finally over and the established conventions of society were changing. Universal rules about fashion no longer applied. With the consumer in charge and style tribes increasing, fashion systems were in need of revamping. The styles from the streets often dictated what fashion would enter the mainstream. With increasing access to world events and news, fashion influences came from changes in political systems, demographics, and changing values. With the economic crisis nearing the bottom, newness was on the horizon. New sophisticated technology and increasing global manufacturing provided a fresh future for fashion.

1980–1989: POSTMODERNISM AND TIME OF EXCESS

identify the "spirit of the time"

This era is known for the movement away from a singular fashion ideal toward an "everything goes" attitude called postmodernism. This decade was all about excess and the mantra was "the bigger the better." Eagerness for new wealth and desire to consume followed the recession of the 1970s. The 1980s were a time of economic growth that was embraced by the baby boomers and yuppies (young urban professionals). Brand names and designer labels became status symbols, and the increased use of credit cards and disposable income gave people the buying power that they desired.

When Ronald Reagan became president, early in the decade, he brought a glamorous sophistication to the nation. Financially, the country emerged from the economic downturn of the 1970s and the stock market soared. People were eager to work hard to make money and were even more eager to flaunt their riches.

World events were still challenging, with violent conflicts in the Middle East and the ongoing Cold War with the Soviet Union. Nuclear weapons jeopardized world peace, and the United States led efforts to control the proliferation of weapons and sign treaties with the Soviet Union. In England, the wedding of Prince Charles and Lady Diana Spencer in 1981 was headline news.

Socially, women made great strides and entered the workplace as "power women," defined as women who could do it all: juggle work, home, and family life. Working women began to establish careers first and have children later in life. Many families enjoyed two incomes with both parents having high-paying careers.

The AIDS epidemic spread dramatically during this decade, resulting from changing sexual practices and increased drug use. The epidemic had

FIGURE 2.15A Computers and video games entered the mainstream, bringing new technology worldwide.

FIGURE 2.15B On the music scene, superstar Madonna pushed the envelope with her rebellious and provocative attitude.

FIGURE 2.15C Bigger is better was the motto for the 1980s, as seen in the wedding dress Princess Diana wore when she married Prince Charles in London.

FIGURE 2.15D Michael Jackson, referred to as the King of Pop, became well known throughout the globe for his dynamic singing, songwriting, dancing, and music videos.

profound effects on the fashion industry as several popular designers and fashion leaders died due to the disease, including **Perry Ellis** and Halston.

Computer use became widespread in the workplace. A new technological age was initiated as the computer began to transform business systems through modernized telecommunication, new design applications, and increasing efficiency. Global manufacturing increased as a result of the new technology. Leisure time was redefined by the computer, which brought new computer games. Pac-Man was introduced as a video game, and the Nintendo Entertainment System was launched.

FIGURE 2.16A
The fitness craze brought athletic wear to the streets that was accepted as day wear.

FIGURE 2.16B
Fashion was inspired by the opulence and over-the-top styles featured in the TV series *Dynasty*.

FIGURE 2.16C
Miami Vice was a TV series that integrated music, visual effects, and fashion, becoming one of the most influential shows of the decade.

FIGURE 2.16D
Claude Montana exemplified exaggerated silhouettes, including massive shoulder pads, tiny waist, and neon colors.

Although there were many influences in the era, pop culture became a powerful way to link people together. With the 1981 creation of MTV, the first wholly music TV channel, musical performers became mega pop stars; for example, Michael Jackson and Madonna. New genres of music were introduced, including rap music and hip-hop. Musicians and celebrities banded together, hosting events to raise funds to benefit famine relief, environmental disasters, and give humanitarian aid. The disco dance craze of the 1970s continued into the early 1980s, and new styles of dance became popular, including break dancing, a dance style that came from the streets.

Television gave viewers the chance to see excess in action in the new evening shows, such as *Dynasty* and *Miami Vice,* which exemplified excess with glitz, glamour, and shoulder pads. Cable TV increased the entertainment selections and CNN launched its all-news network. Important films that showcased the fashion of the 1980s that were made either during the era or later include *Scarface*, *Flashdance*, *Desperately Seeking Susan*, *Goodfellas*, and *Wall Street.*

Some supermodels became more popular than movie stars. Cindy Crawford, Christy Turlington, Naomi Campbell, and Linda Evangelista were a few of the most sought-after icons of the time. Appearing on the runways, on top fashion magazine covers, and in fashion videos, supermodels became recognized worldwide.

By 1987, the affluent times ended with a stock market crash. At the close of the decade, George H. W. Bush was elected president and the mood of the nation changed.

fashion of the time

The economic boom and the attitude of "bigger was better" certainly appeared in the fashions of the decade. First Lady Nancy Reagan brought glamour to the White House in her famous embellished red suits, and in England Princess Diana brought romance to Windsor Palace in her enormous Cinderella-like wedding dress. On stage, Madonna wore her "big hair" and provocative corsets. In music videos, Michael Jackson wore flashy sequined jackets and his famous glove. Larger-than-life extravagance was spotted everywhere.

Women in the workforce dressed for success wearing tailored menswear, inspired suits with powerful shoulders that were polished and professional. Women wore sneakers for fast mobility while commuting to work and replaced the athletic shoes with high-heeled pumps in the office. Men wore sharp-looking suits as they dressed for success.

The desire for luxury brought European designers back into the U.S. market. **Giorgio Armani** was known for his fine-tailored suits and sophisticated evening wear. **Christian Lacroix** was known for his extravagant and theatrical styles. **Jean Paul Gaultier** showed nonconformist and provocative styles, such as the famous corset worn on stage by Madonna during the 1980s. **Claude Montana** and **Thierry Mugler** were known for styles with very broad shoulders, tiny waists, and futuristic silhouettes.

Japanese designers stormed the fashion scene as well. **Rei Kawakubo, Issey Miyake,** and **Yohji Yamamoto** presented designs that were radically different from other current fashions. The oversized garments in nontypical silhouettes hung organically from the body. Colorless, shapeless, and deconstructed, the Japanese collections were admired as brilliant art forms by some and deplored by others.

In the United States, **Donna Karan** and Ralph Lauren continued to focus on lifestyle fashion, as they designed smart, wearable clothing. Licensing agreements between designers and manufacturers boosted business as some designers often created secondary collections that were offered at more moderate prices. **Steven Sprouse** was known for his art-inspired, edgy looks.

As in the early part of the decade, style tribes continued to develop with each having their own view of fashion. The creation of MTV revolutionized fashion, giving each music style its own fashion sense. Some of the pop music styles included jumpsuits, lingerie looks for day, and wedge-shaped dresses worn with tights or colorful stockings. Neon and bright colors were mixed in patterns and worn together. Accessories such as fingerless gloves, big and gaudy jewelry, and extravagant hair accessories were worn. Hair styles were teased, frizzy, dyed, and oversized.

Another influence on fashion was the fitness craze and the public's interest in working out in the gym. Spandex leotards and legwarmers were worn under oversized knit tops. Sneakers and athletic shoes were worn both inside and outside of the gym.

moving forward

The 1980s can be characterized as a time of cultural shift and economic fluctuation. The increased wealth allowed for expansion in industrialized markets and American dominance while causing social shifts in gender roles and ideals. These factors exerted a great change in the fashion industry as it began to grow internationally while boosting the American middle class. After the conspicuous consumption of the decade, the economic downturn sobered society and movement began in a restrained and frugal direction.

1990–1999: GLOBAL FASHION AND INTERNET EXPLOSION

identify the "spirit of the time"

Following the 1980s extravagance, the era of the 1990s was characterized by a sober attitude where minimalism and casualness prevailed. The technology advances in computers, cell phones, and the growth of the Internet allowed for global expansion and revolutionized modern culture. The Internet gave people access to information and the latest trends. Scientific breakthroughs such as genetic modification created ethical concerns about cloning and new medical treatments. The AIDS epidemic continued to spread.

The era was marked worldwide by globalization, following the collapse of the Soviet Union and the end of the Cold War. As a result, the United States emerged at the time as the sole remaining superpower. The Gulf War in the Middle East dominated the era, as well as the rise of international terrorism. In South Africa, equal rights advocate Nelson Mandela was released from prison, elected as president, and became a symbol of the anti-apartheid movement.

Dramatic economic changes occurred all over the world. Global manufacturing and commerce expanded. As China and other less-developed

FIGURE 2.17A
Technological advances continued to affect society as cell phones improved communications and allowed users to be mobile.

FIGURE 2.17B
Globalization and the fall of the Berlin Wall symbolized the end of the Cold War and revealed a more international understanding of the world.

FIGURE 2.17C
Electronic toys became portable entertainment; for example, Tamagotchi was popularized as a handheld digital pet.

FIGURE 2.17D
Beverly Hills 90210 was a TV series about a group of teenagers confronting the social issues of their time in their privileged California neighborhood.

countries increased their manufacturing capacities, U.S. manufacturing continued to decline. The North American Free Trade Agreement (NAFTA) between the United States, Canada, and Mexico phased out a quota system that restricted imports to the United States. In Europe, the adoption of the new European Union currency, the Euro, brought financial strength to European countries.

Successful business attitudes were redefined by Generation X, who rebelled against the excesses of the prior decade. With the computer culture emerging, including the Internet and e-mail, people in society changed the way they worked, shopped, and were entertained. The traditional nine-to-five work schedules in offices were altered to include working from home, flexible timetables, and job sharing. Casual Fridays were introduced, allowing professionals to dress down or wear less formal business attire. eBay, an online auction venue, was founded in 1995 and is known as a leading success of the dot-com era, altering the way retail operations evolved. Mail order catalogs and Internet shopping grew and became more sophisticated and efficient. Video games, DVDs, and home entertainment systems such as Nintendo and PlayStation became popular.

An increasing fascination and accessibility to movie stars, music idols, and superstars created a new type of celebrity fever. Supermodels and celebrities as fashion icons dominated the magazine covers. Reality TV shows and sitcoms became popular including MTV's *The Real World, COPS*, *Melrose Place*, *Baywatch*, *Seinfeld*, *Friends*, and *The Simpsons*. Important films that showcased the fashion of the era that were made either during the era or later include *Prêt-à-Porter*, *Breakin'*, *Boyz n the Hood*, *Jerry McGuire*, *Clueless*, *New Jack City*, *Do the Right Thing*, *Legally Blonde*, and *Menace II Society*.

Huge shopping centers were opened, such as The Mall of America in Minneapolis, Minnesota, spanning 78 acres. Many outlet malls developed offering discounted merchandise. Designers established lower-priced secondary lines to increase their sales volume. Retailers began producing their own brands of private label merchandise.

Feminism became more accepted and publicized as long-established roles were shifting. Even divorce and nontraditional family structures became common. People with disabilities attained equal opportunities.

Similar to the 1960s, new types of music defined the era. Hip-hop, rap, alternative rock, and techno were on the scene providing commentary on the discontentment of the youth and popularizing downbeat attitudes and values. Each music genre influenced its followers and created even more distinctive fashion style tribes. From hip-hop came the "urban trend"; and alternative rock generated the "grunge look." In the later part of the decade, as the economic future brightened, more optimistic pop music entered the scene.

Gianni Versace, a fashion legacy known for ultrasexy collections for men and women that combined street style with high fashion aesthetics, was tragically shot outside his Miami home. Another role model, Princess Diana, was killed in a car accident in Paris, leaving millions of admirers in tears.

fashion of the time

The fashions of the early part of the 1990s reflected the mood of the time with both minimal and informal modes of dress. Most importantly during this decade, individualism flourished. People did not follow fashion as they had in the past; instead nonfashion was hailed as the new fashion. In this "everything goes" decade, lifestyle dressing and dressing to be part of a style tribe led the way.

Black became the main color for **minimalistic** clothing, while accessories and embellishments disappeared. The shapes were simple and clean. **Jil Sander** and Calvin Klein were known for their colorless, streamlined styles.

People in both the workplace and at home adopted an extremely **casual style**. The relaxed attitude mirrored the new work environment, allowing men to wear chino pants, relaxed shirts, and no ties. Stores like the Gap and Banana Republic created clothing to fit this more casual need. Women wore loose-fitting garments often layered on top of lingerie-inspired pieces such as a slip dress or camisole. With the wide use of spandex, comfort stretch was added to many woven fabrics creating easy-to-wear garments. In addition, the fitness clothing of the 1980s evolved into clothing acceptable as day wear, including yoga wear and knit sportswear. Catalog companies including TravelSmith offered easy-care knit separates aimed at the career woman who traveled for business.

The **grunge style** was adopted by the alternative rock musicians from the Seattle scene and is characterized by mismatched and messy

FIGURE 2.18A
Designer Todd Oldham created a heavily beaded and embellished jacket.

FIGURE 2.18B
The Spice Girls, a British pop band, became a global phenomenon as pioneers who paved the way for other teen pop bands. Their "Girl Power" defined the decade with extravagant looks.

FIGURE 2.18C
Followers of alternative rock music adopted an unkempt appearance as a form of rebellion known as the Grunge look.

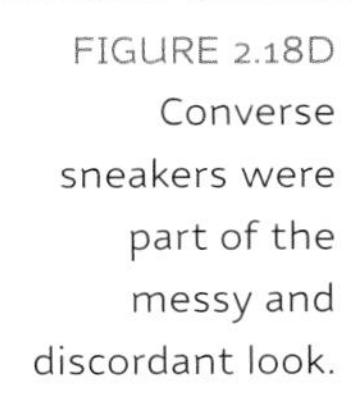

FIGURE 2.18D
Converse sneakers were part of the messy and discordant look.

FIGURE 2.18E
American rapper MC Hammer had great commercial success as a pop icon with flashy dance moves and his trademark Hammer pants.

clothing. Flannel shirts, torn jeans, Converse sneakers, and items from thrift stores were layered together to created this unkempt type of appearance. The grunge followers went against the flashy aesthetic of the prior decade and rebelled against society through music and fashion. Antifashion became mainstream fashion. **Marc Jacobs** initially brought the grunge look to the fashion runways at the time, but he was unsuccessful.

The punk looks of the 70s and 80s morphed into **Goth**. This alternative fashion, also known as *industrial punk*, is characterized by dark leather looks, corsets, and metal studding. Fishnet stocking are worn with platform leather boots. Body art including piecing and tattoos, along with colorfully dyed hair, completed the look.

Hip-hop and rap musicians wore looks from the "streets" that evolved into the **urban look**. Their colorful wardrobes were made up of oversized garments and low slung pants that allowed their underwear to be visible. Huge "bling" jewelry and gigantic gold chains were common accessories. Backward baseball caps and zany sneakers finished the look. Rapper star Sean Combs created a fashion collection called **Sean John** that brought the look from the streets to mainstream society.

Near the end of the decade, **preppy styles** were popularized. **Preppy style** refers to traditional looks that include varsity-style sweaters, classic blazers, button-down shirts, and cardigan sweaters, creating the appearance of young professional adults. Inspired by business attire and school uniforms, the preppy looks were a contrast to the messy grunge look.

With such a wide variety of individual fashion looks, young people began looking back in time to find inspiration. **Vintage dressing** and retro looks included hippie-inspired 1970s nostalgia with garments such as hip-hugging denims and tops that exposed the midriff. The Wonderbra became a sensation, putting great emphasis on the bust.

In Europe, several of the established fashion houses brought in British and American talents to revitalize the couture business, including **John Galliano for Dior, Alexander McQueen for Givenchy,** and **Tom Ford for Gucci.** In addition to fresh talent, large corporations created mergers of design houses to develop new images and identities. Brands and lifestyle dressing became the new focus as secondary apparel lines, cosmetic licensees, and accessory contracts were established. The fashion industry shifted from individual businesses dictated by style to fashion empires dictated by financial goals.

moving forward

During the last decade of the twentieth century, diversity and individualism changed the way that society viewed and responded to fashion. Global changes in politics, economics, and technology allowed the fashion industry access to a larger market than ever before. The industry needed to adapt to the needs of the larger global community. Fashion was no longer dictated from the top, and specific trends that clearly predominated disappeared. Acceptable silhouettes or specific hemlines were no longer clues used to determine what was in fashion or what was passé.

Like the world itself, the fashion industry was transformed. Technology and the rapid expansion of computers changed the ways that designers, retailers, and consumers participated in fashion. In order to survive, the fashion industry developed new ways of satisfying the needs of consumers. With increasing market segmentation dictated by style tribes, the singular approach to fashion trends was replaced by multiple approaches that occurred simultaneously.

The century ended with enthusiasm and trepidation about the upcoming millennium. One thing was certain, fashion would continue to evolve.

2000–2010: NEW MILLENNIUM AND SOCIAL NETWORKING

identify the "spirit of the time"

The new century began with widespread Y2K fears of significant computer failures when the clock struck midnight on January 1, 2000. Fortunately, no major technological problems occurred. But in the following year, society's sense of security and stability was shaken by the terrorist attacks on the World Trade Center in New York and the Pentagon in Washington, D.C. on September 11, 2001. The decade continued with more international terrorist attacks and ongoing Middle Eastern violence. The rise of political and religious ideals fueled the tension between countries. Toward the end of the decade, the United States elected Barack Obama as president along with a call for change. The new president entered office as a global recession worsened, increasing unemployment and creating shifts in international economics. More jobs were outsourced to newly developed countries and manufacturing in China and India increased.

During the decade, increased worry over global warming and environmental issues forced modern society to evaluate progress and sustainability. With new concerns about environmentally sound manufacturing practices, sustainable fabrics such as soy, hemp, bamboo, and seaweed were introduced, and environmental activists found creative solutions for the disposal of waste. Industries responded by marketing and creating products that were "earth friendly." People also became more health conscious and purchased organic products.

Technology made the world more accessible. Internet social networking Web sites such as Facebook and Twitter made it easier for people to keep in touch and informed. Access to celebrity culture inspired people to follow fashion looks of famous stars: musicians, designers, actors, and anyone who caught the spotlight. Artists, socialites, and celebrities began

FIGURE 2.19A
J. K. Rowling's extremely popular Harry Potter books offered an escape into a fantasy world of witches and magic that brought a dark tone of mystery into the era.

FIGURE 2.19B
Global warming and environmental concerns led to the green movement and increasing interest in recycling.

FIGURE 2.19C
Barack Obama was elected the first African-American president of the United States.

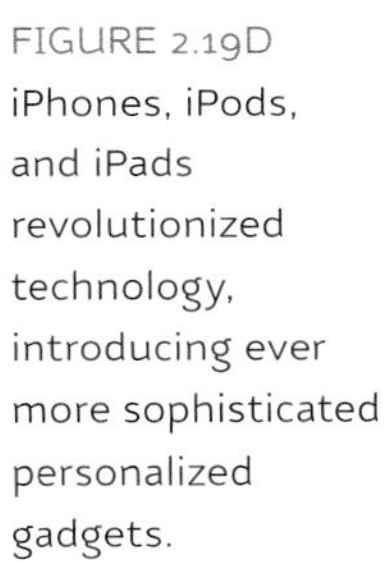

FIGURE 2.19D
iPhones, iPods, and iPads revolutionized technology, introducing ever more sophisticated personalized gadgets.

to launch apparel brands emulating their own sense of style. Even fashionistas could find a following through blogs and Web sites.

The Internet changed the way that people shopped and gave consumers more options, including nearly unlimited choices and access to products from around the globe. Individualism and personal choices led the changes in most industries, and consumers were offered the chance to customize products to fit their desires. "Cause marketing" gave the consumer the opportunity to support specific social or charitable causes through donations derived from their purchases. Retailers and manufacturers began sharing information to spark their businesses.

Although purchasing over the Internet increased, the retail landscape also changed to accommodate the consumer's needs. All-in-one superstores carried all types of products, from clothes to food, allowing for one-stop shopping.

The rise of fast fashion retailers such as H&M, Forever 21, and Zara gave the consumer quick access to fashion looks. Vintage stores and consignment shops provided a way for apparel, accessories, and furniture to have a "second life."

Even the music and entertainment industries experienced substantial change by the introduction of the iPod and iPad, which gave the consumer the opportunity to personalize their entertainment selections. Reality TV shows and movies that featured fantasy and escapism became more popular, and many were viewed in 3D. Important films and television shows that showcased the fashion of this decade that were made either during the era or later include *Lost in Translation*, *8 Mile*, *The Devil Wears Prada*, *Valentino: The Last Emperor*, *Sex and the City*, *Slum Dog Millionaire*, *Confessions of a Shopaholic*, *The September Issue*, *Hannah Montana*, *The Vampire Diaries*, *Project Runway*, *Queer Eye for the Straight Guy*, and *Keeping Up with the Kardashians.*

fashion of the time

The fashions of the new millennium were influenced by celebrity culture, vintage interest, and environmentally inspired "green" fashions. Fashion became consumer-driven; filling the customer's needs and desires became the designer's key to success as they produced looks for niche markets. Fashions became more specific for particular groups as style tribes multiplied. Customization gave the consumer the chance to develop their individual sense of style. Tattoos, piercings, and body art entered the mainstream.

With increasing interest in celebrity culture, people emulated famous stars and trendsetters. With the help of the Internet, nearly unlimited access to style information about celebrities was available. Celebrities were featured on top magazine covers, attended runway shows, and were spotlighted for their styles and lifestyle. Many celebrities created their own fashion collections. The collections often contained looks that the celebrity was known for wearing. **Justin Timberlake** wore urban-inspired clothing, layered separates, and novel sneakers. **Paris Hilton** created collections

FIGURE 2.20A Androgynous elegance is noticed as cosmopolitan women dressed in tailored luxurious suits. FIGURE 2.20B With celebrity worship at an all-time high, singers such as Lady Gaga steal the spotlight with outrageous costumes and a mantra about self-expression. FIGURE 2.20C Enchanting vintage styles with soft ruffles and rich texture achieve a romantic, antique inspired look. FIGURE 2.20D Fashions of the era are dictated by consumers and their personal sense of style as seen in the unusual mix of eclectic items referred to a "soft grunge." The looks are often spotted at music festivals. FIGURE 2.20E A lambskin leather bomber jacket by Sean John is worn over a tunic top and printed legging.

DAVID WOLFE, CREATIVE DIRECTOR, DONEGER CREATIVE SERVICES

End of Trends

Trends are as dead as Latin. Nobody buys trends anymore. In the past, if the trend was Grecian, a woman would wear a draped garment, Grecian-styled jewelry, and gladiator shoes. Specific trends are over! New fashion is all about silhouette, details, and construction. Color palettes are more important than a single color, and one must have a keen focus on textiles.

that emulated her style of effortless extravagance. Plastic surgery, Botox, breast and lip enchantments, and liposuction were used to keep the celebrity look alive. Body conscious garments revealing the midriff and lingerie as daywear were seen. The thong and the push-up bra revived the lingerie market. Status handbags decorated with charms and embellishments made of the finest of materials dominated. Exaggerated shoes were introduced, and **Christian Louboutin** created signature styles with red soles.

At the same time, many designers became so well known that they were celebrities themselves, like John Galliano, Alexander McQueen, and Marc Jacobs. **Michael Kors** became a well-known name after he appeared regularly on the reality TV show *Project Runway*.

Designers came from all around the globe, including Madam Wokie's designer, Mary-Ann Kai Kai from Sierra Leone, Junya Watanabe from Japan; Athens-born London-based designer Mary Katrantzou, and Lie Sang Bong from Korea. With the increasing access via Facebook and Twitter, average people could become "friends" with people who in earlier decades were inaccessible. Designers expanded their notoriety by creating more affordable collections for stores such as H&M and Target to reach their new audiences.

With the global economic recession and the "everything goes" attitude of the era, an increase in interest in fashions of the past surged. Vintage stores and secondhand shops opened. Internet sites such as eBay and Craigslist offered used products and clothing. Fashions from every era were mixed together to create eclectic looks. Long-held fashion rules, such as matching handbags and shoes, no longer applied. The looks were a fusion of daytime and evening looks or sporty and elegant styles mixed together with a modern edginess. Boho-chic became popular with the mix of Bohemian styling and Hollywood glamour. Denim was accepted as an everyday fabric and was worn with embellished and vintage T-shirts by **Ed Hardy**. Skinny jeans and leggings were worn under tunics tops, creating proportions of multiple layers. Short and babydoll-inspired dresses returned, worn with textured tights and elaborate platform shoes or ballerina flats.

Sustainable designs and products were featured in the "green" movement of the decade. Organic products—food, cosmetics, and fashions—became popular. **Linda Loudermilk** established a brand based on changing the planet by changing oneself. She met the needs of the consumer while encouraging awareness of the world that they lived in. Her designs, fabrics, and business model were created with sustainability at the core.

Designers were inspired by the vast advances in technology and began creating clothing with purpose as well as aesthetics. **Hussein Chalayan** was known for his innovative use of materials and progressive innovations using emerging technology. New textile innovations improved quality through gene technology and modernized growing methods. Researchers explored aspects of interactive fabrics infusing the fibers and yarns with sensors and circuits creating fabrics that functioned in novel ways. Fabrics were developed to reduce germs, create a sense of well-being, protect against sunlight, absorb odors, and aid in the circulation of the blood while still having a sense of heightened aesthetic qualities.

Consumers were not satisfied with apparel that just looked good; they wanted the garments to do something for them as well. Utility-inspired trends were popular because consumers wanted function as well as style in their wardrobes. Cargo-pocketed pants, multifunctional jackets, and layered looks gave consumers the comfort and function that they desired.

As the decade came to a close, fashions took a more conservative approach. Fitted clothes became popular with men and slim suits were modernized. The oversized, low-slung pants were replaced by slimmer styles, closer to the body shapes. Women covered their midriffs and less skin was exposed.

moving forward

As the first decade of the new millennium came to a close, fashion continued to change. As global interactions and cultural boundaries shifted, new attitudes influenced the evolution of fashion. Technological advances shaped the new times of the future and things would never be exactly the same again.

SUMMARY

To successfully project future directions in fashion, a forecaster must have a historical view of the past. For example, the 2011 dress worn by Kate Middleton when marrying Prince William was reminiscent of the dress worn by Grace Kelly in the 1950s in its classic attitude, and yet Kate's dress differed with its modern twist. A forecaster must know the specific styles that were popular in each time period and the effect that the spirit of the times had on these styles in order to recognize when elements of these past fashions return to the present. By knowing historical developments and how they affected fashion, forecasters will be able to predict future trends with the help of research, analysis, and synthesis.

KEY TERMS

- Zeitgeist
- Charles Fredrick Worth
- Haute couture
- Jacques Doucet
- Paul Poiret
- Mariano Fortuny
- Amelia Bloomer
- The flapper
- Madeleine Vionnet
- Coco Chanel
- Jean Patou
- Claire McCardell
- Adrian
- Elsa Schiaparelli
- Christian Dior
- Charles James
- Arnold Scaasi
- Bonnie Cashin
- Yves St. Laurent
- Valentino
- Anne Klein
- Bill Blass
- Style tribes
- Mod style
- Mary Quant
- Hippie style
- Space Age style
- Paco Rabanne
- Pierre Cardin
- André Courrèges
- Calvin Klein
- Classic looks
- Ralph Lauren
- Diane Von Furstenberg
- Punk look
- Vivienne Westwood
- Hippie look
- Kenzo

- Disco look
- Halston
- Perry Ellis
- Giorgio Armani
- Christian Lacroix
- Jean Paul Gaultier
- Claude Montana
- Thierry Mugler
- Rei Kawakubo
- Issey Miyake
- Yohji Yamamoto
- Donna Karan
- Steven Sprouse
- Gianni Versace
- Minimalistic
- Jil Sander
- Casual style
- Grunge style
- Marc Jacobs
- Goth
- Urban look
- Sean John
- Preppy styles
- Vintage dressing
- John Galliano for Dior
- Alexander McQueen for Givenchy
- Tom Ford for Gucci
- Christian Louboutin
- Michael Kors
- Zac Posen
- Phillip Lim
- Stella McCartney
- Ed Hardy
- Linda Loudermilk
- Hussein Chalayan

ACTIVITIES

1. Create Fashion Collages

For each era, create a digital (PowerPoint) collage with images that represent the spirit of the time and the fashion of the time. Present the collages. Discuss the images and how they relate to the evolution of fashion fueling the changes for the next era.

2. Visit a Vintage Shop

While at a vintage clothing shop, categorize apparel by era. Investigate which eras are widely represented. Discover what apparel or accessories are prevalent. Create a fashion show highlighting a specific era that is most influencing fashion of today.

3. Watch a Classic Movie

Select a classic movie, maybe from one discussed in this chapter. Watch the movie to identify the spirit and fashions of the time.

4. Create a Historical Fashion Journal

Divide a journal into the eras from the chapter. Place images from each era opposite images of contemporary looks. Discuss which eras most relate to today. Investigate the zeitgeist of the era and consider the similarities and differences compared to today's zeitgeist.

FASHION MOVEMENT

3

Objectives

- Explain the fashion cycle.
- Examine the theories of fashion change.
- Understand direction and speed of change in fashion movement.
- Identify ways fashion moves through society.

How does a fashion forecaster track a trend? How long can a trend last? How do those in fashion know that a trend has reached the point of excess? What changes in fashion movement will occur next? What is a fashion cycle?

Fashion is constantly in motion. This movement occurs in a variety of ways. For fashion forecasters, identifying and understanding the way that fashion moves through society is critical in determining where fashion will go next, which trends will be widely accepted, and what the pace of that adoption will be.

To understand the importance of movement in forecasting, one must recognize that fashion evolves from season to season. Changes in fashion are constant, so to predict future needs and desires of con-

FOWARD THINKER

LILLY BERELOVICH, OWNER, PRESIDENT, AND CHIEF CREATIVE OFFICER OF FASHION SNOOPS

Evolution of Forecasting

The field of forecasting changes moment by moment and must be monitored and watched. In the past, seasonal forecasts were presented by forecasters through books and packets. Today, the speed at which information can be changed and added makes for an on-the-spot, up-to-date report. Sometimes a trend begins to appear but must evolve to become fully immersed into society. This process can take days, weeks, months, or even years depending on the idea. The online services allow the clients to have access to these evolutions from inception to obsolescence.

sumers, forecasters have to consider both the direction of change and speed of change. Retail, design, and trend specialists observe, track, and analyze the changes and look for distinguishable patterns and meaning. Forecasters also use their instincts and experience to sense shifts in preferences and repetition of ideas. However, the tracking of fashion movement today is complicated because some fashions have moved away from the recognizable patterns. Forecasters need to understand multiple theories of how the movement in fashion has occurred in the past to develop new ways to predict fashion transformation. Experience and practice also help forecasters with the complex task of forecasting progress.

To track the movement of fashion, forecasters must be knowledgeable of fashion cycles, fashion adoption theories, pendulum swings, fashion diffusion curves, and the cause of the movements. Fashion can flow, swing, cycle, curve, and repeat.

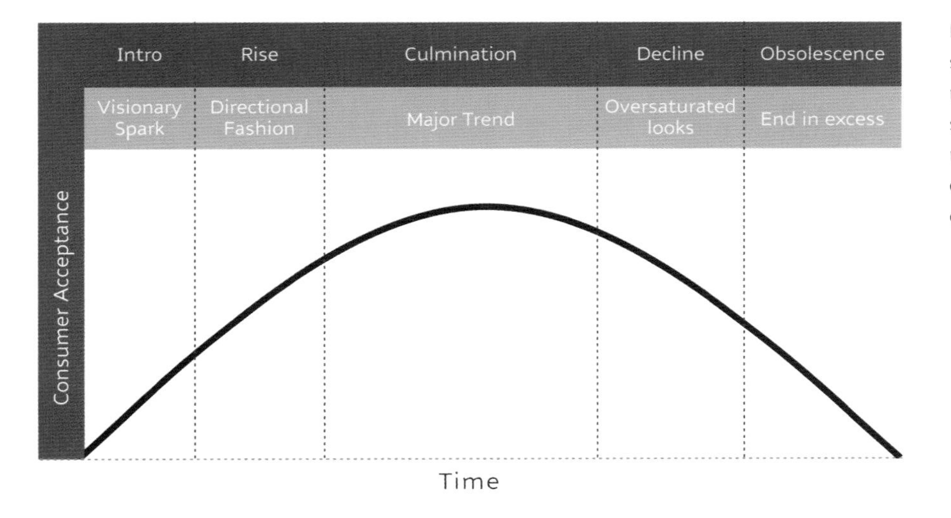

FIGURE 3.1 The life span of a fashion trend moves through five stages: introduction, rise, culmination, decline, and obsolescence.

FASHION CYCLES

Fashion moves in cycles, or it can more accurately be described as moving in waves. Imagine standing at the shoreline watching the waves in the ocean. Some waves are gentle and rhythmic while others are forceful and raging. Some crest at great heights and others form gentle swells. Fashion's cycles can be visualized similarly. A **fashion cycle** is the life span of a style or a trend. The fashion cycle is illustrated with a curve to show the movement that travels through specific stages.

A fashion cycle is the period of time when a fashion trend moves through five stages:

1. Introduction
2. Rise
3. Culmination
4. Decline
5. Obsolescence

For a forecaster, understanding the fashion cycle is needed to help qualify a trend and its movement. Searching for the clues to upcoming trends begins by hunting for emerging information in the introduction stage.

stage 1: introduction

The fashion cycle begins with a visionary spark. The timing of the introduction of a new fashion into the market is crucial—too early and the idea may not be accepted. During this stage, the emerging look begins to move up the curved slope.

- A fashion mood or idea appears on the distant horizon.
- An innovator acknowledges the idea in new fashion.
- Innovators develop concepts containing the seeds for a new fashion direction.
- The style is seen as a possible emerging trend at fashion shows during fashion weeks in major cities, in the media, or on the streets.
- Designers introduce fresh ideas, styles, colors, fabrications, or details.
- Fashion leaders and trendsetters experiment with the new styles.

FRANK BOBER, CEO OF STYLESIGHT

Changes in Timing

The manufacturing process takes less time to produce fashion than ever before, but the decision-making process is what often slows the progress. With validating information available as quickly as a click of a mouse on an Internet-based site, the process can move swiftly.

stage 2: rise

During this stage of the fashion cycle, a new look continues to move on an upward curve. New trends are recognized and copied.

- Styles are accepted by more people because of wider recognition.
- Planning is initiated for mass market.
- Styles are copied by manufacturers, reducing price through fabric and production costs, quality, and limited details.
- Price drops, quantity increases, and sales increase.

stage 3: culmination

The new look reaches the height of the fashion curve and is regarded as a major trend. There is mainstream acceptance of the look, which is recognized as the culmination stage of the fashion cycle.

- Height of popularity and use.
- Accepted throughout multiple markets.
- Mass production with new design details, colors, and innovations.
- Possibility for the style to become a classic.
- Potential for volume sales in mass market.

stage 4: decline

Oversaturated looks are recognized as the beginning of descent on the fashion curve. The principle in effect in this stage is that all fashion ends in excess.

- Repetition of looks.
- Decline of interest and decrease in demand by consumer.
- Market is saturated with fashion product.
- Price resistance by consumer.
- Retailers mark down merchandise and offer price incentives.
- Production slows.

stage 5: obsolescence

The final, obsolescence stage of the fashion cycle is the end of the curve. This stage ends in excess.

- Lack of interest for look and no interest for the product.
- No retail potential at any price.
- Consumer is reluctant to buy.

When beginning a forecast, the forecaster looks for ideas on the horizon or visionary sparks, always looking for new, emerging ideas, concepts, and likely trends. When a new look is noticed, the forecaster observes fashion leaders and trendsetters to monitor the look. By estimating the probable acceptance and calculating the time that the look will take to move to mainstream, a forecaster begins to react to the trends potential identifying the prospective market and consumer. Knowing that all fashion moves forward, forecasters must understand and track the placement of a trend to accurately predict its potential.

THEORIES OF FASHION ADOPTION

Three theories of fashion movement explain the dynamics of fashion adoption. Each theory demonstrates the way that trends are likely to travel in order to aid in more precise predictions of future fashion. Each theory acts as a guide to the process, although each has been disputed or considered outdated based on changing social environments, consumer preferences, and market conditions.

The three theories are:

- Trickle down or downward flow.
- Trickle across or horizontal flow.
- Trickle up or upward flow.

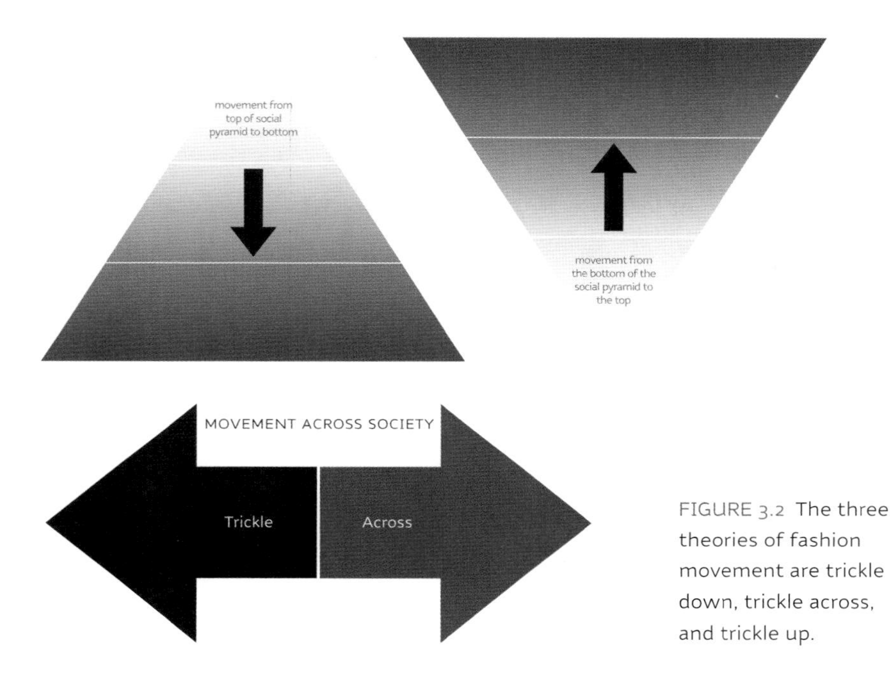

FIGURE 3.2 The three theories of fashion movement are trickle down, trickle across, and trickle up.

trickle down

The **trickle-down theory,** or *downward flow theory*, is the oldest theory of fashion adoption. In this theory, those at the tip of the social pyramid dictate fashion, which is then copied by the people in the lower social levels. People of wealth and prominence adopt a style, and gradually that style spreads downward into the lower classes. Once the lower classes duplicate the look, those in the top classes move on to new styles to maintain social position and power.

This downward movement, fueled by differentiation by the upper classes and imitation by the lower classes, is considered the "engine of fashion" or the force that moves fashion. Those in the elite class strive to be different, but once those in the lower class adopt the same style, the elitists move on to something new. This constant movement fuels the flow.

Fashion analysts both validate and dispute the trickle-down theory today. Some fashions appear to begin in the high-end market and are accepted first by the affluent. Once found and selected by the observant mass-market manufacturer, copies of the styles are made affordable to the mainstream consumer validating the trickle-down theory. Consider the designer handbags that were popular in 2009. Many high-end companies such as Gucci, Louis Vuitton, Chanel, and Fendi made luxury handbags that were trendsetting and extremely expensive. The bags were made of fine materials, oversized, and highly decorated while promoting the logo of the company. Eager manufacturers from the mass market produced lower-priced interpretations or similar copies, making the look available to the mass market. As this occurred, the high-end companies created new styles.

FIGURE 3.3 In trickle-down theory, movement is fueled by imitation, such as high-end designer purses influencing the mass market of lower-priced copies.

LILLY BERELOVICH, OWNER, PRESIDENT, AND CHIEF CREATIVE OFFICER OF FASHION SNOOPS

Pace Changes in Different Market Segments

In some of the lifestyles, the pace of change is slower, and in other lifestyles the speed is greater. For instance, the youth market moves at a much faster pace than the followers of the green movement. The green movement has evolved from the specifics about product to the understanding of cause and effect. People now believe that their own voice can be heard and that each person can truly make a difference, fueling the acceptance of the movement.

Some criticize the trickle-down theory as no longer being relevant because of changes in contemporary social structure and the transformations that have occurred in mass production and mass communication. The elite are no longer the only ones setting fashionable standards or having access to early information and products. The questioning of the relevance of the trickle-down theory is also supported by the speed at which fashion moves through society. Fashion is widely available at multiple price points more quickly than ever before.

trickle across

The second theory is the **trickle-across theory,** or *horizontal flow theory*, of fashion adoption. This theory assumes that fashion moves across groups who are in similar social levels rather than down from a higher level to a lower level. This theory acknowledges that mass production, mass communication, and an emerging middle class contributed to a new dynamic that began after World War II. Different markets and niche markets have requirements for products that are not solely dictated by the upper markets; lifestyle, income level, education, and age are important factors in determining product acceptance.

FIGURE 3.4
In trickle-across theory, similar looks, such as ballerina flats, appear in several markets at the same time.

In the trickle-across theory, the pace of adoption is rapid, almost simultaneous. "Fast fashion" is an example of the way that the trickle-across theory works. Stores such as Zara, Forever 21, and H&M take styles from concept to finished product swiftly, turn over merchandise quickly, and move onto the next items rapidly.

trickle up

The third theory is the **trickle-up theory,** or *upward flow theory*, which is the newest theory of fashion adoption. It is the opposite of the trickle-down theory. According to this theory, fashion adoption begins with the young members of society who often are in the lower-income groups. This theory evolved during the 1960s when the younger generation began to rebel against societal norms and developed looks of their own instead of emulating styles that were considered established or for an older generation. From the miniskirts of the 1960s, to the hippie looks of the 1970s, to the urban styles of today made prominent through hip-hop music, the influences have come from the bottom of the social structure or "the streets." The looks became popular within a specific social group, dictated by age and interests, then eventually moved into mainstream fashion.

The pace of the adoption in the trickle-up theory is difficult to determine. Within the initial group, acceptance is often fast. Depending on the particular look or trend, acceptance in the mainstream can be rapid or it can move slowly. Regardless of pace, this theory is important for the forecaster, designer, manufacturer, and retailer to recognize.

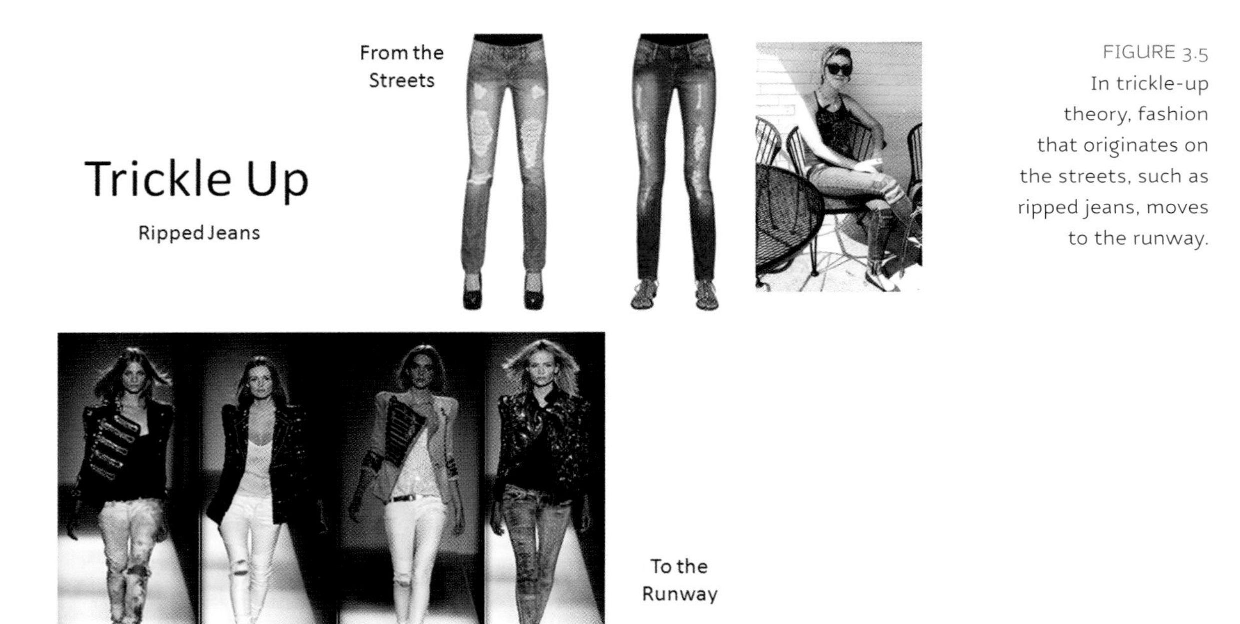

FIGURE 3.5 In trickle-up theory, fashion that originates on the streets, such as ripped jeans, moves to the runway.

PAT TUNSKY, CREATIVE DIRECTOR, DONEGER CREATIVE SERVICES

Colors for Immediate Purchase

I present color palettes to the clients based on specific delivery cycles, when the merchandise will be in the stores available for purchase by the consumer. I encourage the planning to be done based on having apparel in the stores at the time when consumers can wear it immediately. In the past, the timing was based on seasons. For example, initially only spring and fall seasonal palettes were planned. The plans were expanded to Resort, Spring, Summer, Transition to Fall, Fall, and Holiday, allowing for six deliveries per year. Now, stores strive to have merchandise available that is "wear now" or appropriate for immediate consumption with deliveries each month.

All theories of fashion adoption are valid because the flow will continue to move in many directions. The challenge for forecasters is to assimilate the multiple theories and identify what works best for the particular market segment that is being targeted at the time. Shifting between theories or using a combination of theories based on the social, economic, and political climate is necessary to keep tabs on the ever-changing fashion.

PENDULUM SWINGS

The movement of fashion between extremes is referred to as the **pendulum swing**. Changes in style often go from one end of the spectrum to the other. When a trend can go no further, the pendulum begins to swing

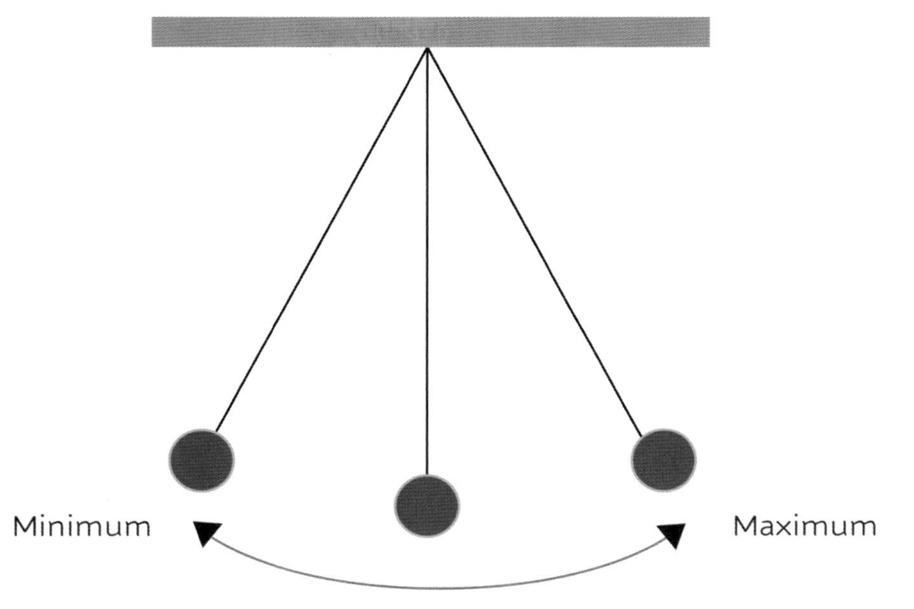

FIGURE 3.6 The fashion pendulum swings from one extreme to the other.

in the opposite direction. The swing can shift slowly or react quickly. A new trend often begins at the exact opposite of an existing trend.

For instance, jeans were traditionally worn at or near the natural waistline. In time, the rise of the jeans started to go lower. Eventually the rise got so low, to a point where jeans could not go any lower, and the pendulum shifted to the opposite extreme, bringing the rise up where the new trend of "high waist" pants emerged. This evolution took more than a decade. In addition, some consumers will continue to wear low-rise jeans even when the look is no longer considered fashionable. Sometimes the swings of the pendulum occur in a season, or the swing can take years.

FASHION CURVES

In tracking fashion movement or fashion curves, it is important to determine the possible pace of a trend and the scope of its impact. Fast fashion or fads change quickly, whereas time is needed for fashion to be adopted as a classic.

fad

A look that swiftly becomes popular, is widely accepted, and then rapidly disappears is called a **fad**. Usually a fad has a prevalent feature or detail that makes it popular. The look seems to appear everywhere in a short time especially in the lower-priced market. Fads often appear in the accessory market; for instance, oversized plastic watches followed the fad of extremely embellished ones. Forecasters must spot a fad at the beginning of the fashion cycle and report it immediately in order to capitalize on the trend.

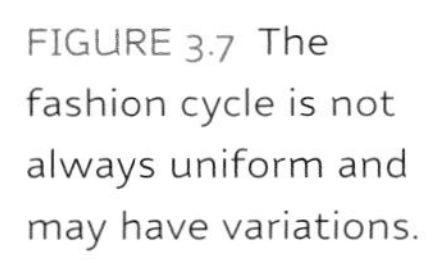
FIGURE 3.7 The fashion cycle is not always uniform and may have variations.

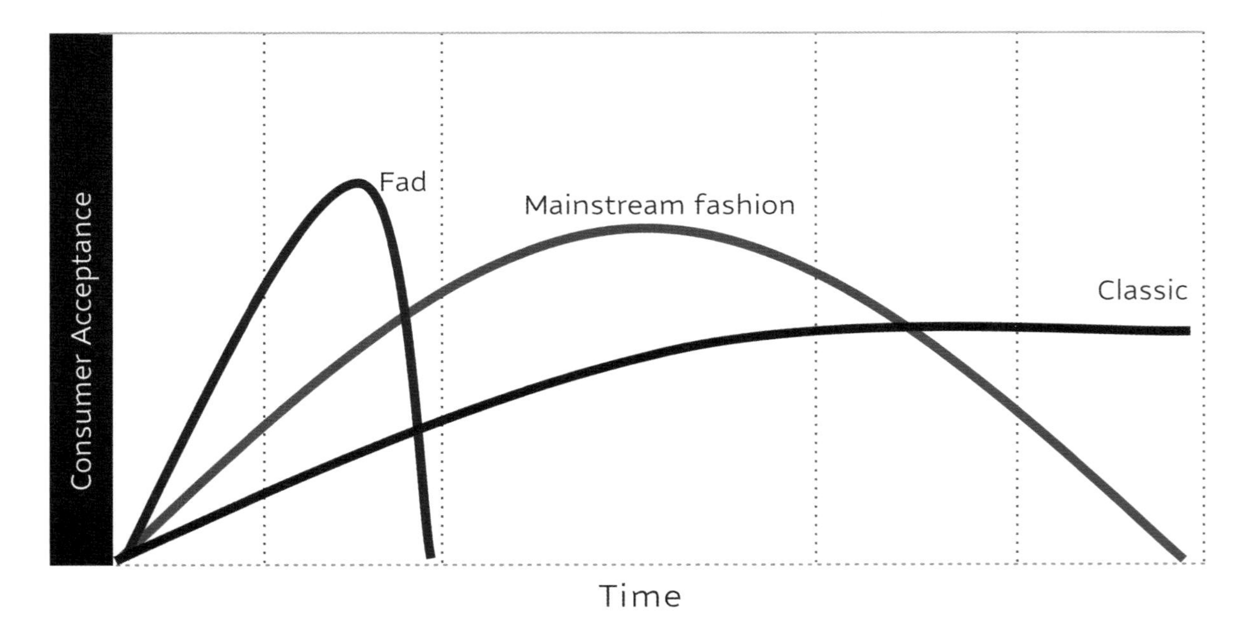

FIGURE 3.8 The quick acceptance of oversized plastic watches was a fad of 2011.

ADAM YANKAUSKAS, DESIGN DIRECTOR AT MAGGY LONDON

Timing of a Trend

Placing new trends into a collection requires awareness of proper timing. For instance, draped dresses appeared throughout the designer collection last year and our designers created their interpretations of the trend. When the buyers first saw the draped dresses, they were reluctant to buy them. In time, the buyers saw similar styles retailing in the designer and bridge markets, saw the trend in other showrooms, and eventually were ready to write orders. Timing is everything, but if I see a major trend, I don't give up. Several seasons ago, brocade fabrics were prevalent at Première Vision in Paris. We added these ornate fabrics to the collection, and it took a few seasons before our customers were ready for the look.

FIGURE 3.9 The "little black dress" is considered a classic in fashion.

classic

A look that remains in fashion for a long time is a **classic**. A classic look is described as a simple design that satisfies basic needs. A classic silhouette is timeless, allowing it to fit into most current themes. For instance, the little black dress is considered a classic fashion. Women with different body types, personalities, and style preferences consider a little black dress as a "must" in their wardrobes. For men, a single-breasted blazer in a basic color such as navy, brown, or black is considered a classic. Classic styles do not have exaggerated details or trims, and that helps them to remain timeless. A classic style moves into the culmination stage of the fashion cycle and continues without declining to obsolescence.

SPEED OF FASHION CHANGE

During the introduction and rise stages of the fashion cycle, the speed is usually faster because consumers desire change. During the middle stages, the consumer is less likely to be interested in change and the adoption process slows. In the obsolescence stage, the fashion style ends due to the lack of interest from the consumer.

The speed of fashion has become increasingly faster through instant access to information through technology and quick production techniques. For a manufacturer, crucial decisions must be made in a timely manner about what to design, manufacture, and promote so that the looks are desired at the correct moment for the consumer.

FORECASTING THE MOVEMENT OF FASHION

For a forecaster, identifying what emerging fashion trends are, estimating the volume and pace of acceptance, and observing the direction of the movement must be determined to begin the forecasting process. Data is collected from manufacturers, merchants, and consumers. Hard facts are collected from a variety of places including:

- News: financial, international, popular culture, and technology.
- Industry coverage: best-selling items, new markets, trade show developments, and retail data.
- Noteworthy shifts: new fashion leaders, products, places, events, technology, and Web sites and blogs.
- Consumers: movements on the streets, new influences, new attitudes, and looks.

DAVID WOLFE, CREATIVE DIRECTOR, DONEGER CREATIVE SERVICES

Pace of Fashion

While we read reports about how fast fashion is now moving, I see fashion moving so slowly that it has almost stopped. I compare the pace to a horse race where the fastest horse has raced around the track so quickly that now it has caught up to the slowest horse and is now behind the pack. In this scenario, all fashion is "in": no leaders, no followers.

The forecasters interpret the research data for the forecast and use their own judgment to identify trends and signals. Forecasters review fashion cycles, theories, and swings to determine if the changes are following an existing model or a combination of patterns.

Forecasters determine what the changes are and what is fueling the movement. Forecasters investigate and analyze the data and use their educated opinion to consider why and how emerging trends or movements will manifest. They also determine who the most likely consumers may be and the tempo at which the concepts may be adopted.

Finally, forecasters make a prediction of the possible outcomes. The direction or trajectory of the movement may have several outcomes, including short-term or long-term possibilities. The further in the future that the forecaster projects, the greater the margin for error becomes as the scope of the forecast widens. With knowledge of fashion principles and their fashion expertise, the forecasters communicate their prediction.

SUMMARY

Fashion movement, with its cycles, swings, and curves, can follow several courses and move at varying paces. Fashion forecasters must understand the theories behind this movement, and their success depends on their ability to observe, analyze, and predict the changes and speed of movement with considerable accuracy and use the findings to plan where fashion will go next.

KEY TERMS

- Fashion cycle
- Trickle-down theory
- Trickle-across theory
- Trickle-up theory
- Pendulum swing
- Fad
- Classic

ACTIVITIES

1. Identify a Fashion Look for Each of the Theories of Fashion Movement

Collect images to illustrate the three theories of fashion adoption—trickle-down theory, trickle-across theory, and trickle-up theory—using photos from today's fashion magazines or from online sources. Create a PowerPoint presentation to show the concepts.

2. Monitor a Blog

Find a fashion blog through the Internet that includes information about a new fashion trend. Monitor the trend from the blog. Report the trend's movement.

3. Track a Look from Visionary Spark to Obsolescence

Identify a look that is near the end of the fashion cycle. Research when the look first appeared. Record the time lapse from the beginning of the cycle to the end.

SOCIAL AND CULTURAL INFLUENCES

4

Objectives

- Develop an understanding of long-term forecasting.
- Identify demographic, economic, political, social, psychological, environmental, and cultural influences on fashion as keys to forecasting.
- Develop an understanding about lifestyle influences on fashion.

How do forecasters predict what will happen two or more years into the future? What are the signals that help them recognize the changes in consumer desires? How do forecasters use cultural relevance as a significant force for success in forecasting? How do forecasters interpret this information into a long-term forecast?

LONG-TERM FORECASTING

Fashion forecasters project long-term social and cultural shifts, population trends, technological advances, demographic movement, and developments in consumer behavior in long-term forecasting or **future studies**. For this type of forecasting, fashion professionals observe the horizon to identify early signs of change. Long-term forecasts extend at least two years in advance or even decades ahead. Forecasters must track the forces that alter society. They monitor the pulse of culture to identify the shifts that occur in society by targeting the wants, needs, and attitudes of consumers to understand what is fueling any movement.

Forecasters seek to understand and identify patterns of the past and present to determine what is likely to happen in the future. Forecasters identify cultural trends that will either continue, change, or yield to what is new or upcoming. They study and analyze the sources, pattern, consistency, and basis of change in the effort to plan possibilities for the future. These futurists strive to identify emerging movements or forces locally as well as globally for their possible implementation in the fashion spectrum.

Three facets to future studies are to:

- Examine what is not only possible but also probable, preferable, or "wild card" futures.
- Attempt to gain holistic or systematic views based on insights from a range of different disciplines.
- Challenge different points of view about the future, whether they are dominant or contending ideas.

TARGET AUDIENCE AND CONSUMER SEGMENTATION

The first question that forecasters must ask is, "Who is the customer?" Identifying the **target audience** or the segment of the population who may adopt new products and ideas at a specific time in the future is crucial in forecasting the evolution of fashion. Particular customers who share lifestyles, preferences, and desires must be identified and targeted. Groups of consumers who share similar demographic, economic, sociological, and psychological characteristics are identified as a **consumer segment.** Once a group of prospective customers is identified as the target market, businesses can plan their products to fill these customers' wants and needs. Questions can be asked and data collected to determine what these customers bought in the past and are likely to buy in the future. Along with other information, the forecaster needs to know the following:

- How many customers are there?
- Where do they live?
- How old are they?
- How much will they spend?
- Why do they buy?

FRANK BOBER, CEO OF STYLESIGHT

Attitudes of Consumers Influence Fashion

The information that we present as forecasters also includes attitudes about anything that is not fashion that undoubtedly influences fashion. For example, lifestyle trends, celebrity looks, vintage items, and images that inspire may not be directly related to a forecast but influence the current mood of the moment.

LILLY BERELOVICH, OWNER, PRESIDENT, AND CHIEF CREATIVE OFFICER OF FASHION SNOOPS

Lifestyle Influences on Fashion

Instead of a particular trend, I focus on lifestyle. If a designer/manufacturer can identify lifestyle currents, then all of the fashion that surrounds a particular lifestyle makes sense and can be adopted and predicted. Through lifestyles, the job of identifying specific trends becomes more manageable. By breaking the fashion structure into lifestyle instead of seasons, information is sorted into different categories.

DEMOGRAPHICS, GEOGRAPHICS, PSYCHOGRAPHICS, AND POPULATION

In order to answer the questions above, forecasters research certain characteristics or **demographics** of their customers. Demographic data includes age, sex, income, marital status, family size, education, religion, race, and nationality. Demographic studies can also divide a large population into smaller segments that can be analyzed separately.

The **geographic studies** focus on where people live, including information about which country, state, city, and the population in each area where the target customers are. Attitudes and lifestyles change depending on location. People who are in metropolitan areas are often more business savvy, therefore their choices in clothing are often more professional and refined. In country or rural settings, casual attire is most predominant.

The studies also take into consideration the climate that can influence the lifestyle of a region. Imagine the types of apparel and acces-

FIGURE 4.1 Teens use social networking to share information about prom dress selection.

LORI HOLLIDAY BANKS, DIRECTOR OF RESEARCH AND ANALYTICS, TOBE REPORT, A DIVISION OF THE DONEGER GROUP

Consumers Set the Tone

Great societal changes are impacting the retailer. The consumer demographic is changing greatly as the population grows. Emerging markets in groups with specific age mixes—such as the Generation Y consumers, the "tweens" and the "moms"—will impact the retailer. For instance, the "tweens" have needs unlike any other demographic. This demographic group shops differently than past generations, relies on new technology for communication, views media differently than previous generations. Many "tweens" use social networking sites when considering retail purchases. For instance, high school girls often post information about the prom dresses that they are purchasing so that their friends and classmates don't end up wearing the same dress.

sories that one would pack for favorite vacation hot spots. For a vacation in Miami, a bright halter bikini that delivers a tropical punch with a multicolored dress, metallic platform sandals, and plenty of gold bangles makes for a day-into-evening look. In Santa Fe, the desert heat calls for a light cotton loose-fitting top embellished with turquoise and stones to coordinate with earth-toned linen capri pants. A western style raffia hat and oversized fringed bag would complete the look. While in Seattle, an outfit is needed that can change as often as the weather. When the sun is out, distressed denim shorts with a boho-chic peasant top and high wedge shoes would work, but as the clouds roll in, a Burberry raincoat and printed rubber boots would keep one chic and dry. For visiting Nantucket Island in Massachusetts, the suitcase would be packed with clothing that could be layered for a whale watching or lighthouse tour, including a nautical-inspired jacket and navy striped T-shirt. Hints of lobster red, traditional khaki, and white accents keep the look clean and classic. It could incorporate an oversized canvas tote or classic docksider boating shoes.

Cities around the globe have also established their own reputations of style. New York is sophisticated, and urban colors such as gray and black often predominate. Los Angeles is known for a more laid-back look with jeans, T-shirts, and surfer-inspired prints and accessories. Paris is recognized for ultimate glamour and chic finery. In London, edgy fashions appear with a spirit of modern youth that contrasts the look of the established conservative regal royals. Milan is known for its rich fabrics and refined leathers that are noticeable in the finely tailored sportswear, shoes, and handbags. Tokyo is notorious for the outrageous outfits that are paraded through the shopping meccas by the teen guys and girls. Minimalism and simple designs are seen in Copenhagen. In New Delhi, traditional saris with embroidery and

FIGURE 4.2 Distinctive looks can be seen in Nantucket, Nairobi, Paris, and Tokyo.

embellishment are fused with Western styling to create a modern Indian look. In Rio de Janeiro, spicy Latin-inspired ruffles and vibrant patterns and colors reflect the year-round spirit of Carnival. Dynamic fashions from Nairobi are infused with color and patterns that reflect African cultures and values. Most cities and regions throughout the globe have style characteristics that make fashions from these areas unique. Through increasing globalization, however, influences from different cultures and geographic locations are assimilating into a new spirit of multicultural fashion.

FOWARD THINKER

PAT TUNSKY, CREATIVE DIRECTOR, DONEGER CREATIVE SERVICES

Worldwide Fashion Market

American retailers have a reputation of being successful and profitable throughout the world. Many international firms from Mexico, Canada, South and Central America, South Africa, Australia, and South Korea look to the U.S. for marketing direction. China is not only producing fashion for the world, they are building their own industry. At this time, in relation to forecasting, China is an upcoming market.

Psychographics are the studies that classify groups according to their attitudes, tastes, values, and fears and are used to identify trends through the research. Individual profiles of potential consumers are identified and tracked to develop a better understanding of their attitudes about image and brands. Behavior of particular consumers or groups can offer clues to the forecaster about why certain products are purchased and why others are not. Once these reasons can be identified, products can be customized to fill their specific requirements and needs. Researchers often survey opinions of consumers in an attempt to better understand and fulfill their desires.

Population is the total number of people inhabiting an area. A forecaster must consider the size of the population, its rate of growth, and the age of the people to project the future demand. The population of an area can also be divided into smaller segments in order to research different style tribes.

SOCIOLOGICAL INFLUENCES

Changes in fashion are directly related to variations in lifestyle and attitudes of customers according to the times. The zeitgeist, or spirit of the time, shifts as consumers' needs and preferences change. Some of the social factors influencing today's changes include:

- Changes in time—both leisure time and lack of time.
- Adoption of casual and simplified lifestyles.
- Greater celebrity influences.
- Changing status of women.
- Increasing methods of communication.
- Greater accessibility to transportation.
- Increasing emphasis on solutions often inspired by creativity.
- Shifting ethnic and racial populations.
- New educational opportunities.

FRANK BOBER, CEO OF STYLESIGHT

Global Fashion

To follow fashion in this new era, one must acknowledge the true size of the market. Information is collected and distributed to all corners of the globe. Many emerging markets at different stages of business development encapsulate the growing fashion world.

LORI HOLLIDAY BANKS, DIRECTOR OF RESEARCH AND ANALYTICS, TOBE REPORT, A DIVISION OF THE DONEGER GROUP

Impact of Informal Business Attitude

Consider the impact that "business casual" had on the fashion landscape. Not only were men not wearing suits to work or women wearing fewer dresses, the consumer's desires changed. Along with these changes came new needs for alternative color palettes, fabrications, and shapes. In addition, attitudes toward professionalism changed. A more relaxed, informal business manner prevailed for over a decade.

PSYCHOLOGICAL INFLUENCES

People choose to wear fashionable apparel for a variety of reasons, including curiosity, a relief from boredom, a reaction to convention, the need for confidence, or the desire for belonging. People participate in the very experience of fashion to "find themselves" and name their place in society. Clothes that are bought and worn are more than just the product or the purchase because fashion is more than just the clothes.

The act of wearing a garment establishes a "moment" or history in the person's life. In modern fashion and design, the object creates an emotional aura. Whether the imprint of clothes on people is loud and obvious or subtle and masked, the moment's emotions have been captured.

In fashion, a person can explore a sense of adventure. Through this journey, a person can escape his or her everyday life and transform his or her reality, experiencing the force of fashion. A designer's or artist's creation can often launch this adventure. It permits order in a disorderly world and allows room for fantasy. Using fashion as a tool, a person can sense the power of transformation as boundaries become bendable. Through awareness, the force of fashion creates an impression in the heart and soul that translates to meaning and power.

LILLY BERELOVICH, OWNER, PRESIDENT, AND CHIEF CREATIVE OFFICER OF FASHION SNOOPS

Global World

With the global access that the citizens of the world have, a breaking down of barriers that make different products exclusive to few is ending. Using Zara or H&M as examples, I see ways for great economic successes in the global world. I was recently approached by many manufacturers from China and other countries that produced fashion for the U.S. who are trying to break into the U.S. market. My suggestion to them is to figure out what it is that they do best—fabric, style, or manufacturing capabilities—and start there, reinforce what they do best.

Fashion forecasters project long-term changes by monitoring changes that are occurring globally in economics, politics, science and technology, and the environment. These forces have significant impact on society. Forecasters study the changes in culture to identify what is causing movement.

GLOBAL ECONOMICS

Global economics play a crucial role in the shaping of today's fashion industry. Forecasters must be aware of the ever-changing economic conditions throughout the world to be able to predict the future accurately. From new markets and increasing trade to a higher standard of living for millions of people, the potential for new consumers is rapidly growing.

In addition, global manufacturing has created worldwide competition. Competitors are always looking for ways to make things faster, cheaper, and better. This competition is advantageous for consumers because it gives them more choices. Forecasters must recognize that globalization has significantly changed the landscape of the fashion world and the changes will continue with new, emerging economies. For instance, as

FIGURE 4.3 Shanghai, China, offers new shopping locations to satisfy the eager consumers.

the manufacturing sector developed in China, millions of people moved from agricultural work in rural areas to manufacturing jobs in cities. Their rising personal incomes from wages, salaries, and investments gave them higher purchasing power and the ability to become modern consumers. With the increase of emerging markets, new customers can be identified and serviced.

FOWARD THINKER

LORI HOLLIDAY BANKS, DIRECTOR OF RESEARCH AND ANALYTICS, TOBE REPORT, A DIVISION OF THE DONEGER GROUP

Global Consumer Changes

With the increase of the global consumer and the changes in worldwide landscape, the growth factor in emerging economies plays a significant role in retailers' perspective. China has enormous retail potential, Japan has a more youth-inspired consumer, and the Scandinavian countries are influential with new design aesthetics. These factors impact the ever-changing fashion needs.

POLITICS

Changes in politics also can influence fashion. Political events, such as elections or leadership shifts, often affect global trade and alliances. The 2008 presidential election in the United States resulted in great societal shifts. The opposing candidates had different societal appeals: one candidate was more conservative and established and the other more liberal and modern. When the American people elected Barack Obama, his spirit of change was felt throughout the world. Not only was his collective consciousness influential and powerful, his modern attitudes appealed to many. In 2009, the new first lady, Michelle Obama, brought a style that was considered innovative, functional, yet fashionable. Her contemporary style is classic and affordable and parallels modern American culture. From changes in regimes to changes in trade alliances, political shifts can greatly influence fashion trends.

FIGURE 4.4 Michelle Obama's contemporary sense of style parallels modern American culture. She recognizes the value of beautiful looks at affordable prices.

SCIENCE AND TECHNOLOGY

Forecasters must understand the force of science and technology in the current era. Like the impact of the Industrial Revolution in the nineteenth century, the future direction of fashion will be profoundly influenced by new technologies that alter the way that members of society fulfill their wants and desires. From new concepts of fashionable technology to alternative methods of manufacturing, the meaning and purpose of fashion is expanding. Garments are designed not only for their aesthetic qualities but also for function and their capacity to perform in alternative ways. New products are being created using new fibers, such as nanotechnology and microfibers, embedded with sensors, or embellished with lights designed to generate power.

FIGURE 4.5
Advances in technology appear in illuminated garments, such as this gown worn by singer Katy Perry to the Metropolitan Museum of Art's 2010 Costume Institute Gala.

In addition, technology affects the ways in which fashion is marketed and distributed throughout the world. The shopping experience is changing as the retail landscape is being altered. Instead of traditional stores, Internet marketing and virtual dressing rooms and customization capabilities are new realities in advancing fashion.

Melissa Lavigne from The Intelligence Group, a research consultant firm, believes that to reach the "tweens" and Generation Y consumers, fashion firms must be more progressive in creating a diverse interactive Internet fashion strategy. Firms need to experiment with social media sites, such as Facebook or YouTube, to reach this youthful group. Lavigne sees success for firms that allow groups like this to be part of their creative fashion process. Instant sales data, inventory control updates, and consumer profiles aid retailers in managing their businesses and predicting future opportunities. With this new technology, goods can be distributed faster and with more proficiency.

Fashion forecasting services are using the newest technology to collect and distribute up-to-date information, making it easier for designers, manufacturers, and retailers to access specific information for their businesses.

FOWARD THINKER

DAVID WOLFE, CREATIVE DIRECTOR, DONEGER CREATIVE SERVICES

Technology

Technology in fashion is like a double-edged sword. With the streaming of fashion shows, immediate Internet access, and the overload of information, consumers don't know what to do with all of the data. The consumer needs to have the information about fashion translated to their level. What will change this trend is the return to thinking with the brain and heightened consciousness using technology as a tool instead of as a creative substitute.

FRANK BOBER, CEO OF STYLESIGHT

Online Forecasting Philosophy

When working to change the world of fashion forecasting, I imagined a plain white board with no boundaries. I filled the vacant space with all of the needs of the fast-moving fashion world. Once the needs were identified, I created a technology-based forecasting hub to house information and create a site that would inspire. I think of an online fashion service like a buffet where each person who visits the site has the opportunity to scan the multitudes of choices and then select only what fits their own needs and tastes. By having fast response from the clients, I modernized the site by adding new features, like a recently launched area where storyboards can be created, saved, and shared.

ENVIRONMENTAL INFLUENCES

Forecasters monitor the changes in society's attitudes about the environment, social responsibility, and the impact of fashion on the ecosystem. With conscious dressing, the consumer seeks a fragile balance between the fulfillment of wearing new apparel, the preservation of the environment, and conscientious social values.

sustainability

Fashion and sustainability are two seemingly contradictory concepts because fashion is always evolving and changing while sustainability is centered on preservation. The "Brundtland Report" from the World Commission on Development and Environment defines **sustainable development** as "development that meets the needs of the present without compromising the ability of future generations to meet their own needs." The UN World Summit Report expresses that any action plan must take into consideration the social, economic, and environmental factors that work together to drive solutions, people, processes, and environment.

Since fashion is a nonverbal response to what is occurring in the world, it offers a tangible tool for communicating new ideas and concepts. Sustainable consciousness allows fashion solutions to be innovated while preserving the environment, establishing a healthier economy, and solving social inequalities. By rethinking the manufacturing process and generating new ideas, fashion can be produced with a sense of ethics, using organic or renewable resources and employing humane work conditions that sustain the environment. The people who design, produce, sell, purchase, and discard clothing are all part of this global environmental consciousness.

FIGURE 4.6 The fashion industry has embraced a sustainability consciousness with environmentally friendly practices to make beautiful clothing and products while supporting ethical principles.

eco-friendly trends

From organic foods to textiles, modern society has been embracing environmentally safe products and goods. International interest and desire for environmental improvements has changed production methods, packaging, transportation, and demand in many industries, including fashion. Julie Gilhart from Barneys New York writes in *FutureFashion White Papers*, "The last ten years of fashion have been propelled and inspired by highly marketed, celebrity-driven luxury brands. This trend is beginning to feel outdated. The consumer is developing a taste for great product with ethical principles. Many people want to contribute to solving the global crisis that is occurring to our environment, but feel paralyzed as to what they can do. By applying their values to the products that they purchase, they feel empowered to contribute."

Reincarnating clothing and Recycling memories...

by Chelsea Rousso

FIGURE 4.7 Using recycled materials, new products can be made not only to be "green" but also to preserve one's personal memories.

waste management

From preconsumer waste to postconsumer waste, recycling trends have been emerging throughout multiple industries. Increased interest in reselling existing products through vintage stores, garage sales, recycling firms, or eBay has spawned new consumer interest. Some companies specialize in exporting items to developing countries while others have found niches in repurposing items into new innovations. Recycling existing fashion items into new usable forms encourages people to explore the relationship that they have with their clothing and the responsibility that they hold when they want to discard the items.

A sustainability process not only aids in the development of new products using recyclable components but provides individuals with an opportunity to consider their responsibility for the product throughout its entire life cycle. Society is developing alternative attitudes toward sustainability by recognizing the crisis of excessive consumption and striving to minimize damage to the environment due to ever-changing fashions.

UNEXPECTED EVENTS

Regardless of all of the research and planning that forecasters can do, unpredictable events occur that disrupt the natural evolution of trends. Wars; natural disasters such as earthquakes, fires, or floods; the death of a well-known person; and financial crises, political upheavals, and terrorism are uncontrollable aspects of the world that forecasters cannot anticipate. These events abruptly change the movement of fashion, sometimes temporarily but often with long-lasting impact. For instance, during the recession of 2008–2010, many jobs were lost and budgets were limited. Spending habits shifted and many people began to buy less new products and instead shopped in used or vintage stores. People began to reassess their priorities, aspirations, and needs.

Possibly the most profound disruption of fashion came from the terrorist attacks on September 11, 2001, in New York and Washington, D.C. The effects from this event not only changed consumers' habits at the time but also substantially altered business practices. Consumers stopped spending, businesses struggled to survive, and many companies were forced to close. Consumers reevaluated their attitudes and made changes.

Whether planned or unpredicted, profound events create a reaction that can be felt throughout all aspects of business. Fashion forecasters must react to these unforeseen events and acknowledge the changing direction and new path.

RESEARCH CONSULTANTS

Independent market consultancy firms study trends and supply recommendations and solutions about the future to the forecaster or client. The firms conduct strategic research to identify emerging movements, obtaining relevant data for analysis. The consultants aim to explain how society is shaped by cultural, social, political, economic, and environmental forces and how these forces can influence future developments. The insights are the starting points used to recognize why consumers behave the way that they do. The consultants offer informed recommendations that are considered necessary to make successful informed decisions. Several firms include:

- Future Foundation. *Web site*: www.futurefoundation.net
- Faith Popcorn's BrainReserve. *Web site*: www.faithpopcorn.com
- The Intelligence Group. *Web site*: www.intelg.com

COLLECTING AND EDITING INFORMATION ABOUT CULTURAL INFLUENCES

Once the data is gathered and the observations have been recorded, the forecaster begins to edit the information. The forecaster looks for clues and patterns. Through media scanning, or organizing signals and information from multiple media sources into categories, similar ideas start to repeat themselves and form themes. By identifying the strength of a theme, forecasters can identify the importance of the idea or potential movement. Several ideas may connect together to create a more significant overreaching theme.

For example, the major concept of escapism can be expressed through multiple smaller ideas. When the minor ideas are identified, they may not appear to be interrelated but when combined, they support a major theme. Consultants may recognize individual ideas such as:

- Desiring to reconnect with holistic roots.
- Redefining goals in search for a simpler life.
- Wanting extreme vacations to exotic locations.
- Indulging in excessive partying and libations.
- Desiring tranquility through pampering and spa treatments.

Collectively, these individual ideas combine to express a more significant theme of escapism. It is the job of fashion consultants to understand how these individual ideas and major themes relate to fashion.

INTERPRETING AND ANALYZING INFORMATION FOR A LONG-TERM FORECAST

The forecaster identifies forces of change and repetitions of ideas and then begins to interpret and analyze the information. In addition to relying on research consultants, forecasters must identify the direction that society is moving in and at what rate. Forecasters use the collected information to generate new ideas, advanced strategies, and plans of action for the future.

Creating scenarios, or summaries of possible future predictions, provides a plan for moving the information into the future. While considering multiple outcomes, forecasters may explore "best case" scenarios as well as "worst case" ones because not all predictions have a positive result. Writing and surveying the scenarios can lead to decision making that will be most pragmatic for the future.

FIGURE 4.8
Forecasters look for the interrelationships of individual ideas and desires with larger movements or themes, such as how fashion may be a part of an individual's search for escapism, entertainment, or even a new approach to life.

Current business practices must be identified, plans developed for repositioning of products, and innovation for new products must begin. The forecaster studies the relationship between fashion and consumer culture and offers design and lifestyle predictions and ways that the new ideas may relate to daily life.

While preparing a forecast, the forecaster strives to deliver information that will have universal appeal, although some forecasts are more appropriate for specific target markets. They identify the type of consumer and the possible scope of acceptance. The conclusions are used to shape the forecast.

When presenting the forecast, the forecaster identifies if a particular theme may have greater impact in a specific market and a lesser impact in another. Depending on the purpose of the research or the particular client, forecasters can present the collected and analyzed data through meetings, workshops, seminars, newsletters, or models. Visualizations, photo collages, and mood boards aid clients in sensing futuristic and conceptual ideas.

SUMMARY

Forecasters use long-term forecasting to identify cultural trends that will affect society in the future. They identify the segments of the population who are most likely to desire specific products and services. Forecasters monitor the pulse of culture to look for clues in the changes that occur in society throughout the years by targeting the aspirations, attitudes, and needs of consumers to understand what is currently occurring and prepare for what is to come. Information is collected, analyzed, and used to plan strategies. Multiple scenarios are explored and used to predict trends that will rise in the upcoming two years or more.

KEY TERMS

- Target audience
- Consumer segment
- Demographics
- Geographic studies
- Psychographics
- Population
- Sustainable development

ACTIVITIES

1. Geographic Wardrobe

Select a geographic location. Plan a weekend wardrobe that would be suitable in that location. Collect an image of each item. Create a collage. Show the collage to others and ask them to identify the location where the wardrobe would be best suited.

2. Identify a Target Market for a New Trend

Name a new trend. Predict the target market for the trend. Include demographic, economic, sociological, and psychological characteristics. Predict the pace and scope of the trend.

3. Memory Apparel

Find item of apparel in your own wardrobe that holds significant memories. Describe the emotions and feelings associated with the item. Write a story describing the item and what makes it memorable.

MARKET AND SALES RESEARCH FOR FORECASTING 5

Objectives

- Understand the relationship between sales and forecasting.
- Examine marketing research and analysis.
- Explore methods of in-house research.
- Discuss importance of the Internet in data collecting.
- Recognize the growing significance of social media and viral marketing.

How do forecasters gather sales information and use it in shaping their predictions? How can information about what has sold in the past be used to anticipate what trends will be desired in the future? Where do forecasters look for sales and marketing information?

Forecasters today depend on a wealth of information to predict future fashion successfully. Combined with artistic and inspirational senses, forecasters use solid, hard facts to research and develop their predictions. Diverse sources of information are accessible, including marketing statistics and sales records. By knowing how to use the technological advances of the information age, forecasters collect and interpret sales and marketing data to help shape their forecasts. Trade organizations, market research firms, and government agencies study and report information related to marketing and sales. In-house studies by independent companies are conducted, and the Internet is monitored.

RETAIL TRADE ASSOCIATIONS, FEDERATIONS, AND ORGANIZATIONS

Many retail trade associations, federations, and organizations conduct extensive research on retailing. They track consumer statistics and sales data from department stores, specialty stores, catalog companies, and Internet marketers that can be used by designers, manufacturers, retailers, and forecasters. These groups offer resources promoting the retail industry. Some focus on international trade and retail trend forecasting.

With increasing globalization, people, businesses, and countries have become progressively more connected. This interconnection includes many groups and cultures that influence the design, manufacturing, and merchandising of fashionable goods and products. The World Trade Organization (WTO) is an organization of more than 150 countries that deals with international or global trade rules among nations. The mission of the WTO is to ensure the free and smooth flow of trade between countries. In addition, the WTO measures the levels of economic development and activity, monitors production, and assesses the value of production from country to country. *Web site*: www.wto.org.

For forecasters, understanding the demands of the global market is essential for success for today's businesses. From emerging economies to different standards of living, forecasters follow global trends to provide a framework for analyzing the needs of the larger consumer base that exists beyond the borders of the United States. This large consumer base is often needed to generate a profit. Forecasters must pay close attention to the complex and changing world markets, taking into consideration not only international political and governmental perspectives but cultural, social, and environmental differences as well. As the global market continues to expand, new consumers desire products not only to satisfy their needs but also to fulfill their desires.

Through newsletters, publications, seminars, webinars, and private meetings, retail trade groups offer guidance to their clients and offer solutions for retailing challenges. Information about how much product has sold, at what price, and at what pace is valuable in forecasting the future. Two major retail trade groups are:

FIGURE 5.1 The National Retail Federation's Web site keeps retailers informed.

- The **National Retail Federation** is one of the largest retailing organizations. Its mission is to help retailers in every segment of their business while protecting their clients' interests. This organization conducts studies on worldwide retail data and provides the information to its members. *Web site*: www.nrf.com.

FOWARD THINKER

SCOTT MARKERT, SALES MANAGER FOR LONDON TIMES

Changing Retail Environment

The biggest change that I have seen in fashion marketing is the reduction of small stores and boutiques and the consolidation of department stores. Now there are fewer stores to sell to in the U.S. The growth is occurring through global expansion and the desire of the international consumer to buy fashion from the West.

FIGURE 5.2 The Fashion Group International's Web site provides up-to-the-minute fashion direction.

- The **Fashion Group International** is a professional organization in the fashion industry that includes members focusing on apparel, home, and beauty markets. The organization provides insights that influence fashion direction for the marketplace, including lifestyle shifts, contemporary issues, and global trends. *Web site*: www.fgi.org.

GOVERNMENT ORGANIZATIONS

Agencies of the U.S. federal government collect data and provide statistics that can be useful for fashion forecasting, including studies on population, retail sales, manufacturing data, and domestic and international trade data. Key economic indicators are provided on a regular basis by the U.S. Department of Commerce and the U.S. Census Bureau. *Web sites*: www.commerce.gov; www.economicindicators.gov.

FIGURE 5.3 Buyers, manufacturers, and designers share information to make educated choices.

IN-HOUSE RESEARCH

data sharing

Many different methods are used to conduct in-house research. Fashion retailers and manufacturers often conduct their own in-house research. **Data sharing** between the designers, manufacturers, retail management, and buyers that is specific to their products is one method.

FOWARD THINKER

DAVID WOLFE, CREATIVE DIRECTOR, DONEGER CREATIVE SERVICES

Sharing Data (Retailer to Forecaster)

By working so closely with retailers, manufacturers, and style-related businesses, I have a considerable edge on other forecasters. The exposure I have reveals the big picture, including how much merchandise is sold at full price, at what pace, and in what quantities. The key is to understand the consumer, data, and timing of fashion simultaneously.

FIGURE 5.4
Retailers collect sales data to be aware of the dynamics of the market.

sales strategy

The retailer collects specific information about a manufacturer's product and tracks performance. An in-house expert or team of experts can track a wealth of data, such as when the merchandise sold, how many pieces were sold, what sizes sold best, what colors sold first, what incentives were offered, and when markdowns occurred. With this understanding of the dynamics of the market, the retailer and manufacturer develop a **sales strategy** so that successes are likely. This information can also be shared with the forecaster.

observation

Observation is a data collection technique that entails watching, photographing, recording, and reporting on consumers' behavior in multiple locations. This process is often done by a team of researchers, trend spotters, fashion enthusiasts, and forecasting experts. The teams strive to discover newness while observing people in their natural settings. They can also observe by immersing themselves into a group, photographing participants, or watching from a distance. While observing, the forecaster looks for similarities, differences, repetitive behaviors, and change.

FIGURE 5.5
Observing behavior and recognizing changes helps forecasters to anticipate the evolution of consumer desires.

FOWARD THINKER

SCOTT MARKERT, SALES MANAGER FOR LONDON TIMES

Sales Strategy

My sales strategy starts with relationships that I have developed over the years. Knowing the buyers, the store management, and the store's philosophy is the key to placing the right product on the selling floor. The buyers have access to concrete sales information, including data from their own area as well as departments that carry more expensive products. Having quick access to sales information helps the buyer and manufacturer supply additional product in a timely manner so that more revenue can be generated. However, to keep the product from looking old or outdated, the color or fabrication may need to be adjusted for the next delivery cycle. Capitalizing on a "best seller" is imperative, but so is bringing in new garments to keep the inventory fresh.

HOME
ABOUT
EVENTS
CONTENTS
CONTACT

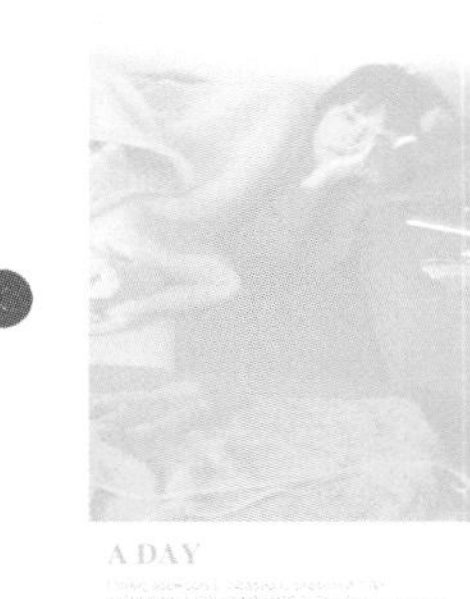
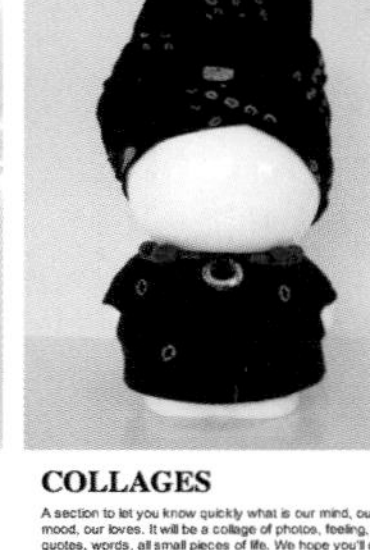

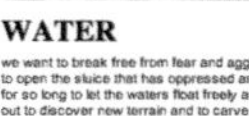

FIGURE 5.6
Trend Tablet is a socially interactive information platform that offers fashion intelligence to help understand current and future trends.

At Cool Hunting, a global team of editors publishes current updates about creative innovations, including information about art and design as well as technology and modern culture. Designers and innovators can follow and contribute ideas through YouTube, Facebook, and Twitter or by subscribing to receive newsletters by e-mail. *Web site*: www.coolhunting.com.

DailyCandy provides an insider's guide to fashion and culturally related information from cities around the globe. Their editors report on topics ranging from fashion, accessories, home décor to food and vacation trends. *Web site*: www.dailycandy.com.

At Trend Tablet, Lidewij Edelkoort, a renowned trend forecaster who anticipates future fashion trends, presents trends as they develop and evolve. This interactive social media platform is designed to help one to understand how the information affects everyday life. *Web site*: www.trendtablet.com.

Fashion Etc. highlights fashion collections, trends, influences, celebrity style, and shopping tips. Topics about trends in beauty and makeup are reported. News and special features including events and parties are also covered. *Web site*: www.fashionetc.com.

questionnaires and surveys

Questionnaires and **surveys** can help researchers in understanding and identifying existing and potential customers. Researchers formulate lists of questions that are designed to elicit the desired information from consumers. Consumers may be questioned about where they live, or their age, gender, religion, and income bracket. This data gives the researcher valuable information to help identify who the customer is and to find clues for new predictions. While questions about past purchases, brand loyalty, and spending habits can provide researchers with a historical perspective on the consumer, determining what the consumer may be interested in purchasing in the future is much more difficult. In order to predict future buying habits, the researcher may focus on aspirations and lifestyle questions.

Whether researchers conduct the surveys by telephone, online, or in stores, a sampling of both existing and potential customers can guide the researcher. Depending on the market segment that is being targeted, specific survey methods may be more appropriate than others, and customers are sometimes offered incentives to participate. The responses can lead to insight about their possible future purchases.

ITAY ARAD, CEO AND COFOUNDER OF FASHION SNOOPS

Global Information

When developing Fashion Snoops, the team chose to create a way to research and report fashion. Currently, trend researchers report style news from all over the globe, from the streets to events, runways to trade shows. The reporting mirrors the needs of designers, retailers, and manufacturers by providing timely reports coinciding with seasonal events.

FIGURE 5.7
Questionnaires and surveys provide valuable data for the forecasters.

LILLY BERELOVICH, OWNER, PRESIDENT, AND CHIEF CREATIVE OFFICER OF FASHION SNOOPS

Online Forecasting Service Fills Needs of Fashion Professionals

Fashion Snoops was created to fill a need. As a children's wear designer, I traveled globally to collect fashion trends to inform my upcoming collections. After years of doing the research, I felt the need for a system that brought all of the information to me. In partnership with Itay, a software engineer and marketing expert, we developed an online forecasting service where information would be accessible to fashion professionals.

focus groups

A **focus group** is a representative group of consumers who are questioned together, through informal conversations or through organized debates, to gather opinions about products, services, prices, or marketing techniques. Researchers ask group participants questions about their needs and desires to collect and summarize potential consumer aspirations and behavior. This data helps forecasters to understand and predict any change in consumer attitudes.

Focus groups also can provide forecasters insight about specific topics beyond fashion, including consumer preferences in music, entertainment, art, and sports. Again, such lifestyle questions may provide insight into future purchases. The focus group provides a sampling of data and, depending on the age, income, or habits of the group, the research may only be relevant for a similar demographic of consumers or may be relevant to a widespread community.

FIGURE 5.8 Focus groups are another way forecasters research consumer attitudes and trends.

WEB AND INTERNET

viral marketing

Viral marketing refers to marketing practices that use existing social networks to spread the word through society. By encouraging people to pass along the marketing message, the information has the potential to spread quickly to a large number of people through Internet videos, interactive Web sites, social networking sites, blogs, or text messages. The goal of viral marketing is to create successful messages that will reach consumers with the highest social networking potential. It relies on a large rate of transfer from person to person, sometimes referred to as the snowball effect.

When viral marketing is successful, the information is transmitted to an even-larger portion of society who will spread the marketer's message. The viral marketers often make the transfer of information easy through links to other sites. A significant difference between viral marketing and traditional advertising is that in viral marketing the consumer participates and contributes to the process. Advertising calls attention to a product through paid announcements, such as newspaper or magazine ads, radio or television spots, or Internet advertisement, but the consumer cannot interact.

social media sites

Social media sites, such as **Twitter**, **Facebook,** or **YouTube,** are fast-growing Internet-based platforms that are being used to broadcast messages, communicate, and hold conversations. These sites are being used as a marketing device to spread viral messages about brands, products, and trends.

blogs

A **blog** is a type of Web site often frequented regularly by individuals who post text, images, videos, and links to other Web sites related to the topic of the blog. This interactive format gives participants the ability to communicate about current trends and events. **Bloggers** are people who post commentary or images about a particular subject on their blog. Many fashion bloggers keep tabs on "up-to-the-minute" ideas about the fashion industry and personal style. A fashion blog

FIGURE 5.9 Students who are fashion enthusiasts can create blogs to share their opinions about style and fashion trends.

can be about specific categories of fashion such as apparel or accessories, or cover various market segments such as couture fashions, ready-to-wear, or street fashions. Fashions from well-known brands as well as emerging newcomers have created blogs to feature their products. Fashion blogs related to fashion and shopping now number in the millions and are created in countries from around the globe. Fashion blogs have become a profitable media business because revenue is made by placing ads on the blogs. Fashion blogs provide a new way to keep a pulse on quickly changing fashion trends and are expected to have a significant lasting influence on the fashion, advertising, and media industries.

There are different types of fashion blogs. Some are written and maintained by insiders from the industry or outsiders who have a strong opinion about fashion or aspiring fashionistas who hope to enter the industry through a nontraditional route.

Fashion blogs are being accepted by the mainstream press as valid media coverage. Bloggers have been invited to attend runway shows and attend exclusive events so that they can post commentary on their blogs. Even street fashions, real people creating or wearing fashion trends, are featured on blogs.

A forecaster can participate in a blog by viewing the site, posting questions, and creating a dialogue in real time with fashion enthusiasts. Forecasters also create their own fashion blogs to stay connected to dedicated followers of style.

FOWARD THINKER

ITAY ARAD, CEO AND COFOUNDER OF FASHION SNOOPS

Influence of Bloggers

My focus is not only on celebrities but also on passionate fashion bloggers. The bloggers have great abilities to influence fashion because they are in touch with the style around them and have the pulse of the technologically savvy generation. A young individual's dream of rising to stardom is not out of reach for the average aspiring fashion follower. A young man who is seventeen years old from Manila has risen to stardom as a fashion trendsetter by posting photos and fashion insight from his perspective. He has even caught the attention of the gurus of fashion, including Anna Wintour.

FIGURE 5.10
Manila-based Bryanboy's home-based fashion blog propelled him into the international spotlight.

MARKET RESEARCH FIRMS

Many independent **market research firms** that focus on the fashion and apparel industries conduct studies and provide information that can benefit forecasters. From reports detailing product and market trends to marketing strategies, research firms analyze and project marketing opportunities. They aim to explain what is being purchased as well as where, when, why, and how consumers are buying. They monitor retail through audits and track Internet purchases. They take into consideration price, promotional incentives, merchandising methods, and distribution. They monitor personal buying habits, demographic shifts, and consumer buying power.

Most market research firms not only provide data based on consumer purchases through technological scanning processes, they offer analysis and solutions through customized research for their clients. The clients need research about brand awareness and customer satisfaction so that they can produce products that the customer will desire and purchase. Market researchers focus on how to turn the shopping experience into an interactive activity, where consumers can immerse themselves into the experience, because filling a consumer's needs by just providing a product is no longer enough excitement for most consumers. Numerous research firms specialize in fashion-related research. *Web sites*: www.marketresearch.com; www.npd.com; www.neilsen.com; www.sri.com; and www.just-style.com.

EDIT, INTERPRET, ANALYZE, AND PREDICT USING MARKET AND SALES RESEARCH

Once a forecaster has collected information from trade or government organizations, through in-house studies, from Internet sources, or with the assistance of sales and market research specialists, the task of interpreting the data is next. The forecaster identifies patterns, signals, and emerging ideas related to sales and marketing trends. Information is ranked in order of importance and less significant data is edited. Knowing what has sold in the past and what is currently selling gives clues to the forecaster about what potentially will sell in the future.

The forecaster analyzes and projects marketing opportunities. Successful forecasters use the data and intuition to evaluate what has happened already in attempts to predict consumers' next desires. They predict if the information will be spread through media, through style tribes, in the clubs, from one group to another, or through word of mouth. They provide scenarios of how the lifestyle or a specific trend will move through society. They offer solutions through customized forecasts for their clients or wide-ranging forecasts that apply to varied markets. The clients use the forecasts to enhance brand awareness and marketing opportunities so that they can manufacture goods that the customer will want and buy.

SUMMARY

By looking, searching, and asking the right questions, forecasters anticipate the potential landscape of future fashion. Researchers collect data by recording consumer profiles, purchasing habits, and sales. Trade associations, market research firms, and information consultants examine and report findings. Consumers can be questioned and surveyed. For more specific information related to a particular business, researchers conduct in-house studies and monitor fashion blogs and the Internet. Market research firms can provide customized forecasts for specific markets. With the increase of information available to forecasters, the challenge more often comes in the analyzing stage rather than the gathering stage. For a forecaster, after collecting, interpreting, and analyzing the sales and marketing data the forecast can be developed.

KEY TERMS

- National Retail Federation
- Fashion Group International
- Data sharing
- Sales strategy
- Observation
- Questionnaires
- Surveys
- Focus groups
- Viral marketing
- Social media sites
- Twitter
- Facebook
- Blog
- Bloggers
- Market research firms

ACTIVITIES

1. Create a Fashion Blog

Develop a fashion blog about specific categories of fashion, such as apparel or accessories. Post images, comments, or questions each day for one month. There are several free blog platforms. See, for example, blogspot.com, from Google.

2. Interview a Sales Associate at a Retail Location

Set up an interview with a sales associate at a local retail store on a specific fashion topic. Research and write up questions beforehand. Gather information about a current trend. Find out what items are best sellers.

3. Conduct a Survey

Identify a topic for a survey for fashion. Create a list of questions related to the topic. Conduct the survey through classmates or actual shoppers. Evaluate the results. Present the findings.

FALL 11/12 I MILITAIRE I COLORS

MILITAIRE

Harkening back to another war pea coat navy and olive drab are paired with felted wool in worn sage. Button brass highlights the military influence.

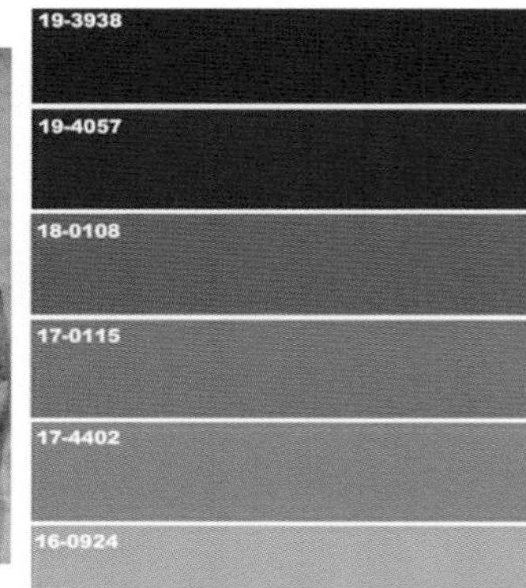

Fashion Snoops "MILITAIRE" forecast was inspired by military influences from the armed forces. The muted color range includes hues such as olive drab and peacoat navy found in uniforms. Rugged fabrics such as twill, leather, and shearling support the functionality and utility of the look. Details include cargo pockets, metal buttons, and epaulettes.

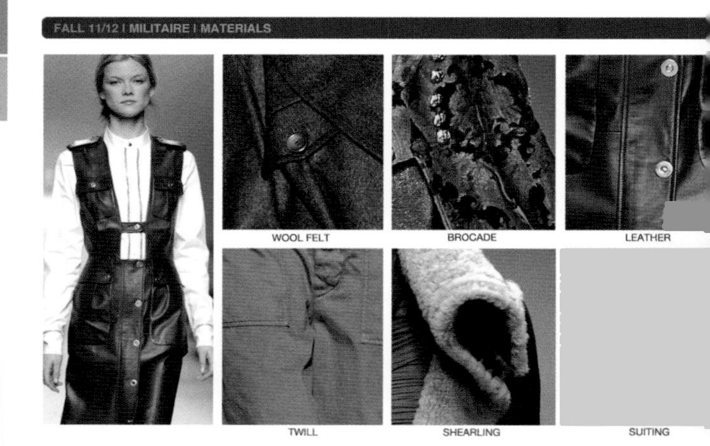

FALL 11/12 I MILITAIRE I KEY ITEMS

Part Two

DEVELOPING AND PRESENTING A FASHION FORECAST

THE SECOND HALF OF THE BOOK is dedicated to learning to develop and present a fashion forecast. Chapters 6 to 9 examine in depth all elements of a forecast, including theme, color, textiles and materials, and the look. The steps in every chapter are provided for researching, editing, interpreting, analyzing, and predicting each portion of the forecast. By completing all steps that appear as the first activity at the end of the chapter, the forecaster will be prepared to finalize the forecast using the directions in Chapter 10, which explain how to incorporate each element into a complete forecast. Instructions are also provided for visual board development, script writing, and forecast presentation. A comprehensive final exercise also appears in the Appendix.

THEME

6

Objectives

- Understand the theme forecasting process.
- Define what a theme is.
- Identify sources of inspiration for themes.
- Discuss how an idea is formulated for a theme.
- Examine how image, title, and tagline contribute to a theme.
- Explain the difference between descriptive and narrative story.
- Understand how story and mood support a theme.
- Learn to develop the theme portion of a forecast.

What is a theme and why is it important in forecasting? Where do the forecasters look for theme ideas and inspirations? How do forecasters develop stories and moods?

IDENTIFY A CENTRAL IDEA AS A THEME

what is a theme?

A **theme** is a topic for a fashion forecast that has a unifying, dominant idea. The central concept will determine the message of the forecast. The job of forecasters is to identify the emerging forces in current society, understand what is fueling the cultural shifts, consider the relevance of the changes, and communicate possible outcomes for the future through themes. A forecaster creates various themes to capture the pulse of contemporary culture and predicts forward by illustrating innovative creative concepts and solutions. These concepts can be translated into design and merchandising ideas for products and businesses.

developing the idea

When developing a theme, forecasters look at a current trend or a recent event and then anticipate the trend or event's evolution. Forecasters focus on the very first signs of change as they attempt to foresee what will fulfill the obvious and unexpressed wishes of the customers that will arise from this trend. Forecasters focus on aspects of a change in human behavior, including changes in attitudes and desires. A prediction of something that is going to happen or some shift that will occur is the starting point of the theme development. With the understanding of fashion and experience, forecasters identify patterns related to a theme. With repetition of similar ideas, a theme can be identified and developed. In a typical forecast there may be several themes developed that define the spirit of the times and prepare for what possibilities may occur. Designers, merchants, or producers evaluate the relevance of the theme concept for their particular market or line of items.

A theme idea can be discovered by watching changes in the lifestyles of trendsetters. New trends often begin with trendsetters and move into the mainstream. An idea that is first accepted by the trendsetters often moves into fashion as it gains momentum throughout society. When trends appear in two or more industries at the same time, the trend has the potential to go mainstream.

inspiration for theme

Some of the factors that are influential are current events, economic and political climate, celebrity influences, and current standards of style.

To find ideas for themes, a forecaster looks to what is in the news, in art, or the world at large. Generally, cultural events and lifestyle have a great influence on fashion.

the news, art, and politics

Newsworthy events, political shifts, architectural innovations, and art shows that well-known museums are planning or exhibiting are important to a forecaster because there is often a relationship between these occurrences and how they influence fashion. For example, in recent years:

- The Metropolitan Museum of Art in New York hosted an exhibit called "*Superheroes*" that highlighted fashion and fantasy. The show influenced fashion with futuristic and technologically driven styles.
- The Tate Gallery in London showed works by Gustav Klimt, Mark Rothko, and Cy Twombly that influenced color, pattern, and design and inspired the themes for the upcoming season.
- The ongoing wars in the Middle East have inspired the combat-ready looks that were spotted on runways, in artists' videos, and on the streets.

FIGURE 6.1 The skeletal structure of Lady Gaga's dress resembles the architectural style of Beijing's 2008 Olympics stadium, referred to as "the bird's nest".

- The fashion world's current focus on sustainable design practices has been influenced by the media and movies such as Al Gore's *An Inconvenient Truth,* which is about respecting the environment and acknowledging the effects of global warming.
- After the election of Barack Obama as president in 2008, the "Obama Effect" has been changing the way that men are dressing, inspiring a more professional look for business.
- Beijing's National Stadium for the 2008 Summer Olympics—"the bird's nest" created by the Swiss firm, Herzog and de Meuron—was designed with the skeleton of the infrastructure on the façade of the building. This unusual look has appeared in the couture collections of Christian Lacroix, Jean Paul Gaultier, and John Galliano.

movies, media, and tv shows

Due to the important role that TV and movies continue to play in society, forecasters have to keep tabs on the newest looks that characters wear.

- In *Sex and the City*, character Carrie Bradshaw, played by Sarah Jessica Parker, was closely monitored and inspired a new sense of style for the modern woman. From Manolo Blahnik shoes to extravagant looks, this theme quickly filtered into the mainstream, redefining women's attitudes.
- Reality TV shows such as *Project Runway* introduced new design ideas and phrases such as "fierce" that later appeared in themes.
- Other important films significantly influenced fashions longing for the past, including *Casablanca*, *Gone with the Wind*, *Out of Africa*, *Bonnie and Clyde*, *The Great Gatsby*, *Titanic*, *The King's Speech*, and *Cleopatra*.
- The vampire obsession, created by movies and shows such as *Twilight*, *True Blood*, and *The Vampire Diaries,* has influenced themes based on everlasting youth, immortality, and romance.
- Recent movies such as *Avatar* and *Alice in Wonderland* inspired themes about fantasy and escaping reality.

FIGURE 6.2 Celebrity style icon Sarah Jessica Parker popularized the oversized flower as a dramatic, trendsetting embellishment.

FIGURE 6.3 Kate Middleton's 2011 royal wedding dress by Sarah Burton of Alexander McQueen was seen worldwide and was likely to influence future bridal fashions.

FIGURE 6.4 Fashion trendsetter Kanye West wears a shocking hot pink blazer at the 3.1 Phillip Lim fashion show.

iconic fashionable women and men

Society's ongoing obsession with celebrities forces forecasters to keep an eye on their changing lifestyles and wardrobes.

- Up until her death in 1994, Jackie Kennedy Onassis, with her Dior suits, sheath dresses, pillbox hats, big sunglasses, and her haircut inspired fashion not only in her day but also years later.
- In the 1980s and 1990s, England's Princess Diana's style influenced fashion in many ways. For example, her ball gown wedding dress, hairstyle, and her one-shoulder dresses defined that era. More recently, the wedding dress worn by Kate Middleton in April 2011 inspired the romantic use of lace, shown not only in wedding dresses but everyday styles.
- Victoria Beckham, from the pop group Spice Girls, continues to be seen as a trendsetter. She has helped spread "Girl Power!" around the world clad in the shortest skirts and highest heels.
- Teenager superstar singer Miley Cyrus became an overnight sensation after *Hannah Montana* debuted in March 2006. With her solo career, Cyrus continues to influence the "tween" and teen markets with her pop style and music.
- Influence of hip-hop artists such as Jay-Z and Kanye West have inspired the urban themes and styles.

HOW TO DEVELOP A THEME FORECAST

step 1: formulate an idea or concept

The first step in formulating an idea for a theme forecast is research. Researching is the process of exploring or investigating to collect information and imagery while looking for new, fresh, and innovative ideas and recognizing inspiration, trends, and signals—both from a scientific approach and an artistic approach. Remembering that fashion and trends evolve, the past, current, and future must be considered to predict what will be next.

A **scientific approach** is when forecasters research and collect tangible data from:

- Past trend information
- Historical records
- New technology
- Existing objects and materials
- Books, magazines, and current events
- Information from trade shows, manufacturers, retailers, and consumers
- Data from specialists and consultants

An **artistic approach** is when a forecaster relies on creativity to access and record:

- Personal knowledge
- Memory
- Observations
- Opinions and attitudes
- Communications
- Intuition
- Instinct

A forecast that includes both research approaches offers variety that appeals to wider audiences. Some people react best to factual information while others understand best with emotional triggers.

A forecaster may notice something a bit different, something new that they have not seen or experienced before. This subtle difference or new concept can be compared to a single thread. Following the thread and seeing where it leads can be the beginning of a new theme concept. By observing as the thread begins to become interlaced with additional threads, the forecaster begins to weave the foundation for a forecast. Another analogy for the theme development process is through the example of boiling water. As water is heated, first it bubbles gently and begins to simmer. Like a theme idea, the simmering is the beginning of the process. With time and more heat, the water begins to rapidly boil. In theme development, the forecaster looks for simmering ideas and anticipates the bubbling up or boiling point of a concept.

step 2: collect the images

An **image** or a collage of images can be used to illustrate a theme. Once the idea is established, the image must be carefully chosen so that it correctly represents the theme. Clippings, sketches, Internet images, ads, runway shows, and photos can supply impact and visibility to the theme. "A picture is worth a thousand words" can be used effectively to convey the theme idea. All image sources must be recorded and added to the bibliography.

KAI CHOW, CREATIVE DIRECTOR, DONEGER CREATIVE SERVICES

Customized Forecasts and Collaboration

I am known to be forward thinking and to have the understanding of trends even before they appear on the horizon. My forecasts are not based on a client's price point but instead on lifestyle, focusing on sophistication, speed, and youth. Other forecasters are known for more conceptual or more pragmatic projections. My forecasts are fashion forward yet extremely tangible. I rely on a team of talented people to work with me. My team consists of five designers, often each one specializing in a category—fabrics, accessories and jewelry, shoes, or on-line expertise. Freelance illustrators, international designers, and students participate in the forecast, bringing freshness to the team. We pay attention to the bloggers as an immediate way to access attitudes and opinions about changing trends.

FIGURE 6.5
A forecaster might use a collection of images such as this to illustrate the emergence of a new effortless and edgy look in unconventional hairstyles.

Images can be researched by collecting:

- Historical/vintage references
- Lifestyle/cultural references
- Runway analysis—name designers or collections
- Retail references
- Celebrity references
- References from interiors
- References from beauty
- Trade show references
- Street scene references
- References based on travel
- References based on art or music

step 3: edit, interpret, analyze, and predict the theme

Once the data is collected, a forecaster or team begins the process of editing the data. Editing is the process of sorting and identifying patterns in the research, data, and images. To edit, a forecaster reviews the data and begins to organize, group, or separate images and information to identify patterns. Each piece of collected information or imagery is reviewed to ensure that it is cohesive to the theme. The unnecessary data can be omitted, and the facts that seem most noteworthy can be highlighted. Several additions and edits to the selections may be necessary to arrive at a unified and synthesized theme. The selections must be arranged by value and significance, taking into consideration the impact that the theme will have on society.

Next, the forecaster interprets and analyzes the components of the theme. Interpreting and analyzing are processes that entail careful examination to identify causes, key factors, and possible results, investigate what fuels upcoming trends, and consider why and how the trend will manifest. The forecaster explains how different forces influence societal changes through the theme's message, sometimes reading between the lines or inferring some significance. Using intuition and decisiveness based on the information, a process of evaluation, comparison, selection, investigation, and experimentation is required to deduce the possible importance of the theme. The forecaster then provides meaning for the theme.

KAI CHOW, CREATIVE DIRECTOR, DONEGER CREATIVE SERVICES

How a Forecast Is Begun

The first step in developing a forecast is establishing a theme, which makes it easier to design and develop the entire forecast. As a trend forms, it begins to call for a name. Once the concept can be articulated, the theme's title is assigned.

Predicting or declaring in advance why future developments or trends may occur is the next process. To predict, a forecaster foretells the possible outcomes and explains why the results may occur. The predicting process is one of problem solving and planning for the future by foreseeing emerging needs and behaviors of consumers. Although not everyone will understand or support each concept, the forecaster strives to create a theme that will have wide acceptance or universal appeal. Offering scenarios or visualizations is a meaningful, engaging way to explore the prediction process.

Since forecasting is based on future likelihoods, success is achieved when the forecaster inspires the audience to contemplate their theme recommendation and consider the probability of the forecast's potential.

The final stage for a forecaster is preparing and presenting the forecast. A forecaster prepares presentation boards and a script for the presentation, then delivers the forecast. (See Chapter 10.)

step 4: create the title

Once the theme idea has been envisioned, a title is needed. The title must capture the spirit of the theme. When naming the theme, a concise but descriptive name is needed. For example, "Island Breeze" is the title of a sample forecast. The theme of this forecast is about getting away and letting go, escaping from hectic everyday life. The inspiration comes from the beauty of the seas and the soothing energy that it holds. The selected title and images reflect the flavor of the islands, tranquil sandy white beaches, gentle wind, crystal clear water, and treasures of the sea.

FIGURE 6.6 In a fashion forecast, the title board represents the inspiration for the theme—illustrated here by an "Island Breeze" theme and title board by Erica Mahmood.

FIGURE 6.7 A catchy tagline further explains the theme—as seen in the "Island Breeze" tagline board by Erica Mahmood.

step 5: develop a tagline

Along with the theme title, a tagline or phrase can further explain the concept. Popular buzz words, song lyrics, or media taglines can be used. For example, the "Island Breeze" tagline is "It cures her soul like medicine that no doctor could prescribe." Other taglines for this forecast could be:

- "Tropical paradise. . . . Some say it's a perfect place with beaches and warm water. I say it's a perfect state of mind."
- "Escaping the concrete jungle to white sandy beaches."
- Or the lyrics from a favorite Jimmy Buffett song.

step 6: identify the mood

The **mood** describes the tone of the theme, which represents the feelings and emotions of the message. Amongst other things, forecasters must think about what sort of emotions they want to elicit. For example, does the theme pique the listener's interest, joy, serenity, unrest, boredom, or nostalgia? Forecasters must be sensitive to how various moods affect people. Some mood descriptions are romantic, rustic, futuristic, lighthearted, sensual, or dark. The mood, tone, and emotional quality of the theme must be compatible with the idea and the story. In "Island Breeze," the tone relates to the escapism theme, creating a mood of relaxation and comfort. The mood conveys feelings associated with the desire to escape from everyday stress to paradise.

FIGURE 6.8 Selecting mood words sets the tone of the forecast—Erica Mahmood's "Island Breeze" mood words convey the feeling of relaxation.

FOWARD THINKER

DAVID WOLFE, CREATIVE DIRECTOR, DONEGER CREATIVE SERVICES

The Big Picture

I focus on the big picture, forecasting tone instead of themes. I focus on the psychology of the consumer instead of the romance of fashion. In the big picture, I see recurring themes that evolve season after season. Escapism, romance, practicality, past reference, and innovation are elements to focus on. Society fantasizes about luxury and shares a common emotional thread and ongoing mentality: trying to dreamscape away.

step 7: write the story for the theme

The written or spoken text of a forecast is called a **story**. A story is developed based on the concept, images, and title that were selected for a theme. The story may identify the past and present associated with the idea and anticipate the future possibilities. The vocabulary for the story must be carefully chosen so that each word describes the intended message and supports the central idea. It is helpful to develop a list of words that elicit the theme. The story can either be narrative or descriptive.

narrative

A **narrative story** is based on the inspirational and artistic influence of the theme. The story can be written based on a theme of fantasy or fiction. Forecasters may chose to write a narrative story to convey the message of the theme. Some designers even use fictional narratives to give meaning and themes to their collections. Some designers are known to create elaborate fantasies for each of their collections. After researching general ideas for the next collections, they develop a story for the upcoming season. Through collaboration, the story line becomes more expressive and is shared among the team, who uses the ideas to inspire their portion of work. The story continues to grow but remains the central idea for all of the designs and the season's fashion show and production. Forecasters and their teams also create a story to provide undertone and explain their message.

In the sample forecast, "Island Breeze," the narrative story tells of a girl escaping her stressful reality as she vacations on a Caribbean island. She strives to find a way to bring the serenity with her when she leaves paradise and returns to her everyday life.

She turns on the ten o'clock news and wonders what is happening to the world.
The good ole days have passed and she knows the time has come.
She left a note, "I hope you understand, I just had to go back to the island."

There on the island she can rule the world. She can watch ships sail out to sea.
It cures her soul like medicine that no doctor can prescribe. She watches the days as they fade away;
she thinks only about the good times. She laughs without worrying about ageing and spends
her days in the Caribbean sunshine.
The seagulls chirp but at least it's not her boss. She enjoys the thunder because she knows it is not bombs.

Life is good on the island.

As her vacation came to a closure, she carefully observed her surroundings.
She wondered how she could bring the island with her. She embraced the beauty
of the ocean, and the softness of the sand. She watched how the birds flew with the wind and
made a decision to be more like them. She created a collection that reminded her of the islands.

Island Breeze
Presented by: Erica Mahmood

FIGURE 6.9 For her storyboard, Erica Mahmood chose to use a fictional narrative to convey her theme.

descriptive

A **descriptive story** is based on nonfictional data and information about the theme. Details about the origins of the idea, the research, the historical information, the cultural influences, or the marketing response can be included. A forecast can be explained based on real situations and facts. In "Island Breeze," the descriptive story could be information pertaining to world news, job statistics, health facts related to stress, and the benefits one experiences while vacationing.

Once the extended story is established, an abbreviated version of the story is needed. The edited story recaps the idea of the theme. The short version of the story often is placed on the presentation board while the elongated narrative or description is presented verbally. During the presentation, the forecaster elaborates on the theme by telling the long version of the story but in the visual presentation, the edited story appears as text.

SUMMARY

In a fashion forecast, theme is the unifying idea that ties everything together. Forecasters can find inspiration or information for a theme from a variety of sources in everyday life. They formulate their ideas for a theme through either a scientific or artistic approach. Creating a title, locating images, writing a story, and deciding on mood are important tasks in refining a theme. All of the ideas, pictures, and words of a forecast must contribute to the whole story and be compatible with the theme.

KEY TERMS

- Theme
- Scientific approach
- Artistic approach
- Image
- Mood
- Story
- Narrative story
- Descriptive story

ACTIVITIES

1. Follow the Steps to Develop a Theme Forecast

Step 1. Formulate an idea.
Step 2. Collect the images.
Step 3. Edit, interpret, analyze, and predict the theme.
Step 4. Create the title.
Step 5. Develop the tagline.
Step 6. Identify the mood.
Step 7. Write the extended and abbreviated stories for the theme.

2. Research and Compare Past Forecasts to a New Theme Idea

Identify three or more themes from past forecasts that are relevant to a new theme concept. Write commentary on the similarities and differences compared to the new forecast concept. Resources can include online forecasting services, forecasting services that are available at a library, Web site suggestions found in the text, Internet searches, magazine articles, and books.

3. Create a Word Collage

Write words associated with the theme on sticky notes. Make a collage of the words, grouping together ones that identify the theme. Use the word collages for inspiration for the title, tagline, and story.

COLOR

7

Objectives

- Understand the color forecasting process.
- Define color terminology.
- Review color theory, color psychology, and color cycles.
- Learn to develop the color portion of a forecast.

Why does a color look new and fresh one season and, just a few seasons later, look old and outdated? Where do color trends begin and what makes the color accepted by consumers? How does a forecaster know what colors will be popular in the future?

WHAT IS COLOR FORECASTING?

Color forecasting is a process of gathering, evaluating, understanding, and interpreting information to be able to predict the colors that will be desirable for the consumer in the upcoming seasons. Forecasters do this by researching and using their creativity, intuition, and experience to sense color shifts. Given the fact that consumers are greatly influenced by color, a forecaster needs to understand the allure that color creates. Forecasting of color is done in many different segments of the fashion and manufacturing industries.

A **color forecaster** is a specialist in the research and development of color prediction and often is associated with a forecasting service, manufacturer, retailer, or a textile producer. Yarn producers, weaving and knitting mills, and dyeing and print converters have designers responsible for color selections. In larger garment manufacturing companies, a design director and his or her team is responsible for color direction. In smaller

PAT TUNSKY, CREATIVE DIRECTOR, DONEGER CREATIVE SERVICES

Future Buying Habits

Data is available about consumer habits and purchases, but the information is about the past and cannot show the future direction. When I present a color forecast to a client who has been very successful selling bright colors, it is difficult to direct them into more subtle colors. The retailers are often reluctant to try newness in color selections until it is too late and the retailer is left with merchandise that must be marked down or sold at a sale price. For the past few seasons, bright colors dominated the stores and sales. The next season, the movement of color became less saturated and softer. I am encouraging my clients to begin to move from the extremely bright shades to this newer, toned-down color story.

FIGURE 7.1 As seen in cosmetics, ranges of blue evoke an exotic feel while softer sea foam green reminds us of the ocean. Celadon calms while crystal blue adds intensity.

companies, the responsibility is often that of the designers. Large retailers plan and forecast their buying using color forecasts.

Sometimes these color decisions are made by fashion directors and management teams, or these decisions are left up to the individual buyers who have been briefed on the intended color direction for their organization. Retailers have the advantage of using hard sales data to track sales statistics. Unfortunately, this information can be misleading, because it can only track the items and colors that a consumer has already purchased. The statistics cannot anticipate what additional colors would have been sold if they had been available or what colors will be sold in the future. Although data is collected about consumers' spending habits, less data is available about specific color choices for each product.

EVOLUTION OF COLOR

To begin to understand the importance of color in forecasting, one must recognize that colors evolve from season to season. Changes are always occurring, so to predict future needs and desires of consumers, both change of direction and speed of change must be considered.

COLOR PALETTE AND COLOR STORY

Several years before the colors are used in products, color specialists predict the fashionable colors of the future. Color forecasting begins two to three years before specific products are available to the consumer. This process starts when forecasters (often in teams) develop their initial concepts and new **color palette,** which is a range of colors. Like an artist's color palette,

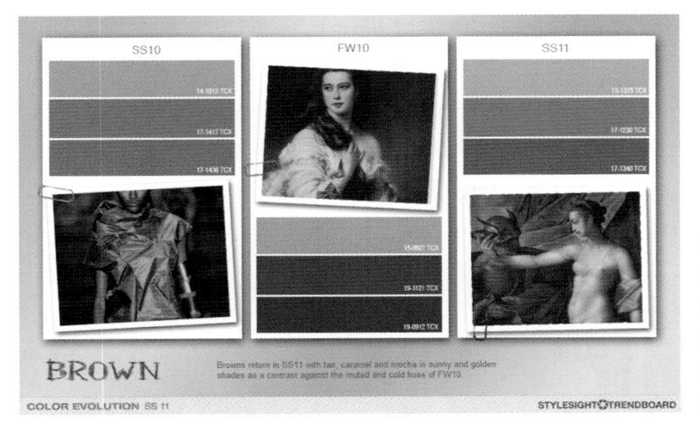

FIGURE 7.2 Color evolves from season to season. By comparing seasons (three brown hues from spring/summer 2010 are the on the far left while three from spring/summer 2011 are on the far right), one can see changes in a color's value, tone, tint, shade, and intensity.

FOWARD THINKER

PAT TUNSKY, CREATIVE DIRECTOR, DONEGER CREATIVE SERVICES

Evolution of Brown

I illustrate this evolution by tracking the color brown from Fall 2010 into the predictions for Spring 2011. In the earlier forecasts, a palette of rich browns, warm tans, and earthy neutrals were presented with accents of spicy mustard, merlot wine, and ornamental rust. The accent colors gave the client an opportunity to introduce the browns while still having the excitement of brighter shades that were familiar and that predominated the past season. By keeping the accent colors in the palette, the brown shades moved into the market giving the consumer an alternative choice to black or navy. The following Spring season's prediction moved the brown and neutral palette forward by tinting the shades of brown to lighten them and by blending the brown shades with additional colors: pinkish brown or a brown shade with a hint of silver. Since the brown palette had already been introduced, the accent shades were no longer needed because the customer was already accustomed to the brown hues.

the group of colors can range from just a few to many colors. A **color story** is a palette of colors that are used to identify, organize, and connect ideas and products for a certain season or collection. An example of a color story that was inspired by the tropics may include colors such as Caribbean blue, parrot green, purple lagoon, living coral, sunset orange, and coconut crème.

Before beginning to create a color forecast, a forecaster must understand color theory, psychology of color, and color cycles.

FIGURE 7.3 The tropical color forecast by Luzmaria Palacios illustrates a vibrant palette with descriptive color names that reinforce the theme.

COLOR THEORY

Color theory is the study of color and its meaning in the worlds of art and design. To understand color theory, basic scientific principles about color and insight are needed. The color wheel, developed by Sir Isaac Newton in 1706, arranges the colors of the spectrum into a circular pattern and is commonly used to understand color. In addition, contemporary color theory focuses on the way that people see, feel, and relate to colors.

A **color wheel** (also referred to as a *color circle*) is a visual representation of colors arranged according to their chromatic relationship.

- **Primary colors** are colors at their basic essence; they cannot be created by mixing others.
- **Secondary colors** are achieved by a mixture of two primaries.
- **Tertiary colors** are achieved by a mixture of primary and secondary hues.
- **Complementary colors** are located opposite each other on a color wheel.
- **Analogous colors** are located close together on a color wheel.

Systems of identifying color use hue, value, and intensity to further describe a color. **Hue** refers to the color itself. **Value** is the lightness or darkness of the color. **Intensity** refers to the saturation or brightness of a color. Tints, shades, or tones of a hue have been altered by the addition of white, gray, or black. **Tint** refers to a hue that has white added, **shade** refers to a hue with black added, and **tone** refers to a hue with gray added.

In addition, color schemes are used to create color combinations. A **color scheme** is a group of colors in relation to each other. **Monochromatic color schemes** have two or more colors from one hue. A **neutral color scheme** is created by white, black, gray, brown, and cream. Neutral colors do not appear on the color wheel. **Discordant color schemes** include colors that "clash."

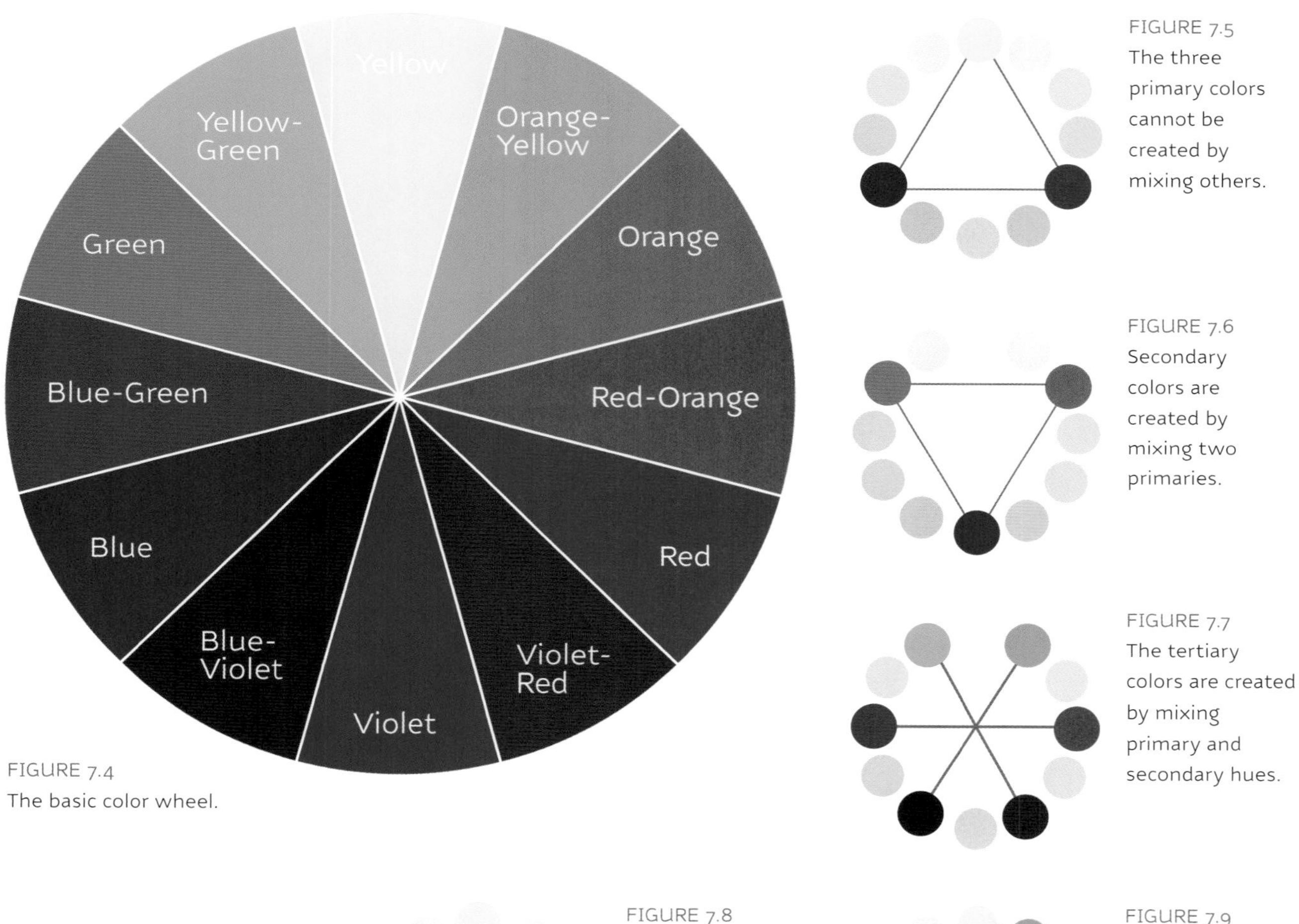

FIGURE 7.4
The basic color wheel.

FIGURE 7.5
The three primary colors cannot be created by mixing others.

FIGURE 7.6
Secondary colors are created by mixing two primaries.

FIGURE 7.7
The tertiary colors are created by mixing primary and secondary hues.

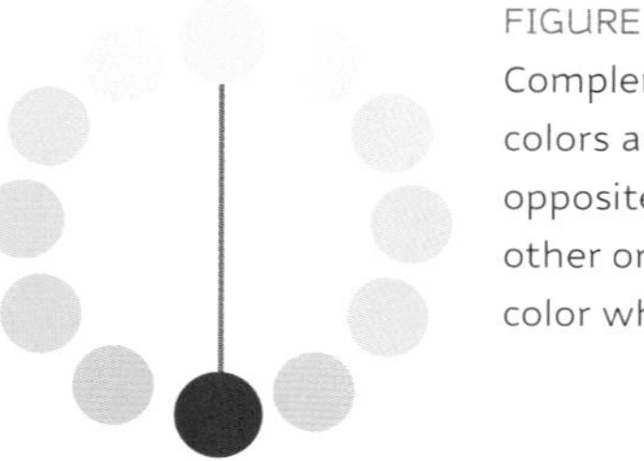

FIGURE 7.8
Complementary colors are opposite each other on the color wheel.

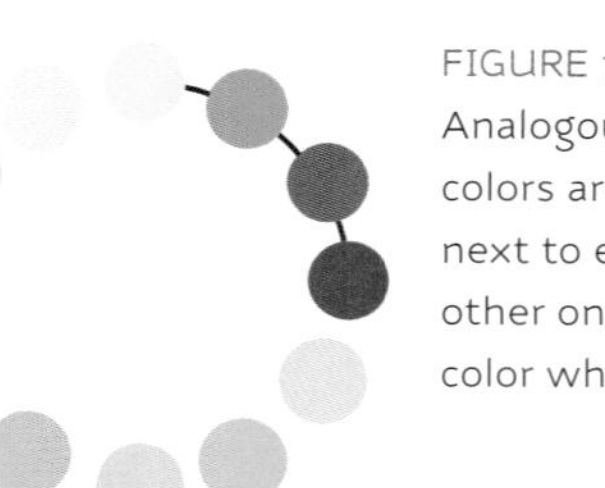

FIGURE 7.9
Analogous colors are next to each other on the color wheel.

PSYCHOLOGY OF COLOR

The psychology of color focuses on the effects related to mood, emotions, feelings, memories, and behavior. Understanding the psychology of color requires recognizing a consumer's communication, association, and reaction to color. Although perceptions of color are individual, some colors have universal meaning. Color symbols appear in our everyday world, and often have associations with an earlier time. In some cultures, colored clothing is worn on certain days to signify celebrations, special occasions, or even political affiliation. The forecaster must recognize the different connotations that each color has in various cultures. To understand the symbolic significance of an individual color or color combination, color forecasters may investigate its origins and then interpret it in a modern context.

In the language of color, **temperature** is a way of describing color (**warm colors**—reds, oranges, and yellows—can evoke emotions of excitement or anger, and **cool colors**—blues, greens, or purples—can be calming and pacifying). Color can also create physiological reactions in humans. Studies have been conducted that show how colors can impact society and consumers. Some of the meanings that the colors evoke are:

- **Red** is the color associated with energy, fire, and blood. The intense color is highly visible and draws attention. Red is used to signify danger or action such as on stop signs and fire trucks. Red is associated with love as seen on Valentine's Day hearts and long stemmed roses. In China, red signifies prosperity, and in India, red is worn by brides. By mixing red with white, pink is produced and is considered to be a feminine color associated with women and girls.

- **Yellow** symbolizes joy and happiness. It is the color of sunshine and cheerfulness. Yellow is also considered the color of wisdom or for stimulating intellectual activity. It is used for legal note pads.
- **Orange** is created when mixing yellow and red. It is associated with the energy of red and joy of yellow. This optimistic color promotes creativity. Citrus orange is considered a healing or healthy color. Golden orange symbolizes wealth and luxury.
- **Green** is the color of nature and symbolizes growth and fertility. Environmental and sustainable initiatives are considered "green." Green is a restful color associated with balance and well-being. In the U.S., green is the color of money. In Asia, jade is a gemstone considered to have healing and protective powers.
- **Blue** is the color of the ocean and the sky. Blue is considered the color of inspiration, loyalty, and faith. To appear trustworthy and dependable, businessmen wear blue suits. Blue is calming as it slows metabolism and is often used in bedrooms to promote peacefulness.
- **Purple** symbolizes royalty and luxury. Purple is the combination of calming blue and energetic red, creating a color that promotes inspiration and imagination. Purple is also considered a magical and mystical color. Light purple or lilac is considered a romantic color and often represents first emotional love.
- **Brown** is the color of the earth. Brown promotes stability and order. The color is worn by those who are genuine and casual. Brown is considered an eco-friendly color.
- **Black** is the color of power and evil. In many cultures, black is the color of death. Mystery and fear are represented using this color. Black is worn for formal or elegant occasions such as "black tie" events. Black has a negative connotation and is worn by "bad guys" or as a form of rebellion.

FIGURE 7.10 Unconventional color and pattern mixes give the South Korean pop band "Wonder Girls" a modern look and exciting appeal.

- **White** is the color of purity and goodness. White is worn by doctors and medical professionals to symbolize cleanliness and safety. In many countries, women wear white wedding dresses because they are associated with innocence and virginity. White light is often imagined on the path to heaven. "Good guys" in movies wear white. In China, white is the color of death.

What makes a person have a favorite color? In addition to a person's response to color, color forecasters are interested in understanding **color preferences**, the tendencies for a person or a group to be partial to some colors over others. Color preferences often come about from personal experience, memory, ethnic identity, or the spirit of the time. Age, income, and gender also play a role in color preferences. Blue is considered the most preferred color. Specific color combinations hold meanings; for instance, the colors red, white, and blue used together signify American patriotism to many. Lifestyle choices or association with a particular style tribe can influence a consumer's color purchase. Someone who chooses a "Goth" lifestyle will buy primarily black or gray items, while a person who has heightened "sustainability values" may choose more neutral, earthy colors. The option of customization of products permits a customer to create personal color combinations to fit her color preferences.

COLOR CYCLES

Color cycles are shifts in color preferences and color repetition. The common factor, though, is change. Colors become fashionable as consumers desire newness. Researchers have found that the color cycle moves from **high chroma** (bright) colors to multiple colors, then to earth tones, followed by **achromatics** (tonal grays and black), next to purple phases, and back to high chroma colors. Color acceptance moves from warm to cool colors, experiences revivals that correspond to fashion history, and is influenced by economic stimulus, but no clear method is in place to fully understand the color evolution process. Like the adoption of trends, different stages of consumers' acceptance of colors can be recognized. For instance, creators and trendsetters are likely to experiment with a new color first, followed by trend followers and mainstream adopters, and finally new color may be slowly adopted by the conservative consumer.

Consumers are likely to experiment with color by purchasing a new color in accessories: jewelry, handbags, or shoes. Once a consumer is confident about the new color, more substantial purchases occur. In home furnishings, a new color can be added to a room by adding pillows, accent rugs, or tabletop items. When color confidence is higher, eventually larger or more expensive items, such as sofas or artwork, may be added.

Certain colors are considered **staple** or *basic* colors and remain consistent from season to season. Black, navy, khaki, and white are examples of basic colors. Fashion colors are the colors that move more quickly and change more often. As color evolves, the fashion colors change by adjustments in value and intensity. After several seasons, a fashion color may disappear from the palette altogether and will be replaced by new ones. In the 1980s, as the economy grew stronger, colors became more vibrant as well. Rich jewel tones, bright bold hues, and vivid color combinations predominated the era of conspicuous consumption. By the 1990s, the downturn in the economy led to a trend for minimalism and the color palette was predominated by black and gray for apparel. The concept of cocooning at home, or spending more quality time at home in the 1990s shifted the color palette from the prior decade to muted, comforting colors, such as gentle neutrals, subtle peach, and soft greens.

In the last chapter, the development of a theme, story, and mood were described. Developing a color forecast is the next step. Along with theme development, a color forecast will aid in capturing the essence of the concept.

HOW TO DEVELOP A COLOR FORECAST

step 1: formulate color ideas

The first step in developing a color forecast is research—both from a scientific approach and an artistic approach. Remembering that color evolves, one must look to the past, identify the current times, and then predict the future.

A color forecaster visits seasonal trade shows, international fabric fairs, and regional textile events to look for clues. Première Vision, held in Paris two times a year, is considered the most important exhibition. A panel of participants prepares the color and textile forecasts for the show over a year in advance. The selected colors are arranged on a color card that is supplied to textile manufacturers, including fiber producers, weavers, knitters, and printers, so that they can coordinate their collections to present unified themes and colors at the show. The themes, moods, stories, colors, and fabrics are used for a presentation that is created and shown for inspiration at the fair. Trend boards are made for the exhibition to help deliver the messages of the evolving trends. Première Vision is attended by manufacturers, designers, retailers, trend hunters, and forecasters. During their time in Paris, most participants also scout the boutiques of the city for new ideas and products, as well as watch the streets for new inspiration. By having so many people from the fashion and design industries in the same place at the same time observing many of the same influences, similar information is assimilated into upcoming fashion.

Data is available noting which were the most sampled or requested colors from the color services and mills. At retail, certain colors from the past season outperformed others, and this information must be considered. Observations are made from the media, runways, and streets to gain insight about color direction. Scanning political, economic, and lifestyle trends is essential. Online resources and design blogs offer color inspiration and ideas. Combining information gives the forecaster a foundation from which to begin to build his or her forecast, which is frequently aimed at specific needs.

Two examples of companies for color reference are CAUS (Color Association of the United States) and Pantone, Inc. Since 1915, The

Color Association has been studying, predicting, and documenting color. Currently, The Color Association consults industry professionals in color selections for their products and brands. *Web site*: www.colorassociation.com.

Pantone, Inc. is known worldwide as a leading color authority due to the technology they use to select and communicate color accurately. Pantone has developed a standard color coding system used throughout the fashion industry to ensure proper color identification and matching. This system is also used to guarantee color accuracy in graphics, printing, and interior design. *Web site*: www.pantone.com.

step 2: develop a color story

After research is completed, the next step is to develop a color story. The colors for the color story can be collected from many sources. Paint chips, yarns, swatches of fabrics, magazine clips, items from nature, and colors from packaging can be used as valuable sources. Color specialists often have a library of color with separate bins holding colors of similar hues. Services are offered on the Internet that provide systems to select, create, and save personally developed color stories. Several online fashion forecasting services include color development areas within their sites where color stories can be created.

The process of developing a color story begins by selecting colors to represent the intended message of the theme. A typical color story consists of five to eight predominate colors. The story may also include accent or fringe colors that enhance the color story. Some color stories include colors of multiple hues while others focus on variations of a particular hue. A color story may be created by using only warm colors such as reds, yellows, and oranges or a neutral story based on beiges and tans.

step 3: edit, interpret, analyze, and predict the color story

Colors are grouped and separated to begin to identify patterns. One must think, reason, and make decisions about each specific color and the relationship of the colors to each other. Larger swatches of color may be included to represent predominate or more important colors for the story, and smaller slivers of color may be included to represent accents. Further examination and organization of the colors to interpret the meaning of the groups is needed to fully represent the theme concept. Editing or revising color selections is done to ensure a refined color story has been developed. Adding additional colors, changing the placement of the colors, or simply resizing the color samples can improve the story.

The mood of the color story must support the theme of the overall forecast. When looking at a group of colors, do they arouse diverse feelings, have a sense of energy, or create a certain mood? Do the colors appear heavy and dark, light and airy, harmonious and soothing, discordant and unsettled? These are the type of questions that forecasters ask themselves when identifying the mood of the color story. Will different consumers view the color moods in the same way? For instance, a classic consumer who is considered a color loyalist (preferring navy, khaki, and black) may be uncomfortable with clashing bright colors, but a trendsetter who is accustomed to pattern mixing, nonmatching of styles, and contemporary trends (preferring neon colors with darks, or vintage and new style mixes) may feel confident.

Still considering the research and data that was collected in earlier steps, the next step of a color forecast is to interpret and analyze causes, key factors, or possible results of research and interpretations. Finally, the prediction of possible outcomes is determined to provide the recommended color story that anticipates future evolution.

The forecasters create color selections based on the point they want to make or particular clients' requirements. Target market and price ranges play an important role in the selections. A forecaster planning for a high-priced designer collection will choose the newest colors and forward color combinations. For a mainstream retailer, the forecaster may choose safer and more widely acceptable colors.

When developing a forecast, one must always ask the question at each stage of the process, "Does this selection support and strengthen the theme?" If the answer is yes, then the forecast can be developed further. If the answer is no, revisions must be made by doing additional research and/or redeveloping the color story.

step 4: assign color names

Once a color story has been selected, a color name is assigned to each color. Keeping the theme and mood of the forecast in mind, color names are selected to identify each of the colors in the story. The language of color, including color names, is linked to color perception and therefore is quite personal. As a color forecaster, choosing names that have a universal appeal yet a sense of newness is the challenge. For instance, if a safari theme is developed, the color names should suggest an expedition or exotic journey. For a beige or tan shade, one may choose a name like desert sand. In a tranquil spa theme, a dusty green shade might be called green tea or eucalyptus. In a theme named "Candy Land," bright pink might be called bubblegum pink and a dark brown could be called chocolate. Color forecasters must always support the theme, mood, and story. Color names from flowers, foods, minerals, metals, gems, locations, or products can be used to create color associations. Beware that some color names hold different meanings for different people. A color named rose can mean a bright red hue to one person but a dusty pink to another. Color names are used as a marketing tool to represent the feel of the color or to revive an outdated color.

In addition to color names, color numbering systems are used in color forecasts. Pantone color numbers are often assigned to the selected colors. By identifying a color with the standardized system, the forecaster is assured that the exact shade of the selected color is represented.

step 5: write details about the color story

The essence of the color story describes the details about the colors. Compiling a vocabulary list of words that articulate the color story is recommended. An overview of the entire color story is written summarizing the color ideas, evolution of the palette, prediction of the color shifts, and details about the selections. In addition, each individual color can be labeled and explained for its relevance to the forecast.

In the sample forecast, "Island Breeze," the color descriptions are inspired by the location; nature, the sea, the sunset, and the beach. The colors are described as vibrant, bleached, and beautiful. With descriptions like "carefree" and "relaxing," the emotional impact or mood is established.

FIGURE 7.11 (*opposite*) In the color portion of the forecast, additional images can support the spirit of the theme. On her color board for "Island Breeze," Erica Mahmood selects photographs of nature to further illustrate her color story. For each color in her forecast, she provides vivid color descriptions.

- *Conch Shell Pink:* Inspired by the beauty of the conch shell. Its light pink glow adds interest to just about anything.
- *Clown Fish Orange:* Inspired by the fun and carefree fish known for its unique color.
- *Sunrise Red:* Inspired by the vibrant red that fills the sky during a beautiful sunrise.
- *Bleached Sand:* Inspired by the white sand bleached by the sun.
- *Aquatic Blue:* Inspired by the sea and its beautiful blue-green color.
- *Salmon:* Inspired by the fish and the color it projects. This pinkish-orange color is a very important and honorable color.
- *Sunset Blue:* Inspired by the sunset and the colors that own the sky. This color promotes relaxation.
- *Palm Green:* Inspired by the island's favorite tree and its vibrant green leaves.
- *Bark Brown:* Inspired by nature and the bark of the trees.
- *Moss Green:* Inspired by the moss that lives within nature and its subtle relaxing color.
- *Stone Gray:* Inspired by stone found on the island, which represents age and relaxation.

Colors:
Bark Brown
Salmon
Palm Green
Moss Green
Bleached Sand
Conch Shell Pink
Stone Gray
Clown Fish Orange
Sunset Blue
Aquatic Blue
Sunrise Red
Island Breeze
Presented by: Erica Mahmood

SUMMARY

A color forecaster collects, evaluates, interprets, and analyzes color data to plan the color stories for upcoming seasons. The color specialist must understand color theory, the psychology of color, and color cycles to create a palette that represents the theme and mood for a forecast. In developing a color forecast, the forecaster identifies the colors through a coding system and by assigning names and detailed descriptions that support each theme.

KEY TERMS

- Color forecasting
- Color forecaster
- Color palette
- Color story
- Color theory
- Color wheel
- Primary colors
- Secondary colors
- Tertiary colors
- Complimentary colors
- Analogous colors
- Hue
- Value
- Intensity
- Tint
- Shade
- Tone
- Color scheme
- Monochromatic color scheme
- Neutral color scheme
- Discordant color scheme
- Temperature
- Warm colors
- Cool colors
- Color preferences
- Color cycles
- High chroma
- Achromatics
- Staple colors

ACTIVITIES

1. Follow the Steps to Develop a Color Forecast

Step 1. Formulate color ideas.

Step 2. Develop a color story.

Step 3. Edit, interpret, analyze, and predict the color story.

Step 4. Assign color names.

Step 5. Write details about the color story.

2. Color Identification

Once the color names have been developed, it is advised to try out the names with others. Put all colors on a board and have the color names separate from the colors. Ask others to match the names with the colors.

3. Research Color Evolution

Select one popular color from the apparel market for the current season and match it to a Pantone color tab. Track the changes in the selected color from the past three seasons and match them to Pantone color tabs. Write descriptions of the color evolution including hue, intensity, saturation, tint, tone, and shade variations.

4. Identify Mood or Emotion Through Color

Name a mood. Create a collage of color tabs or color images to represent a mood or emotion. Show the collage to others and ask them to identify the mood.

TEXTILES, TRIMS, FINDINGS, AND MATERIALS

8

Objectives

- Understand the textiles and materials forecasting process.
- Define textiles, trims, findings, and materials.
- Review the stages of textile production.
- Define textile terminology.
- Identify resources for a textiles and materials forecast.
- Learn to develop a textiles and materials forecast.

What makes a textile, trim, finding, or material the "in" choice for the season? How do forecasters know that a customer would prefer fashions made of textiles that are shimmering and smooth one season and matte and textured the next? Why are findings such as gold zippers dominant as decorative elements one season and trims of colorful braid popular the next year? How do forecasters know what materials will be most accepted for interiors or electronics? Why will shiny polished stainless steel be desired or rustic granite be the look most sought after at any given time?

WHAT IS TEXTILES, TRIMS, FINDINGS, AND MATERIALS FORECASTING?

Textiles, trims, findings, and materials forecasting is a process of collecting, editing, interpreting, and analyzing information to be able to predict the textiles, materials, trims, and findings that will be popular in upcoming seasons. As in theme and color, forecasters research and use their creativity, instinct, and experience to sense tactile shifts. Consumers are greatly influenced by the feel of textiles or the allure of new materials. Forecasting of emerging fabrications aids many different segments of the fashion and manufacturing industries to create products that appeal to a consumer's sense of touch.

Many different textiles, trims, findings, and materials are available for a forecaster to select from at any given time. Considering that a forecast's theme applies to several industries simultaneously, a forecaster may select items for inspiration as well as for functionality. Most fashion apparel is made from textiles, trims, and findings but inspiration for new varieties of textiles may come from alternate materials. Sometimes, the direction of fashion is driven by color or silhouette, but other times the tactile or aesthetic selections are the driving force and a strong **textile story** emerges. Typically in a fashion forecast, textiles, trims materials, and findings are selected to create the third part of the forecast.

TERMINOLOGY

A **textile** is a flexible fabric that is woven, knitted, or assembled using other methods of construction, and often composed of layers. Textiles are made from either natural and manufactured films, fibers, or yarns. Textiles are used to make apparel, home furnishings, floor coverings, and industrial products.

Trim is used to embellish a product. Lace, ribbons, or beads are trims that decorate an item. **Findings** such as zippers, elastic, Velcro, and thread are functional items that add performance qualities to a product. Sometimes the decorative trim or fashionable finding serves a practical purpose in addition to enhancing the look. Unique buttons, colorful snaps, and ornamental belts are examples of trims and findings that serve multiple purposes.

A **material** is the substance of which an item or thing is made. For instance, concrete is used as a material for the construction of buildings, or a twig is used as a material in making a nest. Materials can be manufactured components or items found in nature. Materials are items not typically used to make apparel, but are the building blocks for architecture, interiors, accessories, or cosmetics. Materials can be the inspiration for the development of a new look in textiles. For instance, shards of reflective blue glass could be interpreted for apparel by embellishing a garment with shiny, irregular-shaped beads.

Although the trends in textiles change and evolve, the fundamentals of textiles remain the same. To begin to understand how to forecast upcoming textile and material trends, one must understand the basics of textiles because apparel is made primarily from textiles. Once this information is understood and applied, one can make educated decisions as a designer, manufacturer, retailer, or forecaster.

FIGURE 8.1 On the runway, an air of nostalgia is presented with layers of exaggerated texture, sophisticated patterns, and handcrafted details.

FOWARD THINKER

FRANK IOVINO, PRESIDENT OF MIROGLIO TEXTILES USA

New Fabrics and Innovation

The market for fabrics is less seasonal than in the past. A need for constant newness and innovation leads. Right now, many customers are requesting similar fabrics and patterns. Sheer, printed chiffon fabrics with animal skin motifs mixed with floral patterns are the rage. Paisley motifs are also being requested. The return to classic patterns reinterpreted in new color combinations seems to be the trend.

FIVE STAGES OF TEXTILE PRODUCTION

Textile production can be broken down into five areas of study:

1. Fiber
2. Yarn
3. Fabric structure
4. Color, pattern, and ornamentation
5. Finishes

stage one: fiber

A **fiber** is a hairlike substance that is the basic building block for most yarns and fabrics. Fibers fall into two main categories: natural (from nature) or manufactured (from a chemist's laboratory). Short fibers are called staples and long fibers are called filaments. Fibers can be considered the ingredient for fabric just like flour is an ingredient for bread.

natural fibers

Natural fibers come from plant (cellulosic) or animal (protein) sources. The four main natural fibers are cotton, flax, wool, and silk.

Cotton is the most widely used natural fiber and is derived from the cotton plant. It grows from a seed into a cotton ball that is later harvested and cleaned. The cotton fiber is a staple fiber, short in length. It is a desirable fiber because it absorbs moisture and dries quickly, making cotton care relatively easy. Cotton also has a soft **hand** (feel) and is very versatile. When the trends in fashion are natural, cotton is highly desired.

Flax comes from the stems of the flax plant. The fiber is longer and stronger than cotton. Flax is known for two distinctive characteristics: **slubs** (thick and thin yarns that create unevenness in the fabric) and the tendency to wrinkle. Flax fibers are used to make linen fabric. Linen is considered a luxury fabric that absorbs moisture and dries quickly, making it a great fabric for warm climates.

Wool is a protein fiber that comes from the hair of an animal, most often sheep. The fiber is removed from the sheep by shearing and then graded (categorized) and sorted based on the length of the fibers. Wool is known for its positive qualities of warmth, ability to resist moisture, and elastic-like flexibility, as well as for its negative qualities of scratchiness, tendency to shrink, and susceptibility to damage by moths. Dry cleaning is recommended for wool products. Other specialty protein fibers include alpaca, camel hair, cashmere, llama, angora, and vicuna.

Silk is a protein fiber that is created when a silkworm creates a cocoon. The fiber from the cocoon is detangled into a long filament strand. Silk from filament fibers makes a luxury textile because of its excellent drape, smooth hand, and lustrous appearance. Silk chiffon and silk satin are examples of fabrics made from filament fibers. Short staple fibers of silk used to make silk noil, tussah, and dupioni are produced when the filament is broken or the moth matured and broke out of the cocoon damaging the long continuous strands. Silk is costly, can be damaged easily by chemicals, and requires delicate care or dry cleaning.

manufactured fibers

Manufactured fibers refer to a classification of fibers that are created using science and technology instead of nature. The three main categories of these fibers are manufactured cellulosics, synthetics, and inorganic fibers. These fibers are created to fill specific needs in the market or can mimic the positive qualities of natural fibers without exhausting natural resources. Blending manufactured fibers with natural ones can provide the benefits from both categories of fibers. The negative qualities of manufactured fibers include poor absorbency, static cling, and pilling.

To create most manufactured fibers, **polymers,** which are chemical and molecular compounds, are extruded through a spinneret. The **spinneret** is similar to a showerhead; the liquid polymer is pushed through it in order to create filament (long) fibers. To include color in a manufactured fiber, it is added in the liquid stage. The filaments are hardened through a variety of spinning methods: melt, dry, wet, or solvent. The fibers can be engineered to have different shapes and sizes that make them look or perform in a desired way. The fibers can also be cut and textured to add surface interest.

Some of the most common manufactured fibers include the following:

- **Polyester** is the most widely used, having many outstanding properties. It is affordable, has easy care requirements, and can be modified to meet consumers' needs.
- **Nylon** is the first manufactured fiber produced in the United States, beginning in 1939. Nylon is strong for its weight and has good abrasion resistance and elasticity.
- **Acrylic** is a fiber that often is a substitute for wool. It is less expensive than wool and has easier care requirements. Acrylic possesses a soft, lofty hand. A negative quality of acrylic is that it pills from abrasion.

FIGURE 8.2 Textural and colorful variations of yarn are used to produce eye-catching fabrics.

- **Spandex** is known for its elastic qualities similar to rubber. It is widely used for swimwear and undergarments. Spandex can be blended with other fibers to create "comfort stretch" and is often blended with denim to create close-fitting jeans.
- **Rayon** is a manufactured cellulosic fiber made from wood pulp that is chemically processed into a solution, then extruded or pushed through the spinneret to create filaments. Rayon has many of the same characteristics as cotton. It is comfortable to wear and takes color well, but it wrinkles and stretches out of shape easily.
- **Acetate,** like rayon, is a manufactured cellulosic fiber. Acetate is lustrous, smooth, and lightweight. On the other hand, it shrinks, has poor elasticity, and is not **colorfast** (does not retain color).

stage two: yarn

Yarns are created by spinning and twisting fibers together to create long, continuous strands. Depending on the type and length of fibers used, different varieties of yarns can be made. Some yarns are twisted tightly creating smooth, silky yarns, while others are spun loosely or crimped creating textured or bulkier yarns. The direction that each yarn is twisted also adds diversity to the final product. Yarns can be blended with a variety of fibers to create novelty yarns.

stage three: fabric structure

Fabric structure is the method in which textiles are constructed by assembling yarns and fibers into a cohesive configuration. Depending on the constructions of a fabric, different qualities such as drape, stability, and density are achieved and make certain fabrics more suitable to specific styles. Fabric structure is categorized as woven, knitted, nonwoven, and by other methods of fabric construction.

categories of fabric structure

Woven fabrics, created by weaving—interlacing yarns at right angles—are the most widely used fabrics. Yarns are typically placed on a **loom,** a hand-operated or power-driven device used for weaving fabric. This apparatus holds vertical yarns (warp) and horizontal yarns (weft). Some identifying characteristics of woven fabrics are that they stretch on the bias, fray on the edges, and the yarns can be seen crossing each other at 90 degree angles.

The basic weaves include the plain weave, twill weave, and the satin weave. The **plain weave** is the simplest form, used for many styles of fabric both solid and printed. The **twill weave** is a definitive diagonal line that appears on the fabric surface. A **satin weave** is created by allowing the yarns to float over four or more yarns in either direction. It provides a fabric with luster and shine.

Fancy weaves include **dobby weaves** which have small geometric designs woven into the textile. **Jacquard weaves** and **tapestries** are beautifully patterned, using floats of yarns to create intricate motifs or designs.

Knit fabrics are created by interlooping yarns to create fabric using needles. Knit fabrics fall into two main categories: weft and warp knits. **Weft knits** can be done by hand or machine. Weft knits are interlooped across the fabric. The two main stitches are knit stitches and purl stitches. **Warp knits** are less common and can only be done by machine. In warp

FIGURE 8.3 Fabrics can be woven on a loom or knitted by hand or machine.

knitting, the loops appear along the length of the fabric and they include tricot knits and raschel knits. Many laces fall into the raschel category.

By using yarns that have different weights or textures and a combination of stitches, many varieties of knits can be created. Because of the looping structure, knits are comfortable, having stretch that provides easy fit. Knits also have greater wrinkle recovery than wovens. Problems with knits are that they tend to stretch out of shape, shrink, snag, or run.

Other fabrication methods: **nonwoven fabrics** are created when fibers are held together by bonding, tangling, felting, creating films, or fusing either in an organized or random manner. Some examples are laminated vinyl, tufted fabrics, crochet, or macramé. Quilting also falls into the nonwoven category.

stage four: color, pattern, and ornamentation

Color and pattern are important elements in the marketing of textile-based products. Consumers are attracted to color and pattern first, and that is often the reason that an item is purchased. Color is applied, retained, or removed from fibers, yarns, fabric, or garments at any stage of the textile development process. Dyeing and printing are the most widely used processes. Typically, a fabric is available in assorted colors or **color ways**. A printed motif, or pattern, is usually available in several color combinations.

dyeing and bleaching

Solid color can be achieved by **dyeing** to add color and **bleaching** to remove color. Certain fibers have an affinity to accept dye better than others, creating richer colors and shades.

printing process

Pattern can be added to a fabric in a **printing** process. Printing is a method of applying color and motif to a surface Prints can range from **monotone** (one color) to **multicolored** (many colors). **Application** or *direct printing* is the most common technique of printing pigments on top of fabric in a design or **motif. Discharge printing** is the process whereby color is removed by taking pigment away often in a bleaching process. **Resist printing** is another method that prevents the dyes or pigments from penetrating into the fabric, for example, tie-dyeing and batik. **Digital printing** is done by creating motifs on a computer and printing, using ink-jet technology, which gives greater design flexibility and is cost-effective.

FRANK IOVINO, PRESIDENT OF MIROGLIO TEXTILES USA

Ink-Jet Printing as Innovation in Printing

Ink-jet printing has become a new source of innovation, allowing for the creation of complex motifs printed from computer-generated designs. Fabric designs can be developed and printed on just enough fabric to create a mock-up sample, so that the designer can visualize the printed design on an actual garment without incurring enormous expenses. Earlier methods of printing require the motif being engraved before it could be printed, which requires a costly commitment. This innovation not only saves time and money, it allows for greater customization in the world of textiles.

FIGURE 8.4 Ink-jet textile printing at Miroglio Textiles allows for complex computer-generated patterns and motifs.

yarn-dyeing

Weaving colored yarns together creates a yarn-dyed pattern, such as a plaid or stripe. By changing the color selections or layout, many variations of yarn-dyed patterns can be achieved.

other methods of creating patterns

Other methods of creating designs on fabric:

- **Flock printing** is a technique that uses an adhesive to create the motif, and then short fibers are attached to create a velvety surface.
- **Burn-out printing** is a process that employs a chemical to destroy fibers, creating a semitransparent design.
- **Embroidery** can decorate a fabric by stitching yarns, stones, or sequins into a design on top of fabric.

FIGURE 8.5 Varieties of finishing techniques are used on denim to strip the color and distress the fabric to give a worn effect.

stage five: finishes

Before a fabric is ready to be made into a garment or product, it first must be finished. **Finishes** are any chemical or mechanical process that a fabric undergoes to alter its inherent properties. Like color, finishes are added at any time during textile production. The finishing processes are classified into three main categories.

preparatory finishes

Preparatory finishes are applied to fabrics so that they can be further processed. Some examples are mercerizing to add strength, bleaching before dyeing to add optical brightness, degumming or scouring to remove unwanted particles or substances, or delustering to remove excessive shine. Most of the preparatory finishes are not visible by the consumer.

functional finishes

Functional finishes change the performance properties of a fabric. Common functional finishes include those that protect from fire, water, and soil. In addition, finishes to control shrinkage, static electricity, and wrinkles can be applied to fabrics. New finishes, such as antibacterial and antiseptic finishes, are being used in health-related industries.

aesthetic finishes

Aesthetic finishes change the appearance or hand of a fabric. Examples of application techniques for these finishes are brushing, glazing, embossing, sueding, stiffening, stone washing, or acid washing. Solid fabrics, such as denim, may be presented with multiple finishes or washes to offer variety to the customer.

TRIMS AND FINDINGS

In addition to textile and fabric trends, innovations in trims and findings can affect the direction of fashion. Trims such as braid, lace, or novelty appliqués are used to create newness. Findings such as buttons, zippers, Velcro closures, and belts can be both functional and decorative. Some seasons, the color of the findings and trims are selected to complement the color palette, and other seasons they conflict. Just as accessory trends change, the acceptance of large ornamentation may be stylish at one time, and little ornamentation may be in vogue at another. During the 1990s, modest trim or findings were visible in fashion as the minimalist look was most acceptable. In 2010, large "statement jewelry" was most desired, and this trend appeared in apparel and home furnishings as well by adding extravagant findings and trims.

FIGURE 8.6 Feathers used as a trim detail are clustered and layered to bring emphasis to the exaggerated shoulder.

FIGURE 8.7 Sustainable fabrics have been introduced to lessen the harmful impact from textile production on the ecosystem.

TEXTILE INNOVATIONS

sustainable fabrics

With increasing interest in natural and **sustainable fabrics**, organic cotton, hemp, bamboo, eucalyptus, pineapple, soy, and seaweed are fibers that have become alternatives. Several of the fibers are considered sustainable because they grow quickly and require little pesticides or water. From the antibacterial qualities to nonpolluting manufacturing methods, the impact of textile fiber choices is being addressed. Textile manufacturers are implementing changes to decrease the negative environmental impact from the production of textiles. The subject of sustainable textiles is being discussed and implemented all over the world.

technological advances in fabrics

Recent technological innovations have brought advances in fabrics, often referred to as smart fabrics, including spider silk fibers, wicking jersey, electrotextiles, textiles with nanotechnology, fiber optic fabric, and temperature-sensitive textiles:

- **Spider silk fibers** are extremely strong fibers, as Randy Lewis, professor of molecular biology at the University of Wyoming in Laramie, explains: "There's a lot of interest in spider silk fibers because they're stronger than almost any other manmade fiber and they're also elastic." These fibers can be used to create various biomedical devices of extraordinary strength. Technology has enabled the genetic manipulation of spiders with other creatures, such as goats, to produce this type of fiber in large quantities. A possible application for spider silk fibers is in the manufacturing of bulletproof apparel that is lighter in weight and more flexible than the materials currently in use. *Web site*: www.nsf.gov.
- **Wicking jersey** is a stretchy performance fabric that has fibers included that have the ability to pull moisture away from the body and leave the skin feeling cool and dry. *Web site*: www.coolmax.invista.com.
- **Electrotextiles** have been developed by covering polymer fibers with a metallic coating, producing strong and flexible strands. Once thought to be unsuitable for clothing, the textile industry is embracing the new technology. The wearer can experience a variety of functions, from controlling temperature to the monitoring of medical conditions. In the future, this innovative technology may allow people to wear clothing wired with electrical devices, such as cell phones, computing devices, or music players. Research is ongoing to provide electrotextiles for applications for space travel, military uses, and for the increasing needs of law enforcement. *Web site*: www.sti.nasa.gov.

FIGURE 8.8 During the 2011 Super Bowl half-time show, The Black Eyed Peas wore garments made with fiber optic fabrics.

- **Textiles with Nanotechnology** add functionality and value to traditional textiles by creating nanolayers that control the movement of chemicals through the layers of fabric. This technology may be used in the manufacturing of protective clothing to shield the wearer from the effects of biological warfare. *Web site*: www.nanotextiles.human.cornell.edu.
- **Fiber Optic Fabric** is a unique fabric made from ultra-thin fibers that allow light to be emitted through advanced luminous technology. The fibers are connected to LEDs and the light travels through the length of the fiber producing a glowing effect. When the optic fibers are woven together with other manufactured fibers, many colors can be made.
- **Temperature sensitive textiles** are not only extremely breathable and lightweight but can also regulate body temperature. This material is treated with paraffin, and as the body becomes hot, the paraffin becomes more liquid, which lets heat pass through the garment. The paraffin solidifies as the body gets cold, keeping the heat near the skin. The fabric can expand or contract to properly fit to an individual's body. *Web site*: www.sti.nasa.gov.

HOW TO DEVELOP A TEXTILE AND MATERIALS FORECAST

step 1: formulate textiles and materials ideas

As in theme development and color forecasting, the process for developing a textile and materials forecast begins with research. By understanding the basics of textiles, the terminology, and the details about fabrications, the forecaster begins to look for newness to add to his or her information. Forecasters also consider trims, findings, embellishments, and materials for the forecast.

Fiber producers, textile manufacturers, and trade associations present the latest developments in fabrics and textiles at trade shows and fabric fairs. Trade shows can focus on seasonal themes or innovations in fibers, yarns, textiles, prints, color processes, and new finishes. Fashion professionals attend the fabric fairs to view innovative collections of fabrics and surface designs for a variety of fashion markets. Designers and manufacturers can also discover new suppliers, source materials, learn of new developments, and order samples. At the shows, forecasters and consultants display trend information and offer presentations on color, fabric, new looks, and silhouette. In conjunction with the fairs, leading industry professionals in fields of technology and marketing often hold seminars.

Some of the leading shows include:

- Premiére Vision in Paris
- Premiére Vision Preview in New York
- Interstoff Asia Textile Fair in Hong Kong
- Ideacomo in Como, Italy
- Pitti Filati in Florence, Italy
- Yarn Fair International in New York
- Yarn Expo in Shanghai
- International Fashion Fabric Exhibition in New York

FIGURE 8.9 The fabric display at Premiére Vision highlights new textile trends.

FRANK IOVINO, PRESIDENT OF MIROGLIO TEXTILES USA

American Manufacturers No Longer Produce Domestically

The office of Miroglio Textiles is the only Italian fabric company that still has permanent representation in New York. Although the desire for manufacturing in the U.S. is apparent, the factories that produced American garments are nearly all gone. Design and marketing responsibilities for garment companies continue to be based in the U.S., but much of the manufacturing has moved to other global locations.

Following the shows, most fabric firms host clients in their showrooms or send representatives to follow up on products of interest. The agent also keeps clients up to date on information generated from the show, including the most-desired products and items that produced the most interest. Since textiles and apparel are produced in countries all over the world, the exhibitions showcase the newest apparel fabric collections and make them available to diversified global clients.

Runway shows also give the forecaster insight about upcoming textile, material, trim, and findings trends. When new innovations are spotted from the collections, the forecaster identifies if the newness is because of new fibers, finishes, or any other changes related to the textile process. Changes in the texture often give clues to upcoming textile trends. Sometimes the novelty is created when different fabrications are combined in original ways. Other times the innovation is derived from inspiration from past eras.

Fashion Snoops observed changes in textile trends following the Paris runway collections in 2011: "In our last look at the major fashion weeks, Paris proves that sheer fabrics are the most important expression of the season. As we've seen in the other cities, silk chiffon, organza and netting are all part of sheer, and in Paris, tulle becomes its own topic. Lace is also a big deal from panels and overlays to trim." This observation was later used to develop the textiles portion of a fashion forecast.

Textile organizations, fabric producers and councils, trade publications, and fabric libraries also offer information and ideas for the forecaster. Forecasters develop their own reliable sources for research.

Retail fabric stores, vintage stores, or used clothing outlets are places where a forecaster researches. The materials can also be found in unlikely places such as nature, the hardware store, or the supermarket.

PAT TUNSKY, CREATIVE DIRECTOR, DONEGER CREATIVE SERVICES

The Design Library for Research and Swatches

When preparing a forecast, I rely on the Design Library for textile ideas and swatches. The Design Library has an extensive historical collection of antique and vintage swatches that have been collected from mills around the world in addition to modern and contemporary designs. I cannot rely on today's mills for upcoming textile ideas, instead the fabric producers rely on my information to begin their new collections and textile developments.

FIGURE 8.10 The Design Library is one of the finest designer resources in the world, with vast historical collections of antique, vintage, modern, and contemporary textiles for present-day use.

step 2: collect fabrics and materials

Swatches are sample pieces of fabric or materials that are collected for a forecast. Textile firms show their fabrics using **swatch cards**, **types**, or **head ends** to display the available selections or developmental fabrics. Forecasters collect any textiles or materials of interest, including ones that performed well in the past, or are commonly used, or are new to the market. Forecasters gather textiles and materials that fit best into the theme and color stories. Sometimes the textiles, prints, patterns, or textures inspire a new theme or an alternate color story. The materials can be artistic creations

FIGURE 8.11 Fashions made of brightly patterned and colored fabrics are worn by the four members of 2NE1, the South Korean hip-hop/pop girl band.

using surface design techniques such as hand painting, batik, or mixed-media collages. Materials can also be inspiration for the development of new textiles and the forecaster includes the items in the presentation.

step 3: edit, interpret, analyze, and predict the textiles and materials story

Once the fabrics, materials, and trims are collected, they are organized and categorized. Related items are grouped together and replication of ideas becomes apparent. Attention to the variety of fibers, fabric construction, textures, and colors keeps the story's appeal. Similarities in look, color, and pattern start to be recognizable and trends emerge. Lone items are often edited as cohesive stories are developed. The selections must then be interpreted and analyzed as the forecaster strives to understand why particular fabrications have the potential to become widely accepted. Finally, the forecaster makes a prediction, showcasing the textiles and materials that encapsulate the concept of the theme.

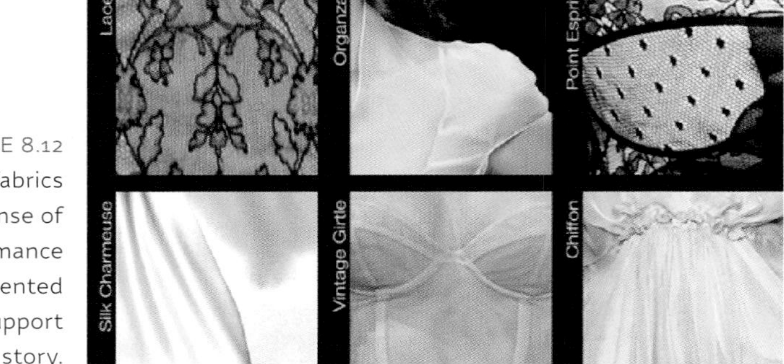

FIGURE 8.12 Dressmaker fabrics that evoke a sense of enchanting romance are presented together to support the fabric story.

Depending on the theme, a fabric story contains materials that are specifically suited to the idea or lifestyle. For instance, in the story "Parisian Romance," fabrics such as sheer chiffon, silk satin, delicate lace, openwork crochet, and transparent netting are appropriate for a lingerie-inspired trend.

step 4: identify fabric and materials

Once a fabric story has been selected, forecasters must conveyed the story through vivid descriptions and accurate information about the materials. Using textile terminology and vocabulary helps the forecast to be understandable. Forecasters describe the materials using details about fiber, yarns, fabric structure, color, and finishes as detailed in the earlier part of this chapter as the more scientific approach to communicate the forecast. A forecaster also describes the aesthetic qualities of the materials, such as look, feel, and texture, to convey the more artistic aspects of the selection. Details about performance qualities of the selections can give insight about how a textile will function or act. Through the combination of descriptions and the development of appropriate wording, a textile forecast is written.

step 5: write story about the textiles and materials

The story about the selections of textiles, materials, trims, and findings describes the information about each item and provides a summary for the selections as a whole. Each item is named using the style name associated with the item, or explained by its inspiration. Reference of past use of particular items can be included to convey the evolution of a textile or to name the historical time when the textile was last popular. For instance, the story can explain a prediction of materials inspired by the glamour of old Hollywood from the 1930s noting the return of embellished satin. The reemergence of textured, multicolored patchwork patterns can be described in the story focusing on fabric trends inspired from the 1970s.

As each component of the forecast is developed, the forecaster must continuously reaffirm that the new information that is being added about color and textiles helps to support the overall theme.

In the sample forecast, "Island Breeze," the textiles, materials, trims, and findings that appear on the board are natural and sustainable fabrics, including organic cotton, hemp webbing, bamboo dobby, and

FIGURE 8.13 The seemingly unrelated mixes of texture and color are masterfully combined to create a modern patchwork dress.

PAT TUNSKY, CREATIVE DIRECTOR, DONEGER CREATIVE SERVICES

Utility Trend

One of the major movements that I forecast for the next several years is the trend that I am calling "utility." The utility trend can serve as a denim replacement because denim has oversaturated the market. The utility trend can be described as an alternative to denim, having a blend of military styling and casual wear through color and fabrications.

FIGURE 8.14 For her "Island Breeze" textiles and materials board, Erica Mahmood provides supporting ecofriendly examples.

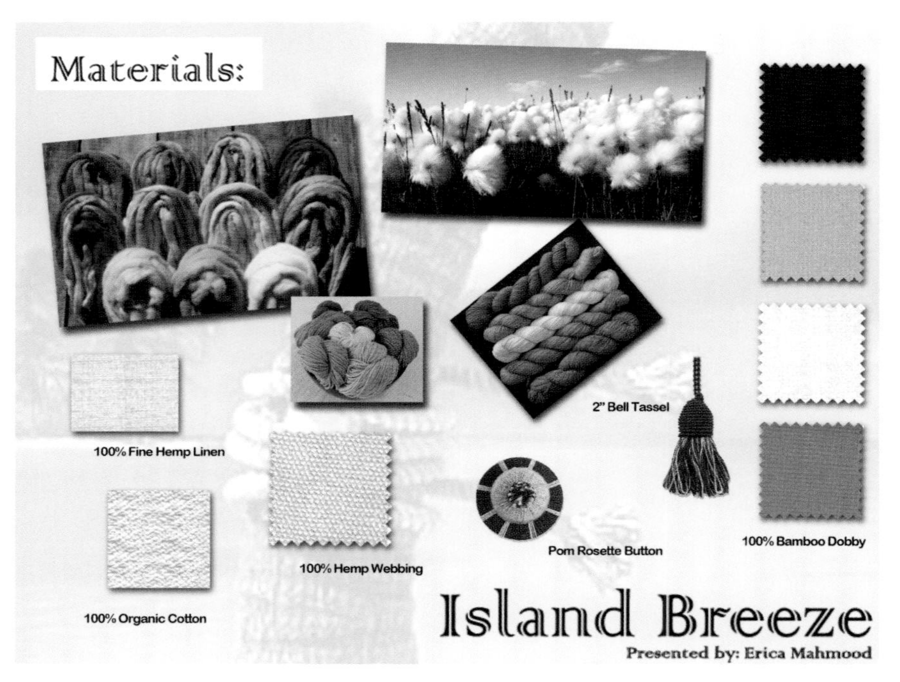

an ecofriendly pom rosette button. The image of cotton growing in the field reinforces the natural focus of the theme. Using earthy selections create a comfortable, relaxing, and airy feel.

SUMMARY

Forecasters need to have an understanding of textiles, trims, findings, and materials, including how they are produced, in order to articulate a textiles and materials forecast. Forecasters need to develop a vocabulary and language of textiles to properly predict the subtleties of change in future fashion and report these findings effectively. Not only is it important to understand the established basics of textiles, but knowing the history of textiles along with the awareness of new technology and emerging fabrics keeps a forecaster current.

KEY TERMS

- Textile story
- Textile
- Trim
- Findings
- Material
- Fiber
- Cotton
- Hand
- Flax
- Slubs
- Wool
- Silk
- Manufactured fibers
- Polymers
- Spinneret
- Polyester
- Nylon
- Acrylic
- Spandex
- Rayon
- Acetate
- Colorfast
- Yarns
- Fabric structure
- Woven
- Loom
- Plain weave
- Twill weave
- Satin weave
- Dobby weaves
- Jacquard weaves
- Tapestries
- Knit fabrics
- Weft knits
- Warp knits
- Nonwoven fabrics
- Color ways
- Dyeing
- Bleaching
- Printing
- Monotone
- Multicolored
- Application or direct printing
- Motif
- Discharge printing
- Resist printing
- Digital printing
- Flock printing
- Burn-out printing
- Embroidery

- Finishes
- Trims
- Sustainable fabrics
- Smart fabrics
- Spider silk fibers
- Wicking jersey
- Electrotextiles
- Textiles with nanotechnology
- Fiber optic fabric
- Temperature-sensitive textiles
- Swatches
- Swatch cards
- Types
- Head ends

ACTIVITIES

1. Follow the Steps to Develop a Textiles and Materials Forecast

Step 1. Formulate textiles and materials ideas.
Step 2. Collect textiles and materials.
Step 3. Edit, interpret, analyze, and predict the textiles and materials story.
Step 4. Identify textiles and materials.
Step 5. Write details about the textiles and materials.

2. Visit a Fabric Store for Fabric Trends

Visit a local fabric store. Search for fabrics that were recently displayed in the store. Look for merchandised groups of fabrics. Identify the themes of the newest arrivals. Is the newness based on fiber, color, pattern, or innovation?

3. Create a Fabric Journal

Create a fabric journal. Divide the journal into sections that correspond to specific themes. Identify emerging fabrications and collect images. Note different types of texture. Provide names or labels for each selection.

4. Identify Fabrics as Classics or Fads

Gather fabric swatches that are considered classics. Gather fashion swatches that are considered fads. Identify the names.

5. Research New Fabric Technology

Find information about new fabric innovations. Contact suppliers of new fabrics for information and/or swatches. Report new technological advances.

Objectives

- Understand the look forecasting process.
- Review design elements and principles.
- Explore innovation through design.
- Develop a vocabulary for describing styles and details of garments.
- Learn to develop the look forecast.

How do forecasters sense the shifts of design aesthetics? How does the shape of a product contribute to the look? How do the silhouettes of garments change so that sensuous hourglass shapes predominate one season and angular minimalistic shapes the next? Why is the look of popular furniture geometric and sleek one year and cozy and soft the next? Why are architectural styles characterized by simplification of form and minimal ornamentation during one period and characterized by organic floral-inspired motifs and flowing forms the next?

WHAT IS A LOOK FORECAST?

The portion of a forecast that focuses on design elements, principles, and innovations is the "look" segment of the forecast. A forecaster identifies shapes, silhouettes, and combinations of features that contribute to the total look. The process consists of researching the similarities and differences across different design practices and then editing, interpreting, analyzing, and predicting the upcoming direction of looks to come. By observing design changes, a forecaster can formulate predictions of what looks will come next.

DESIGN ELEMENTS

Design elements are the building blocks for designed products. The elements include line, silhouette, shape, and details as well as color, texture, and pattern (discussed in previous chapters).

line

A **line** has many qualities that can affect the look of a design. Lines have direction—horizontal, vertical, or diagonal—as well as qualities such as width and length. The different types of lines used in a design can affect the character of the piece. For instance, vertical lines can create an elongated, slimmer look while horizontal lines draw attention to width.

Diagonal lines create a sense of motion by allowing the eye to travel. Lines on the outside of a garment identify the shape or silhouette.

FIGURE 9.1
The use of bold lines brought graphic excitement to the Missoni 2012 resort collection.

silhouette

The **silhouette** is the overall outline or outside shape of a design or a garment. The silhouette is the one-dimensional figure used to create a look using form and space. The silhouette of a design can be classified using geometric terms such as circle, oval, rectangle, cylinder, sphere, cone, triangle, or square. Silhouettes for garments can also be described using letters of the alphabet: A or A-line, T or kimono-shaped, or V or wide at the top and narrow at the bottom.

Having the vocabulary to describe the overall silhouette is necessary to convey the specific look of the design. Like the shapes themselves, the terminology used to describe the silhouettes is always changing. Using the correct buzzwords help forecasters to convey subtle changes and newness. A forecaster can describe a rounded silhouette as cocoon-shaped. The lamp shade skirt or bubble skirt describes volume. Cylinder-shaped sportswear can be described more effectively as long, straight tunics over slim, narrow skirts. Using terms such as slouchy sweaters, simple sheath or shift, traditional Asian-inspired kimono-style wrap dresses, or elegant columnar shapes with a body-skimming fit conveys the silhouette's description with more flair. In architecture, columns help to define order as a vertical support element giving the feel of strength and organization. Garment silhouettes that have been used in certain periods of history or culture also are ways that one describes shape: flapper, empire, or harem.

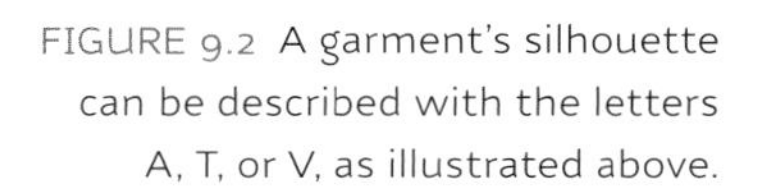
FIGURE 9.2 A garment's silhouette can be described with the letters A, T, or V, as illustrated above.

details

The lines on the inside of a garment provide **details,** such as collars, necklines, sleeves, pleats, darts, pockets, and contour seaming. Several lines together, or asymmetrical lines, can create optical interest. Embellishments and trims, such as embroidery, buttons, zippers, appliqués, and ribbons, can further enhance a garment's look. Details for peasant blouses are a ruffled neckline, gathered neckline, novel halter neckline, off-the-shoulder asymmetrical neckline, flowing bishop sleeves, or elbow-length sleeves with flounces. Details for coat dresses may include a structured notched collar with ornamental stitching, draped lapels, brass zip closures, menswear-inspired welt pockets, ornamental buttons as double-breasted closures, or vintage-inspired embroidery placed near the hem. Details for new accessories include multicolored woven leather looks, luggage-style stitching, bright gold buckles and magnetic closures, and industrial-imitated screws and rivets.

DESIGN PRINCIPLES

Design principles use design elements in combinations to create aesthetically pleasing looks. Proportion, balance, focal point, and harmony are design principles.

proportion

Proportion is the scale used to divide a garment into parts. For instance, horizontal lines are used to break designs into sections, such as waistline, hip line, or shoulder line. Equal proportions can be created

FIGURE 9.3 On this J. Mendel skirt from the 2012 resort collection, the asymmetrical pleating detail creates a chic, modern look.

in a short dress by creating a line at the waist, while an exaggerated shoulder yoke line creates unequal proportions by positioning the line close to the top of the garment instead of the center. Proportions for pants can be described with wording such as higher waistlines, hip-slung styles, or extra-long lengths to further explain the looks. A description for a dress could be: a shift with ornamented shoulder yokes and a dropped waist or short tulip skirt.

FIGURE 9.4 For the 2010 Academy Awards, actress Charlize Theron wore a gown nicknamed the Cinnabon with an unmistakable focal point at the bust.

balance

Balance is a state of equilibrium or equal distribution. A symmetrical design is equally balanced, or the same on each side, but an asymmetrical design is different on each side. An asymmetrical design can become balanced by adding details, such as bolder shapes and colors, to shift the balance. Graphic stripes and color blocking can add a playful mood to a design. Incorporating brightly colored plaids and delicate minifloral motifs into patchwork dresses gives the overall look a sense of balance.

focal point

The **focal point** of a design is the area to which the eye is drawn. A designer may use line or color to direct the viewer to a certain aspect of the design. Jil Sander's Raf Simons used a contrast peplum as a focal point in a recent collection. Optic stripes were the eye-catching areas of the shift dresses as well. Beading or shiny embellishments are often the focal point in evening wear. In interior design, the focal point of a room can be created by proper placement of artwork or accessories.

FIGURE 9.5 Avril Lavigne is known for her mismatched rock- and punk-style clothing.

harmony or discord

Harmony is achieved when all design elements and principles work successfully together to create an aesthetically pleasing design. **Discord** is created by a lack of harmony and is often used to intentionally break the acceptable rules. Examples of discord would be the "grunge look" of the 1990s and the "deconstruction movement" of the early twenty-first century when the fashion went against societal norms. These radical shifts in design principles change the way one thinks about and views the rules of design.

DESIGN INNOVATION

Design innovation is a process that takes into account what a product can do for an individual. Through modern understanding of design potential, a person can find meaning and create personal connections to the product. Consumers can explore their desires and attitudes through designed products. Phrases such as "experiential design," "lifestyle," and "memory and meaning" are new buzz phrases in the current business vocabulary for a fresh standard of innovation in the design and marketing of products. With consumers striving to find meaning and a sense of belonging, the visionary design futurists examine the influence and create designs beyond trends or silhouettes that have power to change culture. Since the "global world" is connected by technology, the future is about design excellence that is culturally important and accessible to all.

HOW TO DEVELOP A "LOOK" FORECAST

step 1: formulate look and silhouette ideas

Each part—the design elements, principles, and innovations—contributes to the total look when cumulatively added together. To fine-tune a look forecast, one must find the repetition of a shape or detail. When certain silhouettes reappear or subtle shifts in shapes of garments are noticeable, this can be the beginning of change and the evolution of the look. As in theme, color, textiles and materials, a "look" forecast begins with research. Runway shows, fashion magazines, retail stores, Internet Web sites, blogs, vintage collections, and the streets are filled with examples of looks. Forecasters research look concepts in nonapparel markets as well. Research into new technologies can guide the forecaster. Shifts in styles of art, architecture, and interiors give clues to the forecaster. Often information is shared between the creative teams, data specialists, and retailers, who give insight about the shifts in fashionable shapes.

FIGURE 9.6 The look of the traditional Louis Vuitton luggage collection took a modern turn with the introduction of graffiti-style letters and motifs.

By identifying the emerging looks and lifestyle trends, forecasters can begin to sense the looks that will become widely accepted in the future. Different designers, fashion houses, and retailers have style characteristics, brand recognition, and specific target markets that help to identify their look and define the spirit of the products. For instance, the Ralph Lauren label, Polo, is known for preppy patterns, vintage-inspired silhouettes, and classic colors that define the lifestyle and mood of the collection. The urban fashions made by companies such as Baby Phat or Rocawear first appealed to the followers of hip-hop music and culture. The reversed hat, low-slung pants, and graffiti-inspired prints have evolved into mainstream fashion, catering to meet the needs of urban fashion followers.

There are places and events that all fashion forecasters must search for information, but knowing where to look for the particular customer or target market is crucial in finding the best information. For newness in the youth market, clubs that feature underground bands, innovative cafés and restaurants, artistic new galleries, viral videos, and blogs are monitored. Cool hunters or teams of trend consultants research new and emerging spots and relay the information back to forecasters.

step 2: develop a look and silhouette story

Forecasters use a variety of methods to collect the information: collecting pictures and magazine clippings, sketching, or taking photographs. Using personal notes, memories, and conversations combined with instinct and intuition helps forecasters notice and examine signals of change. Once the information and images are collected, the story is developed. Groups of images that show apparel and nonapparel items are included.

ADAM YANKAUSKAS, DESIGN DIRECTOR AT MAGGY LONDON

Understanding Target Market by Exchange of Information Between Retailers and Designer

Knowing my markets and customers helps me to select appropriate looks. I travel to the retailers, often attending meetings that highlight the best-selling items, or working with them developing products. The retailers and I do a "walk through" of their stores, identifying what is selling, and I take this information back to my team. The communication between the stores and the manufacturer is the key to knowing what to produce next. I also educate the buyers about upcoming trends by showing them the runway photo collages. Sometimes the buyers are reluctant to experiment with new styles and the photo images help them to understand the importance of a trend, and this gives them the confidence to step ahead.

step 3: edit, interpret, analyze, and predict the look and silhouette story

After the research is completed, forecasters begin the editing process. By grouping looks together that are similar, one can begin to see the repetition of fashion shapes and details. The goal is to create classifications of the looks. Are garments draped, ruffled, or tucked with excessive volume, or are the looks sleek, simple, and classic? Is the emphasis on the bust, waist, or hips? What embellishments are reoccurring—embroidery, stones, or lace? What findings are seen—buttons or zippers? Is a particular fit recognizable? Are certain shapes appearing in home furnishings? Are particular forms reappearing in the newest technological gadgets? Once forecasters determine the classifications, the looks that are aligned with the theme, color, and textile forecast can be selected to support the message of the overall forecast.

While keeping in mind the purpose or market for the selections, forecasters hone the most significant looks or creative ideas. A trendy, fast-fashion manufacturer or retailer requires looks that appeal to its customers that are different from the looks that appeal to more conservative ones. Regardless of market, certain looks become the "big picture" looks and others become the "fringe" news. One can think of this editing process as the condensing of the latest trends with a pointed focus while keeping in mind that some fashion will become long-term movements and others will be short-lived fads. To make the final selections for the forecast, forecasters must be skilled editors.

The interpretation and analysis begins by asking what is causing society's desire for change or by considering the motivation behind the trend. The forecaster strives to explain why the changes are likely to occur. There is always a reason for the evolution of fashion—a cause and effect.

MAGGY LONDON + LONDON TIMES SPRING 09 TREND REPORT: PENCIL THIN

MAGGY LONDON + LONDON TIMES SPRING 09 TREND REPORT: BARE NECESSITIES

MAGGY LONDON + LONDON TIMES SPRING 09 TREND REPORT: SARONG SONG

MAGGY LONDON + LONDON TIMES SPRING 09 TREND REPORT: RUFFLE MY TIERS

FIGURE 9.7–9.10
At Maggy London, collages are created to categorize popular looks and identify trends from the runway shows.

For instance, one of the significant trends that recently appeared on the runways and the streets is a tribal global fusion, a mixing of African and Native American cultures into a modern-day look. A desire to maintain roots, customs, and identities as a people is fueling this tribal trend that makes use of rich ethnic patterns and references from indigenous cultures, such as Native American motifs, batiks, ikats, and mudcloths. Kaftans and ponchos are key fashion items, appearing in a saturated palette of rich browns, indigo blues, and intense African-inspired primary pigments. The looks have appeared on the runways from Gucci, Missoni, and Louis Vuitton as well as at the Coachella music festival.

ADAM YANKAUSKAS, DESIGN DIRECTOR AT MAGGY LONDON

How to Forecast Fashion?

Knowing that trends continue, I watch for the changes and evolution of fashion. The most important place to see fashion is on the runways. As Creative Director, overseeing eight designers and five textile designers, one of the most successful ways to determine the major trends is to view every photo from the runways of the world, categorize the images, arrange them into collages, and identify the trends. Of course, my focus is on dresses and there are certain designer collections that I currently pay close attention to: Lanvin and Dries Van Noten. Understanding that the collections that Maggy London and London Times produce are derivative lines that follow the influences of the bridge and designer markets, I identify the silhouettes that are translatable to my markets.

The youth of today are also influenced profoundly by media and celebrities. By emulating the lifestyles of celebrities and following their fashion leadership, the looks for the "tweens" and teens have become seemingly more appropriate for the stage than the classroom or street. Costume-like attire that calls for attention has been accepted as typical day wear, including hot pants, see-through tops, overembellished apparel, lingerie as day wear, and eccentric shoes. The costumes that singer Miley Cyrus wears when she performs, for example, can later be spotted in the streets as girls try to imitate her. The effect created by the extravagant looks on teens is a manifestation of their desire to be noticed and their need for attention.

FIGURE 9.11 At the spring 2011 ready-to-wear show, the Missoni collection was full of vibrant colors and tribal shapes that fused multicultural looks from around the globe.

FIGURE 9.12 Singer Miley Cyrus's provocative stage costumes are often imitated and worn on the streets.

The other important analysis is to establish the tempo or speed of the trend and the range of its impact. One must ask: Is the look a visionary spark, directional fashion, an oversaturated look, or a trend ready to end in excess?

FIGURE 9.13 Apple's well-crafted, wildly successful iPad quickly became a "hot item" desired by people of all ages.

In addition to identifying the motivation, timing, and potential impact of a look, a forecaster must also identify if the look will become a minor trend or a **"hot item."** A minor trend may appeal to fashion followers of a specific style tribe or lifestyle. Although the look may be accepted by most of the members of that group,

FOWARD THINKER

LORI HOLLIDAY BANKS, DIRECTOR OF RESEARCH AND ANALYTICS, TOBE REPORT, A DIVISION OF THE DONEGER GROUP

Questions a Forecaster Asks When Analyzing the Runway Shows

When viewing the runway shows, the questions that one must ask are:

- How does the current collection differ from the past collection?
- Have the looks appeared on the streets?
- What is the projection of the looks?
- Will the looks have longevity?
- How will the looks evolve?

DAVID WOLFE, CREATIVE DIRECTOR, DONEGER CREATIVE SERVICES

Innovation Will Lead in Future Fashion

Innovation of the industry and products, methods, and ideas is where I see the future of fashion. Imagine if an apparel manufacturer came up with a clothing innovation as impacting as the iPhone was to communication and technology. Every customer would race to buy the newness. Possibilities in the textile sector could be the area of fashion where such a phenomenon may occur.

the group itself may not be large enough to support the look in the larger, mass market. An item is a specific design or product that is a "must have" and can create interest among several markets and appeal to customers with different demographics. The iPad is an example of such an item because it has been accepted by people of different ages and socioeconomic groups.

Once the analysis is completed, the silhouette forecasts can be finalized based on each theme. Forecasters select the images or the illustrations that are the best possible examples to convey the message of the forecast. Flats, or flat drawings, may be created to show the look of the forecast in addition to photos. Images from several different markets help show universal possibilities of the theme and support the theme's possible impact on multiple industries. Groups of apparel images for different target markets may be planned for a portion of the presentation. These may include women's wear, children's wear, and menswear from the designer level to budget market. To illustrate the possibility of the forecast in nonapparel markets, interior design, architecture, accessories, cosmetics, art, and industrial design images are included.

FIGURE 9.14 Erica Mahmood's first silhouette board for "Island Breeze" reflects the casual mood of her apparel presentation.

FIGURE 9.15 The second silhouette board for "Island Breeze" shows earthy, natural accessories and shoes.

FIGURE 9.16 The third silhouette board for "Island Breeze" illustrates the way that the theme can be translated to the interior design and the home furnishing markets.

step 4: assign look names

Once the images have been selected and the reason for including the selection is clear, the forecaster describes the look. Using specific established terminology clearly defines the images and ideas. Throughout history, already-established silhouettes and details have been named, and a forecaster must be familiar with them and use the names to accurately identify the looks. For looks that are new innovations, original vocabulary, or expressions are needed. In recent years, for example, the "geta shoe" became the name associated with footwear inspired by Chinese and Japanese platform shoes that is a cross between a clog and a flip-flop. The "boyfriend blazer" became the catch phrase associated with the look of a man's jacket worn by a woman. The forecasters must be able to identify the looks and develop vocabulary to articulate each look.

step 5: write details about the look and silhouette story

The final step in preparing a look forecast is to write the information for the presentation. A well-scripted, written explanation of the shapes includes the naming of originators of the creations, the descriptions of the silhouettes, and the call out of the details. When used properly, a well-developed vocabulary of silhouette and shapes not only articulates the specifics of a look forecast but also connects the memory and mood of the entire project.

In the sample forecast, "Island Breeze," the silhouettes for the apparel that are shown are very flowing and relaxing. Whether it is a sundress or a bathing suit, the looks give off a vibe of being earthy and relaxed, a feeling of being complete. An asymmetrical one-shoulder top is embellished with a soft floral appliqué. The linen drawstring pants and casual shorts with a self-tie belt are sporty and easy. Several of the dresses, skirts, and tops allow for movement with A-line shapes and ethnic-inspired embroidery at the hem. The looks have very flattering silhouettes that conform to many body shapes and make any woman feel feminine in what she is wearing.

FOWARD THINKER

ADAM YANKAUSKAS, DESIGN DIRECTOR AT MAGGY LONDON

Fashion Vocabulary

Along with knowledge of the history of fashion, having a vocabulary of fashion terms is crucial. Being articulate with fashion terms develops a language of fashion that is universal. For example, one must know the difference between a shift and a sheath. A shift is a loose-fitting dress and a sheath fits closer to the body.

FIGURE 9.17
The highly stylized geta sandals by Kenzo in spring 2011 were inspired by Japanese platform shoes.

For nonapparel items, such as accessories and shoes, the "Island Breeze" silhouettes are meant to complement the already tranquil look. The earthy earrings use shapes that originated in nature, and the organic necklaces are made with collected stones and sea treasures found at the beach. The shoes are made to look and feel effortless yet modern, connecting one to the island surroundings. These items enhance the carefree look and style. The bits and pieces found in home furnishings and interiors combine all of the elements of the trend. Natural and organic cotton bed linens and earthy inspired motifs on pillows create an inviting setting for the home. Weathered wood, fresh flowers, and beach-inspired botany adorn the eco-friendly island look.

SUMMARY

In developing a look forecast, a forecaster must take into consideration design elements, principles, and innovation. Shapes, silhouettes, and design features contribute to the total look. The forecaster seeks out clues about emerging looks and collects evidence to support the theme. Through editing, the forecaster organizes the selected looks. Through the interpreting and analyzing process, the forecaster questions why fashion looks evolve and then predicts the changes. The look forecast is developed showing visual imagery that reinforces the theme concept and further defines the look. Using fashion vocabulary of existing fashion terminology and contemporary buzzwords, the forecaster names the looks in the forecast. A written portion of the look forecast is prepared to become part of the script for the presentation.

KEY TERMS

- Design elements
- Line
- Silhouette
- Details
- Design principles
- Proportion
- Balance
- Focal point
- Harmony
- Discord
- Design innovation
- Hot item

ACTIVITIES

1. Follow the Steps to Create the Look Forecast

Step 1. Formulate look and silhouette ideas.

Step 2. Collect images, sketches, or create flats.

Step 3. Edit, interpret, analyze, and predict the look story.

Step 4. Identify the looks and silhouettes.

Step 5. Write details about the looks and silhouettes.

2. Create Collages of Looks

Collect images of apparel and home furnishings from magazines. Group garments with similar looks or silhouettes together. Create a collage of the images.

3. Develop a Vocabulary of Fashion Looks

Name the looks with existing fashion vocabulary and create new buzzwords to describe the looks. Create your own fashion dictionary.

4. Create a Look Journal

Place images of fashion looks in a journal. Add new items each week including ideas, drawings, and comments. Use the journal to track the evolution of looks.

CREATING AND PRESENTING A FORECAST

10

Objectives

- Understand how to create a unified final forecast.
- Identify keys to a successful forecast.
- Learn how to create the visual presentation.
- Outline script development.
- Learn to present the forecast.
- Show examples of fashion forecasts.

Forecasters spend all of their time working toward one basic goal: creating and presenting their forecasts. Here forecasters gather all of the completed components (research, editing, interpretation, analysis, and predictions) for a successful presentation. What is the best way to present the information? How do forecasters successfully convince others to follow their prediction? What makes a successful presentation?

WHAT IS A FINAL FORECAST?

The two portions of a final fashion forecast include a visual portion and a written portion. To create a professional-quality forecast, a visually stimulating product and a compelling script must be developed. The visual portion is made up of presentation boards, computer-generated slides, or imagery created for the Web. The written portion can be verbally presented to an audience through a script, recorded as part of a webinar, or appear as text on the presentation boards. A combination of methods for presentation may be required so that the forecast can be presented in different settings. Forecasts may be offered through forecasting books, forecasting presentations, online forecasting sites, and webinars. The message of the forecast is understandable when both components fuse together to produce a strong point of view.

The process of creating a fashion forecast requires a combination of tools from either the scientific and objective approach or the artistic and subjective approach. By fusing the two approaches, a forecast can be filled with information and inspiration. Forecasters combine these approaches and create their own style of forecast that works best for their listeners and viewers.

KEYS TO A SUCCESSFUL FORECAST

A successful forecasting presentation must create meaning by transforming the forecasting data into knowledge that is applicable for the audience or client. All parts of the forecast (theme, colors, textiles and materials, and the look) must be presented so that they can be understood. Besides being practical and understandable, the forecast message must be communicated to stir emotions as well.

FRANK BOBER, CEO OF STYLESIGHT

Successful Fashion Formula

I believe that the successful formula for the shifting world of fashion is: Art + Technology = Action. In other words, starting with creativity and imagery, then adding information and tools gets the job done.

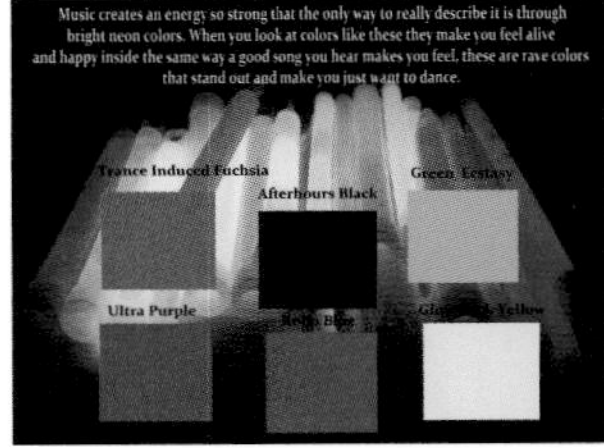

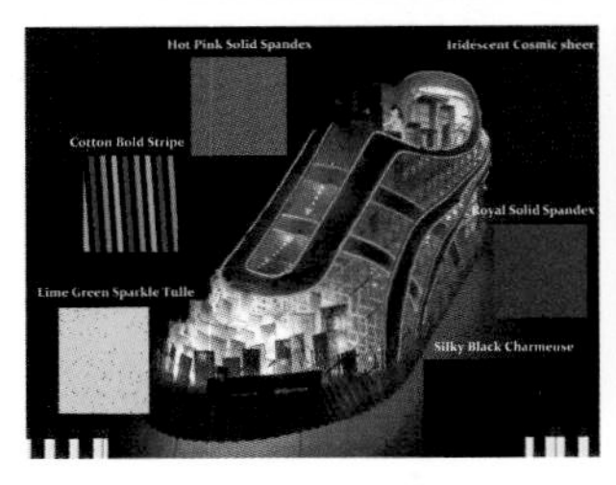

"I Can Feel The Beat"

Imagine a world where a die hard electro fan wakes up one day and sees that everyone is dressed like they are going to a rave and jamming out to house music. This is the future, the future of house music. Miami, a city that never sleeps is home to events such as Ultra Music Festival which has a huge impact on everyday things such as music and fashion. House music is growing rapidly because of these events and with it comes the bright neon colors, outrageous patterns, and unique sunglasses that create a different yet trendy new fashion look. Every year more and more people are excepting this crazy Miami lifestyle. It's only a matter of time before this raver's dream becomes a reality.

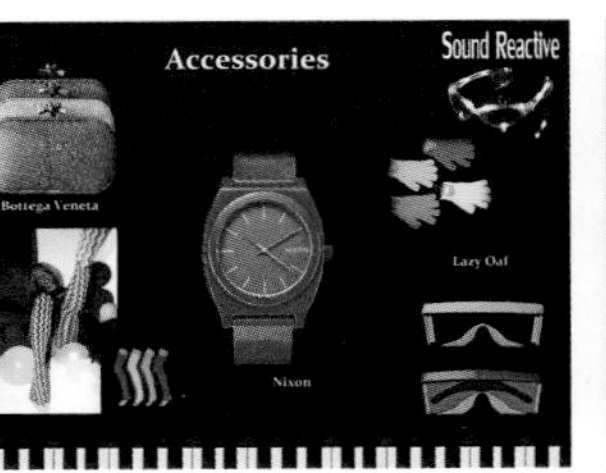

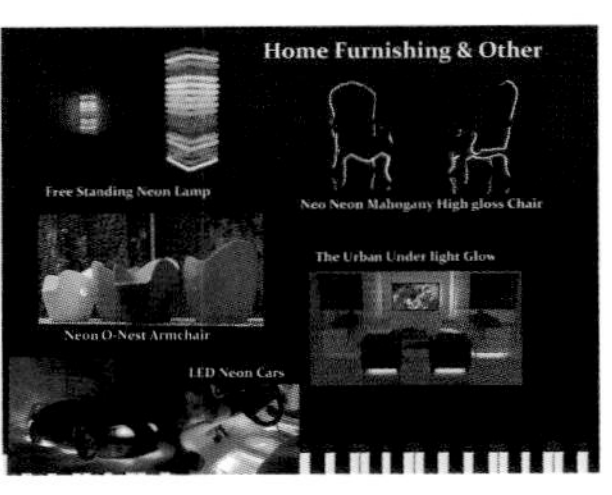

FIGURE 10.1 In Camila Nageva's fashion forecast, entitled "A Raver's Dream," the inspiration, title, mood, story, color palette, textiles, and the looks are presented for apparel, accessories, and home furnishings.

When audience members can anticipate the way that the forecast can be implemented into their businesses, the forecast effectively offers guidance and direction. Because each audience member or client has specific needs, the impact of the forecast may vary from person to person, but it should have a sense of universal appeal. For instance, if a forecaster is describing a theme or lifestyle, audience members

FOWARD THINKER

LILLY BERELOVICH, OWNER, PRESIDENT, AND CHIEF CREATIVE OFFICER OF FASHION SNOOPS

Intuition Then Research

I emphasize the need for designers and forecasters to listen to their own voices and follow their intuition first; then rely on research to back up their ideas. Without the creative impulses and ideas, fashion becomes the same and without character.

from a variety of markets should be able to find ways to execute the forecast for their market whether it is for apparel, home furnishings, or accessories.

A successful forecast inspires the audience to customize the message and find ways to apply the information into their own products. When the forecaster leads the client to his or her own discoveries, the impact of the forecast and variety of outcomes can create individual opportunities. Visually appealing boards and clearly edited information support a well-crafted presentation.

A forecast fails when the audience is left confused and uninspired. If the forecast does not effectively communicate the idea or purpose of the theme, the message is lost. For an audience to understand the significance of the idea or theme, a forecast must be carefully narrated and clearly focused. Too much information or visuals that are too complicated can cloud the impact of the forecast.

FIGURE 10.2 This "Save Me" forecast by Christina Rondinone was inspired by a 2008 exhibit at the Costume Institute at the Metropolitan Museum of Art that featured garments illustrating the influence of popular themes and characters from comic books. Following the exhibit, "superhero fashion" trickled into the mainstream in the form of comic book graphic T-shirts—most recently being referred to as "Geek Couture."

HOW TO CREATE A FORECAST

visual portion

The process begins by selecting, editing, and assembling the components into a forecasting board for each part of the forecast. Detailed information about developing each component appears as steps in Chapters 6 through 9.

The components are:

- Theme: idea, visionary theme imagery, interpretations, analysis, predictions, title, tagline, mood, story, and abbreviated story.
- Color: color inspiration ideas, color story, interpretations, analysis, predictions, color names, written descriptions for each color, color numbers, and color story summary.
- Textiles, materials, trims, and findings: ideas, textiles and materials samples, interpretations, analysis, predictions, identification of samples, and textiles and materials story summary.
- The look: ideas, apparel and nonapparel images and flats, interpretations, analysis, predictions, descriptions of looks, and the look story summary.

Once all components for the forecast have been prepared, the visual presentation can be created. At this stage, fashion and graphics can communicate the intended creative solutions, forecasting information, and future prediction. The information needs to be clearly displayed to deliver the intended message. Through layout, typography, background, color selection, and assembly style, the significance of the forecast can be delivered. The amount of boards needed to successfully show the imagery for a forecast can vary: Some forecasts are created by merging all of the components of the forecast onto two or three boards. Other presentations expand the amount of boards so that each component of the forecast is displayed on several boards, usually six to ten. Some forecasters even expand the forecast further with each theme presented in twenty to thirty boards.

FIGURE 10.3 Jaclynn Brennan's student project, titled Futuristic Glam, communicates her concept using bold graphics, strong colors, and dynamic layouts to help the viewer identify with the powerful futuristic forecast. In her own words, "[It] fuses classic elements with modern structures. This trend is inspired by technology, globalization, and the future of fashion. The trend is about shielding the body from the natural elements."

layout

The layout of a trend board or digital forecast directs how the viewer perceives and understands the message and meaning of the prediction. The board can be set up with either a horizontal or vertical layout (landscape or portrait). A focal point, or the area where the viewer's eye is first attracted, will give the viewer a place to start looking, so plan the most important item to represent the theme as the focal point. By dividing the layout into sections, the presentation can have several focal points that create a more visually dynamic view. The structure of the layout relies on fundamental graphic concepts: grids provide a structure used in magazines and books, groups define relationships of items, or paths highlight visual movement between objects.

The goal of a successful board is to guide the viewer through all of the images on the board. A forecasting board may contain all of the visual segments of the presentation: theme, color, materials and textiles, and looks or each of the segments can appear on separate boards. Consider placement, positive and negative space, and color relationships and begin to create a layout that is visually appealing and effective in delivering the intended message.

typography

Selection of **typeface** or *font* can connect the message of the text with the concept of the theme. A mood can be created by using size (point), font (style of lettering), and effects (such as bold, pictorial, or disorder). For the best results, choose type that is legible, well-spaced, and coordinates with the theme. The type used should include the title of the theme and any key words that are descriptive to the story. Do not include excessive amounts of type on the visual portion of the presentation.

background and color selection

Plan the background of the board, making certain that it will enhance the overall theme. Borders, backdrop, and decorative elements added to a presentation board often help to support the theme. Choose a color or texture that acts as a unifying force. For instance, a romantic theme may be enhanced by using an ivory lace background, pastel flowers, and pearls to support the theme.

assembly

With all of the components prepared for the board, begin the layout. Shift the items around the board, searching for the best possibilities for conveying the essence of the theme.

Choose a technique for cutting or cropping images. For a traditional board, cut the images accurately. For instance, for a theme dealing with a return to classics, all components should be cut precisely and neatly. For a theme dealing with vintage recycling, uneven or torn edges would be appropriate to further support the mood of the story. Attach items to the board using appropriate adhesives, making sure that the items are properly mounted. Spray adhesives and rubber cement are effective in securing the items without creating unevenness.

PAT TUNSKY, CREATIVE DIRECTOR, DONEGER CREATIVE SERVICES

Realistic Forecasting Method

The type of direction or forecast that I give to my clients is based on a realistic approach. My pragmatic information is very specific to the market. Other forecasters focus on the tone of fashion or the fashion on the horizon aimed at the creative designer. I begin with an analytical approach to the runway collections and, with a strong intuitive sense, I edit for precision. I focus on delivering information that will be usable by the clients to help them make clear choices and potential profit. With each client, I deliver information that is specific to their company's needs and market.

Creating a mood board digitally, using computer programs, is done in a manner similar to a traditional one. Boards can be created with a variety of programs, including PowerPoint, Photoshop, Illustrator, and InDesign. Most fashion forecasting services have an area where storyboards can be created, saved, and shared. Other sites, such as Polyvore.com, offer the user a place where they can collect, import, and use images to build and share mood boards.

To assemble the visual portion of the presentation, follow the instructions below to create the final forecast boards.

create theme board(s)

Begin the layout of the theme information. Take time to look closely at the selected images and explore the emotions and meaning that they are meant to elicit. Select the best inspirational theme images and plan them as the focal point of the presentation. Be sure that the selected theme image or images convey the story and mood of the project. Explore each image, color, shape, or line and its relationship to the theme.

Rate the importance and address the scale and clarity of the images, making the most important ones predominant. Choose an appropriate font style, size, and color for the title. Place the title of the theme on the first board. Additional text may also be added to board number one, including the tagline and mood words.

In the example below, "Inventive Vintage" is the theme title, with a tagline: "The fusion of modern edginess and the comfort of old." Vintage is always a popular trend, but what makes this different from past seasons is the mixing of old and new aspects of fashion.

For the opening board, the forecaster selected a series of images to illustrate mixing distressed old-world charm with a modern feminine feel. "Inventive Vintage" was inspired by the sort of decorations found in British cottages that are tattered and faded but achieve a fashionable overall effect. The shabby chic style is vintage but modern at the same time. Recycling old furniture and fabrics into contemporary creations is an important aspect of the theme. Vintage furniture, gardens of flowers, and the earth were inspiration for this theme. The font and colors support the theme. The ivory-carved frame creates the focal point for the collage of images. Floral motifs and butterflies support the delicate mood of innocence.

The second board continues the theme explanation. The story of the theme is included on the board surrounded by modern images filled with clothing and accessories. "Inventive Vintage" is inspired by a style of living that embraces its own slightly less-than-perfect attitude. "Inventive Vintage" is delicate, soft, romantic, relaxed, and feminine with a modern twist in the look.

The subtle frame, dusty floral patterns, and tinted color choices bring attention to the descriptive story that explains the modern approach of "Inventive Vintage."

FIGURE 10.4A Jenna Simon's opening board for her "Inventive Vintage" forecast includes a title, tagline, mood words, and imagery for the theme. Courtesy of Jenna Simon.

FIGURE 10.4B The story of the forecast "Inventive Vintage" is narrated on the second board, giving context to the theme. Courtesy of Jenna Simon.

create the color board

Begin the layout of color selections. Colors can be paper tabs, paint chips, yarns, fabric swatches, or miscellaneous items. It is important to note that flat color sources are needed to duplicate the exact shade for mills or printers. Cut the color tabs into consistent sizes and shapes to give equal value to each color in the palette. If the palette contains a selection of colors that are the predominant ones and additional colors that are planned as accents, the color tabs can be cut to special sizes to differentiate them, using proportion as a visual guide. Experiment with the color placement and the order in which the colors are placed. The arrangement can change the perception of the palette. Always place the color selections on a white or black background so that the perception of the color is not distorted by other colors.

As the color story is developed, the mood of the colors helps to further support the theme. Evaluate the colors and the meanings that they evoke. Remembering that color evolves, investigate past color palettes to track how the colors have changed.

Creating a color story digitally can be done by selecting colors from Internet sites or by downloading color images. Many forecasting companies provide libraries of colors that provide a place to collect and manipulate color stories. Circles, squares, or shapes can be filled with color for the board to indicate the color selections.

Naming the colors can be suggestive and communicate the theme, so choose the color names carefully. Consider categories of color names that support the theme. Using an established color identification system like Pantone, color numbers are often assigned to correspond with the color selections. Label the color names and/or numbers for the board.

FIGURE 10.4C The color story selected to represent "Inventive Vintage" is based on the theme of vintage femininity and a summer's English garden—which is supported by the color names being found in aspects in nature. Courtesy of Jenna Simon.

The colors chosen for "Inventive Vintage" are dusty and muted. The selections evoke the type of colors found in country houses filled with faded and worn decorations. Bleached-out pastel colors found in dried flowers or in aged paint support the theme. Muted floral colors tinted with gray form a palette that reflects a late summer's English garden. Moss green is an understated color that is filled with an antique sense of elegance, femininity, and innocence. Beige tones in all nuances evoke a sense of innocence and mystic feelings. Dusty rose and dried hydrangea in several different soft tones with ashy, muted color will replace the more vibrant fuchsia tones of past seasons. Elements from nature are included with color names like butterfly blue. The text included on the board describes the essence of the entire color story, including a reference to a romantic walk around a beautiful foggy garden.

create the textiles and materials board

Begin the layout of the swatches collected to represent the textiles and materials for the forecast. Cut the swatches neatly and consistently. The fabrics can be mounted onto a backing to make cutting easier. Pinking shears can be used to add a decorative edge to the swatches. Fabrics can be folded and then mounted leaving the edge loose so that the fabrics can be touched and felt.

To create a digital textiles and materials forecast, the swatches must be photographed or scanned, then included in the forecast. In a digital presentation the swatches cannot be touched, so it is recommended that actual swatches are available for closer inspection. If the forecast is delivered to an audience, swatches of the actual textiles, materials, trims, and findings can be passed around to the audience. A swatch ring or a swatch card works well for small audiences. A presentation board can also be created so that the audience can look and feel the swatches at the end of the presentation.

Label the textiles, materials, trims, and findings by style name, content, and construction, and identify techniques used to create pattern, finishes, and novelty features.

Romantic Garden, Antique Sunflower, and Butterfly Netting are the textile groups highlighted in "Inventive Vintage." Jersey, lace, chiffon, and silk are the main fabrics used for the "Inventive Vintage" theme. Chiffon becomes particularly relevant for the season because "Inventive Vintage" uses sheer transparent fabrics to accent the garments. The femininity of lingerie influenced the use of lace and silk in an assortment of applications from panels and overlay to inserts and trims.

Antique Sunflower is light and silky chiffon in sun-burnt shades of yellow and beige that brings the "vintage" in "Inventive Vintage."

Romantic Garden contains prints with the colors of romance and the calm and serenity of a garden. Muted floral prints in chiffon and jersey are reminiscent of the past and make an antique impression.

FIGURE 10.4D The textiles and materials for the "Inventive Vintage" forecast show a combination of romantic patterns, textures, and embellishments. Courtesy of Jenna Simon.

Butterfly Netting is delicate like a butterfly but durable like a net. A knitted material is great for layering over other fabrics and to use as accent pieces on the garment. Lace is light, fragile, and feminine and allows the fabric underneath to show through.

Trims and findings including antique gold rose buttons, romantic flower appliqués, and butterfly lace bows are used on the garments—which is what makes this different from past related trends. Silk cords and pleating are to be used for trims. The ornamentation gives the garment or accessory a vintage inspiration.

The images for this board were scanned from actual swatches and placed within the same delicate frame that was also used for the color board. Since floral motifs are an important element in this textiles forecast, a background was selected of aged, muted flowers.

create the look board(s)

Begin the layout of the look photos and sketches. Sort the photos, identifying the leading images for the forecast. Remember to include images from several markets, such as apparel, accessories, industrial design, interiors, architecture, or beauty. Display photos from different target markets, such as women's, men's, or children's. Include different lifestyles, such as designer runway shots, street images, and magazine editorials. Select images that imply shape direction through intuition of what may likely happen next based on the cyclical nature of fashion. Keep in mind that the photos that are selected are of items and ideas that are already available, so choose the newest and emerging looks. Edit the images to create the strongest visual impact. Images may need to be resized or recolored to best fit the presentation.

Black and white sketches, or flats, can be added to the presentation, showing detail and shape information. Illustrations can be added evoking lifestyle through the context of the drawing. For instance, the styling of the illustration may give clues about age, attitude, and preferences of the forecast. Illustrations can be hand rendered and scanned or created digitally using programs such as Adobe Illustrator.

Once the images have been selected and adjusted, prepare them for the board. Cut the images neatly or arrange them on a digital board, preparing a suitable layout. Borders around the images add additional color, texture, or line that guide the viewer through the board.

The apparel images selected for "Inventive Vintage" are a combination of modern romantic looks and delicate feminine silhouettes for both women and girls of all ages. Using semi-sheer lace, garden-inspired minifloral, ribbons, bows, and feminine embellishments, the look of the images support the theme. The silhouettes in "Inventive Vintage" are fun and flirty. The main garments are skirts and dresses. The outfits are mixed, with one item being a solid fabric with elegant details paired with

a printed fabric to give the outfit the "Inventive Vintage" feeling. Adornments include ruffles and lace, bows, buttons, beads, and flowers used as trim, belts, and necklaces for a fresh and modern approach. Shoes are an important part of the collection, and include both vintage styles made current with wedges, platforms, and bows, and contemporary designs made to appear antique with heel shapes, buckles, and straps. "Inventive Vintage" is timeless and ageless.

FIGURE 10.4E–F The looks represented on the "Inventive Vintage" apparel boards are fun and flirty with a hint of vintage yet modern sense of romance. The outfits include layers, ruffles, and flowing silhouettes. Courtesy of Jenna Simon.

"Inventive Vintage" shows up in other aspects of life, not just fashion. The design elements appear in home furnishings such as floral print pillows and upholstery, bed linens, lamp shades, and vintage dressers in antique dusty floral colors.

"Inventive Vintage" elements are also illustrated in fashion accessories such as shoes, belts, handbags, jewelry, and head wear. Each selection supports the mood, colors, and fabrications of the theme. The items are displayed on several small boards within the same frame that was used earlier in the presentation. By grouping the smaller items, the viewer is given clues about the relationships of the items to each other. If the items were not in groups, the board would become too busy.

FIGURE 10.4G This "Inventive Vintage" board was developed with several different types of accessories: shoes, belts, bags, and jewelry were placed in separate groups representing specific categories. Courtesy of Jenna Simon.

FIGURE 10.4H Home furnishings, interiors, and architecture markets rely on trends forecasts for inspiration. This forecast shows how the "Inventive Vintage" theme can easily translate into other markets. Courtesy of Jenna Simon.

The final nonapparel board includes images of home furnishings, interiors, and architecture. The look further supports the "Inventive Vintage" theme. The new items are distressed to achieve the appearance of something old. The tea-stained colors and old-world fabrications suggest a relaxed, romantic lifestyle.

"Inventive Vintage" is an original and innovative way of dressing that expresses both the old and comfortable, and new and fresh aspects of style. The sentimental yearning for a former time contradicts contemporary and emerging lifestyles. The societal changes that thrust "Inventive Vintage" forward include a nostalgic longing for the return to a past time when life was simpler, friends and family were closer, and comfort and happiness were felt while at the same time rejecting tradition by emphasizing instead individual experimentation and modern sensibilities.

written portion and script requirements

For the final forecast presentation, a written portion of the project must be developed. The narrative portion of the forecast offers a way to explain the forecast and predict the future of the idea. After collecting generous amounts of information and facts pertaining to the forecast, place the facts in the context that allows for the greatest impact. The story of a forecast should deliver facts while unleashing emotions, giving a deeper understanding of how the pieces fit together in the forecast and why it matters.

Successful script development requires organization of information. The script is developed with an introduction, the body of the forecast, and a conclusion. At the end of the script, a bibliography containing sources for all research and images is included. In addition, the script explains each portion of the visual forecast, including each board's images, words, or call-outs, and summaries. Throughout each segment of the script, the forecaster conveys the facts, her insight, and her prediction.

The forecaster customizes the information to be delivered through presentations ranging from one-on-one consultations, large speaking engagements, panel discussions, or Web sites. Although each method of presenting the forecast differs, the preparation of the text or script is similar for any forecast.

introduction

The introduction portion of the script serves several purposes. First, the script is written with the forecaster's introduction, explanation of his or her expertise, and welcoming remarks for the audience. Secondly, the forecaster briefly describes the topic of the forecast. The forecaster tells the audience what they are about to experience. The text explains the first board(s) of the visual presentation that includes the title, tagline, inspirational and mood images, and descriptive mood words.

body of the forecast

The body of the forecast describes the forecaster's research, inspiration, investigation and analysis, ideas for solutions, and evaluations. The script for the presentation makes clear the details on each board. The body of the script explains further the purpose of the selected images, color story, textile and material choices, and the look selections that appear on each board. The text also encourages and inspires the audience to consider the possible future outcome of evolving ideas. Often a story that connects the past, present, and future helps the audience to have confidence in the prediction. Sometimes the narrative explains ideas that are on the far-off horizon, the big picture. Other forecasts are extremely pragmatic—providing explicit details about specific themes, trends, colors, looks, details, and timing. Using current buzzwords and specific vocabulary to articulate the forecast makes for a more professional script.

KAI CHOW, CREATIVE DIRECTOR, DONEGER CREATIVE SERVICES

Customized Forecasts and Presentations

Each presentation is customized to the particular client. Using the themes of the season, I extrapolate information that will be helpful for the particular needs of the client. My clients are typically the creative individuals from a variety of markets, including home, shoes, cosmetics, men's ties, accessories, technical firms as well as apparel manufacturers. For instance, I prepared a presentation for a nail polish manufacturer. The client needed information about upcoming trends in finishes and color. I showed mood photos that conveyed lifestyle ambiance as well as runway photos that identified the texture, sheen, and surface of fabrications that will appear in the retail stores. I guided them to recognize a prevalent trend that included a regal, antique appeal with shine, richness, and glimmer.

The body of the script includes:

- Title/story/tagline
- Mood
- Color names
- Color descriptions
- Textiles and material names
- Textile descriptions
- Look names
- Look descriptions
- Analysis of the forecast
- Prediction

conclusion

The conclusion of the narrative reviews the most important points of the forecast and inspires the audience to continue thinking about the new ideas and possibilities. In the conclusion portion, the information in the script retells the most significant parts of the forecast, highlighting the most important elements and stressing the message and significance. Throughout the body of the forecast, the interpretation, analysis, and prediction are stated, supported by the imagery. The conclusion of the forecast should: (1) explain why the forecast is probable, (2) what is fueling the prediction, and (3) what the societal implications are, so that the meaning of the forecast is clear. By providing the information several times, the audience is more likely to understand and remember the purpose of the forecast.

sources

When researching and creating a forecast, all sources must be collected and added to the script. List all resources in a bibliography. Create an image log with image sources, including Web site information.

SAMPLE FORECAST WITH SCRIPT—FEMININE EVOLUTION

The forecast "Feminine Evolution" is presented through visual boards and a well-developed script. The forecaster begins with an introduction, takes the audience through the body of the forecast, and ends with a compelling conclusion. The following is taken directly from that script.

"Hello my name is Lindsay Smolinski, and I am here today to talk to you about 'Feminine Evolution.' 'Feminine Evolution' is more than just the way fashion is evolving; it's a way of life. How many women in this room have ever felt inferior in any situation simply because you're a woman? Chances are most of us have or will experience this feeling. Women have 'fought' and pushed for so many years to free themselves of the rule of man. We saw it in the Roaring Twenties with the Flappers, and strongly again in the Seventies. These events have had a huge impact on where women stand in the world today.

"There has been so much in history that women have accomplished in order to change the views of a woman's worth. Women have broken free from the shackles that once tied them down and stepped out to show the rest of the world what they're made of. I have a story that I'd like to share with everyone to help explain how 'Feminine Evolution' was born.

"In such a fast-paced world, getting faster and faster by the minute, she rebels against society's views. She is strong and independent, capable of anything that presents itself, and she can always do it the same as he can! In her world she is the ruler of all, and no man can tame this beautiful mysterious creature.

"When she walks into a room her presence is felt by all who surround her. She conforms to no rule dictated by man. She exudes the effortless, sophisticated silhouette of a real woman, and her sense of casual classiness is hard for anyone to ignore. Her style is bold. The colors that accent her personality are bright but neutral, vibrant and timid at the same time. Her mystifying persona allows no one to know what she will conquer next. She is strong enough to rule the world but as delicate as a dancer.

"The colors that have been selected are inspired by the painting, *Sea Serpents IV,* done by Gustav Klimt. The painting consists of a woman who is naked and in her rarest form. She is surrounded by beautiful, warm, multihued flowers. Most people think of pinks, reds, purples, pastels, etc. when asked to think of feminine colors. This does not always have to be true. 'Feminine Evolution' consists of beautiful colors that have been specially selected to complement the delicateness of a woman and represent her boldness through the richness of the colors. Color names have been carefully selected and named after gemstones. Some examples are Citrine, which is considered the success stone, and the Chrysolite, known to be the world's third-hardest frequently encountered

FIGURE 10.5A Lindsay R. Smolinski's "Feminine Evolution" forecast is an example of a complete forecast including the script. Courtesy of Lindsay R. Smolinski.

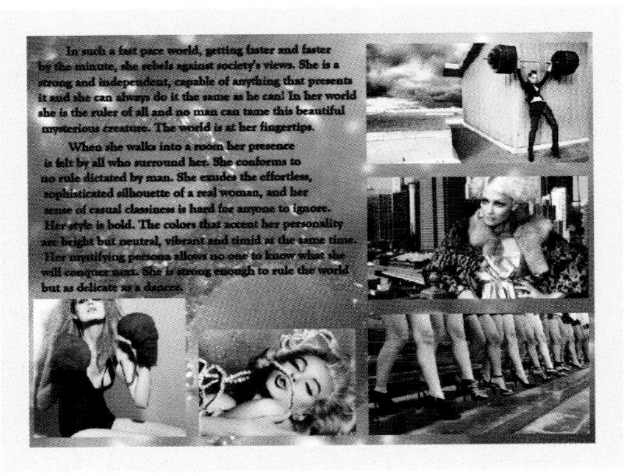

FIGURE 10.5B From the introduction to the forecast: "Many of you will hear this and believe that I'm talking about an actual woman; in fact, I'm actually talking about the concept of 'Feminine Evolution.' This is the attitude, the look, and the idea of what 'Feminine Evolution' is all about." Courtesy of Lindsay R. Smolinski.

FIGURE 10.5C "Feminine Evolution" illustrates how paintings and art can also be a source of inspiration for the color story. Courtesy of Lindsay R. Smolinski.

FIGURE 10.5D
The fabrics and materials play along with the concept of "Feminine Evolution"—the idea of conflict, of not conforming to what society wants women to become. Courtesy of Lindsay R. Smolinski.

FIGURE 10.5E
Forecasters sometimes focus on one aspect of the silhouette. This "Feminine Evolution" forecast focuses on the shoulders. Courtesy of Lindsay R. Smolinski.

natural gemstone. Each color has been named after a gemstone, because after all, aren't all women just as precious as a gemstone?

"For the hand (feel) and visual appeal of 'Feminine Evolution,' several fabrics have been chosen that are heavy but have a sense of softness, and are warm but have a cooling lustrous finish. A lot of fabrics have a lustrous shine to them to give a soft rounded appeal to the feminine physique. Also chosen are fabrics that are thicker and durable to exaggerate the thick-skinned attitude of a strong woman.

"The look of 'Feminine Evolution' is all about the attention to detail of the shoulders. It's all about shoulders! Whether it's exaggerated or very detailed shoulders, one shoulder, or simply missing shoulders, the attention is being drawn to this erogenous zone. Big-shoulder dresses, jackets, and blouses are showing up all over the runways and in the streets. It's the modern-day shoulder pad without letting the hideous shoulder-pad trend of the past haunt the fashion of the future. Bringing attention to detail in the shoulder naturally draws the eye to the area instead of other places on the body. Broader shoulders tend to be a sign of authority and empowerment, and this idea is exactly the role that women possess in the world today.

"Many of the color palettes shown earlier are showing up in upcoming seasons for cosmetics. Orange lips, blushes, and eye shadows

FIGURE 10.5F The cosmetic industry relies on forecasters for directions on the upcoming seasonal trends. Courtesy of Lindsay R. Smolinski.

FIGURE 10.5G Forecast themes are often translated into lifestyle settings, such as interior design. Courtesy of Lindsay R. Smolinski.

are becoming a big trend. Orange is a great play on color for the warm months and great for creating warmth in the cold months. Purples are huge for the up-and-coming year as well! The color is vibrant and can be worn to be flirty or deep to exude sophistication and seriousness. Another color that is making a huge push this year is gray. Many designers were using gray in their shows this year, such as Chanel in the Spring 2011 collection, as well as Rag & Bone and Oscar de la Renta in the Fall 2011 collection.

"In interior design, many of these same colors are beginning to pop up. In kitchens there is an enormous trend of adding more of a feminine feel to this particular room of the house. This trend is staying away from the stainless steel kitchens everyone has become used to. Instead of resembling such an industrial look, these rooms will have more of a feminine touch to them by including color and more delicate features. These qualities are popping up in many other rooms, such as living rooms and bedrooms.

"'Feminine Evolution' is a shift that we will be seeing not only in apparel but also in the attitudes of women and the attitudes of the way the rest of the world views women. 'Feminine Evolution' is more than a trend, it's a lifestyle."

PRESENTING THE FORECAST

The presentation begins with the forecaster's personal introduction. In addition to his or her name, a forecaster may include a brief biography, educational background, and professional affiliations. The introduction can also include specific credentials related to forecasting. The introduction should get the audience's attention, acknowledge the reason for the meeting or presentation, and prepare the audience for the forecast. During the introduction segment, the concept, mood, tone, and idea of the forecast are introduced. A hint of the theme's concept can unleash the audience's mind and imagination as they use their own human experience to guide them into the prediction, sense the atmosphere, and prepare to engage.

After the introduction, the forecaster shows each board and guides the audience through each image and word, explaining why the visuals impact the idea. When each board is shown, the forecaster elaborates by revealing the information that appears in the script. The forecaster uses the script as a guide to tell more extensive details about the colors, fabrications, and looks. The forecaster guides the audience through each board, explaining what the images are, why they were chosen, how they impact the forecast, and why they are important. The forecaster presents his or her analysis and prediction of the theme's future. Providing examples to further illustrate a concept helps the audience to connect already-accepted knowledge with possible outcomes.

To conclude the forecast presentation, the speaker reviews the most significant information that was presented. A recap of the data, intuition, interpretation, analysis, and prediction finishes the presentation. The speaker may encourage the audience to ask questions, give comments, ask for opinions, or open a discussion about the forecast.

presentation tips

practice the presentation

When the visual portion of the forecast is completed and the script is written, the forecaster must practice the presentation. The script must be studied and learned so that the forecaster can deliver the information with confidence and ease. Note cards may be used during the presentation to keep on track but, for a successful presentation, the forecaster should not read the information. Even the most seasoned public speaker can experience anxiety when preparing for a presentation. To ensure a smooth performance, the forecaster must be prepared. Practicing in front of a mirror, before friends, or in the actual location helps the presenter to feel ready.

Even an experienced forecaster may experience problems during the presentation. From forgotten lines to equipment malfunctions, the show must go on. The speaker must strive to maintain composure and move forward.

prepare setting

To deliver a successful presentation, the forecaster must be comfortable with the location and the setting. The location may include a stage, podium, and projection screen, a conference room with a large table in the center, or a classroom. The forecaster needs to review the space and consider how he will move throughout the presentation. Chairs may be rearranged; closing window shades, adjusting lighting, or making other physical changes may be possible to enhance the presentation. If props are used in the forecasting presentation, such as boards, swatches, or handouts, the forecaster must have easy access to the props. An easel may be needed to hold boards, or an assistant may be needed to help. A garment rack of actual garments or textiles may be set up for the audience to experience. Displays with items from the forecast may be made available.

test equipment

Prior to his appearance, the forecaster must test any equipment that is planned for the presentation to ensure that everything is working properly and that she knows how to use the tools. A digital forecast that has been saved on a flash drive or CD must be checked to ensure that it opens properly. Boards must be projected to see that the images are in focus. An audio set must be tested if the forecast requires sound. A forecaster must practice switching from one board to the next so that when presenting, the transition is smooth. If an assistant helps in the presentation, cues must be established so that the assistant shifts boards at the appropriate time.

speaking clearly

Forecasters need to articulate the information correctly, making sure to use the proper pronunciation of details, especially designer names, locations, and fashion vocabulary. Credibility can easily be lost when the speaker misstates or mispronounces information.

connecting with the audience

If the presentation is live, the forecaster should find ways to connect with his audience. Using eye contact, body language, and eliciting responses and participation are ways to capture and hold the attention of listeners. To engage viewers, handouts of information, color cards, swatches, or physical items can be presented. The presenter must be careful not to create too many distractions in order to maintain the focus of the audience.

For an online presentation, or webinar, it is more difficult for a forecaster to personally connect with the viewers, and the presenter must rely on visual and narrative elements.

Audience members may ask questions during or after the presentation. The forecaster may prefer to have the audience hold all questions until the presentation is completed, or they may encourage active audience participation throughout. At the conclusion of the presentation, the forecaster may speak individually to participants.

avoiding traps

By being prepared for a presentation, the speaker can avoid uncomfortable or embarrassing moments. Even with the most diligent preparations, sometimes things do not go exactly as planned. Flexibility and maintaining composure is essential to keep the audience engaged. Forecasters should not apologize or offer explanations of why their forecast is inadequate; they should instead keep the focus on positive intentions.

Since the forecast is a prediction of things to come, forecasters must not overstate the accuracy of the information. Suggesting that the forecast could happen or may happen gives forecasters flexibility and credibility.

FRANK BOBER, CEO OF STYLESIGHT

Personal Contact in a Technology-Based Service

Many critics of online services believe that all of the information can be overwhelming and impersonal. Through a variety of service levels, my clients can have a variety of customer service features, including one-on-one consultations, webinars, and product development seminars. Specialists who help to navigate through the information and help select specific data or imagery for a client are called site geniuses.

FIGURE 10.6 Luzmaria Palacios's "Chillex" forecast is a well-crafted example of the relaxed eclecticism of a free-spirited lifestyle. Courtesy of Luzmaria Palacios.

SUMMARY

Forecasters present their fashion predictions using visual and verbal techniques. They create boards, or digital presentations, using graphic skills involving layout, typography, background and color selection, and numerous assembly techniques. Along with the visual presentation, a forecaster writes a script that becomes the commentary for the forecast. The presentation includes an introduction, the main body of the forecast, and a conclusion. Forecasters prepare by practicing the presentation, preparing the setting, and testing equipment. The forecaster works to connect with the audience while conveying the information. Remembering that a forecast is a prediction, the forecaster avoids traps while delivering the message.

KEY TERMS

- Typeface or font

ACTIVITIES

1. Create a Complete Visual Portion of a Forecast

Create the visual portion of a forecast by (1) creating the theme board(s); (2) creating the color board; (3) creating the textiles and materials board; and (4) creating the look board(s).

2. Write the Script of the Forecast

Write a forecast script that includes (1) introduction; (2) body of the forecast; (3) conclusion; and (4) sources.

3. Present the Forecast

Deliver the forecast in a professional manner in front of an audience. The presentation can be in an auditorium, on the Web, or in a classroom. The steps should include the following: (1) personal introduction and the introduction of the topic of the forecast; (2) presentation of the body of the forecast; and (3) conclusion.

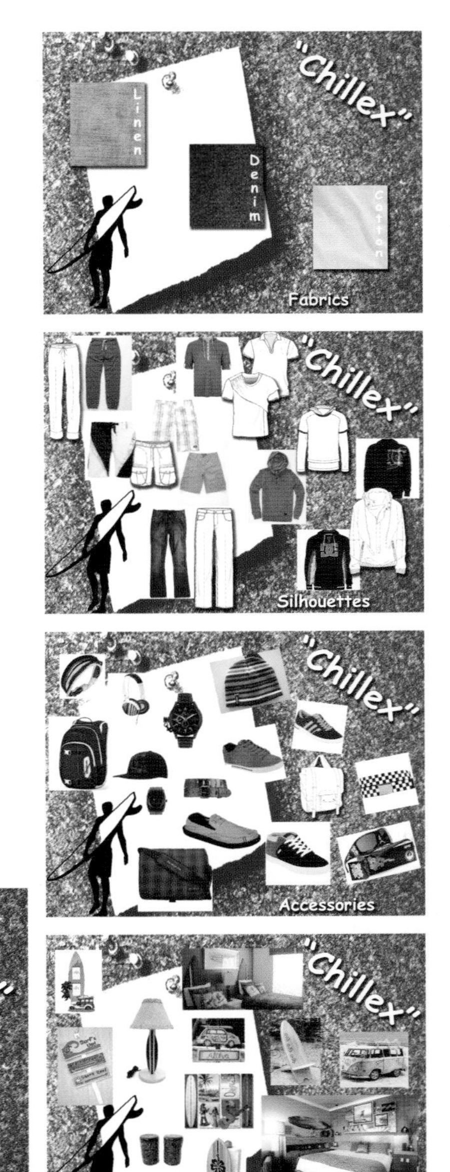

ASSIGNMENT: DEVELOP A FASHION FORECAST

The following is an all-encompassing assignment to follow the steps in creating a fashion forecast. This assignment requires creating six to eight boards, writing a script, and delivering the forecast.

The five processes that are followed to develop a forecast are:

1. **Researching** is the process of exploring or investigating to collect information and imagery looking for new, fresh, and innovative ideas including recognizing inspiration, trends, and signals.
2. **Editing** is the process of sorting and identifying patterns in the research, data, and images.
3. **Interpreting and Analyzing** are the processes of examining carefully to identify causes, key factors, and possible results while investigating what fuels upcoming trends considering why and how the trend will manifest.
4. **Predicting** is the process of declaring or telling in advance potential outcomes by developing scenarios to foretell projected possibilities.
5. **Communicating** is the process of conveying information, thoughts, opinions, and predictions about the forecast through writings, visual boards, and verbal presentations.

The student forecast "Out of This World" by Katherine Galarragga provides an example of a successful forecast that includes theme development, a color story, textile and material selections, and apparel and nonapparel looks.

BOARD 1 (THEME FORECAST—TITLE, TAGLINE, AND MOOD)

- Develop concept/idea for a forecast using scientific and artistic research.
- Select trend clues and collect data.
- Select images to illustrate theme. Begin a collage of images and add to the board.
- Create a title.
- Develop a tagline.
- Identify the mood.

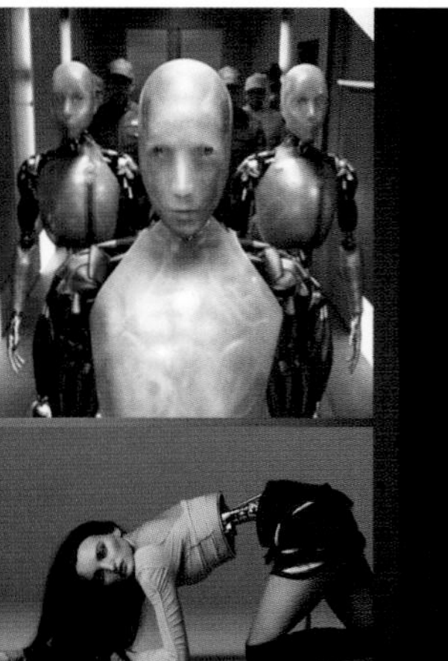

BOARD 2 (THEME FORECAST—STORYBOARD)

- Write a descriptive or narrative story.
- Place abbreviated story on the board with creative visuals.

BOARD 3 (COLOR FORECAST)

- Research past color stories.
- Devise a color story for selected theme—collect color chips or yarns.
- Identify the mood of the color story.
- Assign color names/numbers and add to board.
- Write color descriptions and color story summary.

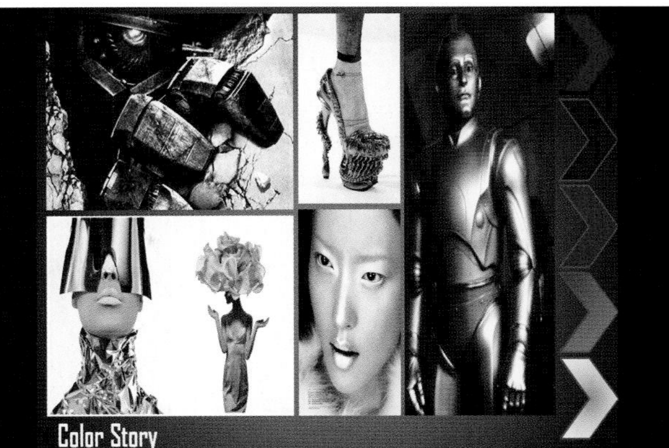

BOARD 4 (TEXTILES AND MATERIALS)

- Research new textiles, materials, trims, and findings.
- Collect swatches and/or materials.
- Prepare swatches for board.
- Name textiles, materials, trims, and findings.
- Write summary for the materials. Add to board.

BOARD 5 (LOOK OR SILHOUETTE—FOCUSING ON APPAREL IMAGES)

- Research emerging looks and lifestyle trends in fashion apparel that support the theme.
- Collect images and/or flats.
- Create visual presentation using apparel images.
- Write explanation of selections, shapes, and details.
- Include images and key words on board.

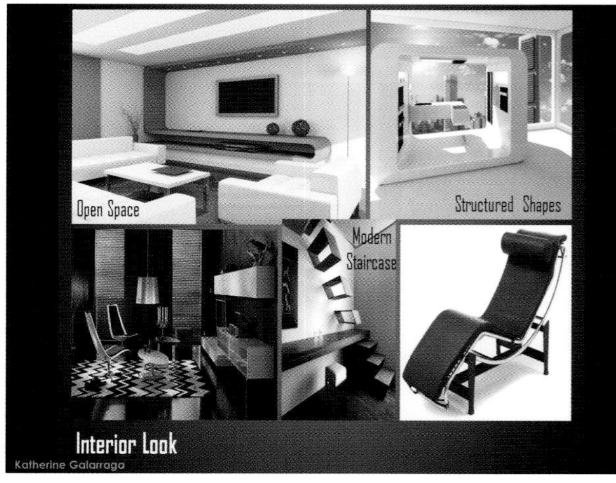

BOARDS 6 TO 8 (LOOK OR SILHOUETTE—FOCUSING ON NONAPPAREL IMAGES)

- Research emerging looks from other industries that support the theme.
- Collect images.
- Create visual presentation on the board using nonapparel images.
- Write explanation and key words on board.

SCRIPT (WRITE THE PRESENTATION)

- Introduction
- Body
  - Title/story/tagline
  - Mood
  - Color names
  - Color descriptions
  - Textiles and material names
  - Textile descriptions
  - Look names
  - Look descriptions
  - Interpretations and analysis of forecast
  - Prediction
- Conclusion
- Sources

PREPARE AND DELIVER THE FORECAST

- Practice presentation
- Prepare setting
- Test equipment
- Present the forecast
- Begin with personal introduction and overview of the topic
- Present the body of the forecast using visual images, swatches, and prepared script
- Finish with a conclusion explaining why the forecast is possible

Glossary

A

ACETATE is a manufactured, cellulosic fiber. Acetate is lustrous, smooth, and lightweight, but it has poor stability and elasticity and is not colorfast.

ACHROMATICS are tonal gray and black colors.

ACRYLIC is a manufactured fiber that often is a substitute for wool. It is less expensive than wool and has easier care requirements.

ANALOGOUS COLORS are colors located close together on a color wheel.

APPLICATION or *direct printing* is the most common technique of printing pigments on top of fabric in a design or motif.

ARTISTIC APPROACH is when a forecaster relies on creativity and intuition to create a forecast.

B

BALANCE is a state of equilibrium or equal distribution. A symmetrical design is equally balanced, or the same on each side, but an asymmetrical design is different on each side. An asymmetrical design can become balanced by adding details such as bolder shapes and colors to shift the balance.

BLEACHING is used to remove color from a fabric.

BLOGGERS are people who post commentary or images about a particular subject on their blog.

BLOGS are types of Web sites often frequented regularly by individuals who post text, images, videos, and links to other Web sites related to the topic of the blog. This interactive format gives the ability of participants to communicate about current trends and events.

BURN-OUT PRINTING is a process that uses a chemical to destroy fibers, creating a semi-transparent design.

C

CASUAL STYLE means comfortable, easy-to-wear garments. The style includes chino pants, relaxed shirts, and no ties for men, and yoga wear, and loose-fitting garments often layered or with comfort stretch added to woven fabrics.

CLASSIC is a style that remains in fashion for a long time.

COLOR CYCLES are shifts in color preferences and color repetition.

COLORFAST refers to fabric that retains color.

COLOR FORECASTER is a specialist in the research and development of color prediction and often is associated with a forecasting service or a fiber producer.

COLOR FORECASTING is a process of gathering, evaluating, understanding, and interpreting information to predict the colors that will be desirable for the consumer in the upcoming seasons.

COLOR PALETTE is a range of colors.

COLOR PREFERENCES are the tendencies for a person or a group to prefer some colors over others.

COLOR WAYS refer to the assorted colors, motifs, or patterns in which fabric is available.

COLOR SCHEME is a group of colors in relation to each other.

COLOR STORY is a palette of colors that are used to identify, organize, and connect ideas and products for a certain season or collection.

COLOR THEORY is the study of color and its meaning in the worlds of art and design.

COLOR WHEEL or *color circle* is a visual representation of colors arranged according to their chromatic relationship.

COMMUNICATING is the process of conveying information, thoughts, opinions, and predictions about the forecast through writings, visual boards, and verbal presentations.

COMPLEMENTARY COLORS are colors located opposite each other on a color wheel.

CONSUMER SEGMENT is a group of consumers who share similar demographic, economic, sociological, and psychological characteristics.

COOL COLORS are blues, greens, or purples.

COTTON is the most widely used natural fiber and is derived from the cotton plant. It grows from a seed into a cotton ball that is later harvested and cleaned.

D

DATA SHARING is the sharing of consumer research on specific products between research firms and designers, manufacturers, retail management, and buyers.

DEMOGRAPHICS are studies of the statistical data of a population that divides a large group into smaller segments that can be analyzed. The data includes age, sex, income, marital status, family size, education, religion, race, and nationality.

DESCRIPTIVE STORY is based on nonfictional data and information about the theme. Details about the origins of the idea, the research, the historical information, the cultural influences, or the marketing response can be included. A forecast can be explained based on real situations and facts.

DESIGN ELEMENTS are the starting point for designed products. The elements include line, silhouette, shape, and details as well as color, texture, and pattern.

DESIGN INNOVATION is a process that takes into consideration what a product can do for an individual. Through modern understanding of design potential, a person can find meaning and create personal connections to the product.

DESIGN PRINCIPLES use design elements in combinations to create aesthetically pleasing looks. Proportion, balance, focal point, and harmony are design principles.

DETAILS are items such as collars, necklines, sleeves, pleats, darts, pockets and contour seaming. Several lines together or asymmetrical lines can create optical interest.

DIGITAL PRINTING is done by creating motifs on a computer and printing using ink-jet technology, which gives greater design flexibility and is cost effective.

DISCHARGE PRINTING is the process whereby color is removed by taking pigment away, often in a bleaching process.

DISCO LOOK refers to a clothing style from the 1970s that used Ultrasuede, platform shoes, leotards, and androgynous looks. This style created the halter dress and simple body-conscious dresses often worn for dancing.

DISCORD is the lack of harmony in a piece and is often used to intentionally break the acceptable rules.

DISCORDANT COLOR SCHEME means the purposeful inclusion of colors that "clash."

DOBBY WEAVES are fancy weaves with small geometric designs woven into the textile.

DYEING is the process of adding color to a fabric.

E

EDITING is the process of sorting and identifying patterns in the research, data, and images.

ELECTROTEXTILES have been developed by covering polymer fibers with a metallic coating, producing strong and flexible strands created to control temperature or monitor medical conditions.

EMBROIDERY can decorate a fabric by stitching yarns, stones, or sequins into a design on top of fabric.

EYELET is a woven fabric that has a pattern made by creating holes that are surrounded by stitches to prevent fraying.

F

FABRIC STRUCTURE is the method in which textiles are constructed by assembling yarns and fibers into a cohesive configuration. Depending on the construction of a fabric, different qualities like drape, stability, and density are achieved that make certain fabrics more suitable to specific styles. Fabric structure is categorized as woven, knitted, nonwoven, and other methods of fabric construction.

FACEBOOK is a social media Web site also used as a marketing device to spread viral messages about brands, products, and trends.

FAD is a style that swiftly becomes popular, is widely accepted, and rapidly disappears.

FASHION can be defined as that which characterizes or distinguishes the habits, manners, and dress of a period or group. Fashion is what people choose to wear.

FASHION CYCLE is the life span of a style or a trend.

FASHION FORECASTING is the practice of predicting upcoming trends based on past and present style-related information, the interpretation and analysis of the motivation behind a trend, and an explanation of why the prediction is likely to occur.

FASHION GROUP INTERNATIONAL is a professional organization in the fashion industry that includes members focusing on apparel, home, and beauty. The organization provides insights that influence fashion direction for the marketplace, including lifestyle shifts, contemporary issues, and global trends.

FIBER is a hairlike substance that is the basic building block for most yarns and fabrics. Fibers fall into two main categories: natural or manufactured.

FIBER OPTIC FABRIC is a unique fabric made from ultra-thin fibers that allow light to be emitted through advanced luminous technology.

FINDINGS are add-ons to clothes—such as buttons, zippers, Velcro closures, and belts—that can be both functional and decorative.

FINISHES are any chemical or mechanical process that a fabric undergoes to change its inherent properties.

FLAPPER was a nickname for free-spirited young women during the Roaring Twenties and their style of dress.

FLOCK PRINTING is a technique that uses an adhesive to create the motif and then short fibers are attached to create a velvety surface.

FOCAL POINT of a design is the area that initially draws the eye. A designer may use line or color to direct the viewer to certain aspects of the design.

FOCUS GROUPS are a representative group of consumers that are questioned together to gather opinions about products, services, prices, or marketing techniques.

G

GEOGRAPHIC STUDIES focus on where people live, including information on the population in the state, country, city, and select target areas.

GOTH refers to an alternative fashion style, also known as *industrial punk,* that includes dark leather looks, corsets, fishnet stockings worn with platform leather boots, body piercing and tattoos, and colorfully dyed hair.

GRUNGE STYLE refers to a fashion style from the 1990s that included mismatched and messy clothing, flannel shirts, torn jeans, sneakers, and items from thrift stores layered together to create an unkempt type of appearance.

H

HAND is the feel of a fiber or textile.

HARMONY is achieved when all design elements and principles work successfully together to create an aesthetically pleasing design.

HAUTE COUTURE literally means "high sewing" and refers to exclusive, made-to-order and trend-setting fashion, specifically from French fashion houses.

HEAD ENDS are small samples of fabrics used by textile firms to show available or developmental fabrics.

HIGH CHROMA are bright colors.

HIPPIE STYLE or *hippie look* refers to a "free" clothing style from the 1960s that used bold colors and mixed wild patterns and was often influenced by the infusion of diverse cultures. Clothing was often loose and made of natural fibers in gypsy-like styles. This style also included peasant tops, Chinese quilted jackets, Indian cotton voile dresses, and mood rings.

HOT ITEMS are "must have" designs or products.

HUE is another name for the color itself.

I

IMAGES are photos, illustrations, or drawings used to illustrate a theme. The Internet, ads, or runway shows can also supply images.

INTENSITY refers to the saturation or brightness of a color.

INTERPRETING AND ANALYZING are processes that entail careful examination to identify causes, key factors, and possible results; investigate what fuels upcoming trends; and consider why and how the trend will manifest.

J

JACQUARD WEAVES are beautifully patterned fabrics using floats of yarns to create intricate motifs or designs.

K

KNIT FABRICS are created by interlooping yarns using needles. Knitted fabrics fall into two main categories: weft and warp knits.

L

LINE has many qualities that can affect the look of a design. Lines have direction—horizontal, vertical, or diagonal—as well as qualities such as width and length.

LINEN is made from the flax fiber and comes from the stems of the flax plant. The fiber is longer and stronger than cotton.

LONG-TERM FORECASTING, also known as future studies, seeks to understand and identify long-term social and cultural shifts, population trends, technological advances, demographic movement, and developments in consumer behavior. Long-term forecasts extend at least two years in advance. Long-term forecasting is less about specific details and more about positioning one's business for long-term growth.

LOOMS are machines that interlace at right angles strands or yarns to make cloth.

M

MANUFACTURED FIBERS are man-made fibers or synthetics that are created using science and technology instead of nature. These fibers are created to fill specific needs in the market and can mimic the positive qualities of natural fibers without exhausting the natural resources.

MARKET RESEARCH FIRMS that focus on the fashion and apparel industries conduct research studies and analyze and provide information on product and market trends and strategies.

MATERIALS are the substance of which an item is made. Materials can be manufactured components or items found in nature.

MINIMALISTIC refers to a clothing style that is simple and clean with little or no accessories and embellishments.

MOD STYLE refers to a fashion style from the 1960s that, for women, included the miniskirt with accessories, tights, and go-go boots. Men wore Edwardian styles, longer hair in a bowl cut, and glasses.

MONOCHROMATIC COLOR SCHEMES have two or more colors from one hue.

MONOTONE refers to one color.

MOOD describes the tone that represents the feelings and emotions of the message.

MOOD BOARDS or *forecasting boards* are where items (images, illustrations, slogans, and color samples) of the fashion forecast are placed.

MOTIF is a repeated design, element, form, or shape.

MULTICOLORED refers to multiple colors.

NARRATIVE STORY is based on the inspirational and artistic influence from the theme. The story can be written based on a theme of fantasy or fiction.

NATIONAL RETAIL FEDERATION is an organization that helps retailers in every segment of their business by conducting studies about worldwide retail and provides the information to its members.

NEUTRAL COLOR scheme is created by white, black, gray, brown, and cream. Neutral colors or natural colors do not appear on the color wheel.

NONWOVEN FABRICS are created when fibers are held together by bonding, tangling, or fusing either in an organized or random manner. Some examples are laminated, tufted fabrics, crocheting, or macramé. Quilting and embroidery also fall into the nonwoven category.

NYLON is the first manufactured fiber produced in the United States, beginning in 1939. Nylon is strong for its weight and has good abrasion resistance and elasticity.

O

OBSERVATION is a technique used that entails watching, photographing, recording, and reporting on consumers' behavior in multiple locations. This process is often done by a team of researchers, cool hunters, and forecasting experts.

P

PENDULUM SWING refers to the movement of fashion between extremes.

PLAIN WEAVE is the simplest form used for many styles of fabric, both solid and printed.

POLYESTER is the most widely used manufactured fiber because of its affordability, easy care requirements, and ability to be modified to meet consumers' needs.

POLYMERS are chemical and molecular compounds.

POPULATION is the total number of people inhabiting an area. A forecaster must consider the size of the population, its rate of growth, and the age of the people to project the future demand.

PREDICTING is the process of declaring or telling in advance potential outcomes by developing scenarios to foretell projected possibilities.

PREPPY STYLE refers to traditional looks that include varsity-style sweaters, classic blazers, button-down shirts, and cardigan sweaters, creating the appearance of young professional adults.

PRIMARY COLORS are blue, red, and yellow: those colors that cannot be created by mixing others.

PRINTING is a method of applying color and motif to a surface and can range from monotone (one color) to multicolor.

PROPORTION is the scale used to divide a garment into parts. For instance, horizontal lines are used to break designs into sections, such as waistline, hip line, or shoulder line.

PSYCHOGRAPHICS are the studies that classify groups according to their attitudes, tastes, values, and fears and are used to identify trends.

PUNK LOOK refers to an extreme clothing style from the late 1970s that included the use of black leather, stud embellishments, outrageous hair and makeup, and distressed shirts held together with safety pins.

Q

QUESTIONNAIRES and surveys help the researcher in understanding and identifying existing and potential customers. Lists of questions are formulated to help the researcher elicit responses from consumers.

R

RAYON is a cellulosic fiber made from wood pulp that is chemically processed into a solution, then extruded or pushed though the spinneret to create filaments. Rayon has many of the same characteristics as cotton. It is comfortable to wear and takes color well, but it wrinkles and stretches out of shape easily.

RESEARCHING is the process of exploring or investigating to collect information and imagery while looking for new, fresh, and innovative ideas and recognizing inspiration, trends, and signals.

RESIST PRINTING is a method that prevents the dyes or pigments from penetrating into the fabric, for example: tie-dyeing and batik.

S

SALES STRATEGIES are developed by retailers and manufacturers to achieve success in the market.

SATIN WEAVE is created by allowing the yarns to float over four or more yarns in either direction. It provides a fabric with luster and shine.

SCIENTIFIC APPROACH is when a forecaster relies on research data to create a forecast.

SECONDARY COLORS are colors achieved by a mixture of two primary hues.

SHADE refers to a hue with black added.

SILHOUETTE is the overall outline or outside shape of a design or a garment. The silhouette is the one-dimensional figure used to create a look using form and space. The silhouette of a design can be classified using geometric terms such as circle, oval, rectangle, cone, triangle, or square.

SILK is a protein fiber that is created when a silkworm creates a cocoon. The fiber from the cocoon is detangled into a long filament strand. Silk is considered a luxury fiber because of its excellent drape, smooth hand, and lustrous appearance.

SLUBS are thick and thin yarns that create unevenness in the fabric.

SOCIAL MEDIA SITES are Web sites such as Twitter or Facebook that are fast-growing Internet-based platforms used to broadcast messages, communicate, and hold conversations. These sites are being used as a marketing device to spread viral messages about brands, products, and trends.

SHORT-TERM FORECASTING focuses on identifying and predicting possible trends that are presented through themes, color stories, textiles, and looks up to approximately two years in advance.

SPACE AGE STYLE refers to clothing that uses futuristic synthetic fabrics made into geometric silhouettes. Materials such as metal, paper, or plastic and metallic colors such as silver and gold often are used.

SPANDEX is a manufactured fiber known for its elastic qualities similar to rubber. It is widely used for swimwear and undergarments. Spandex can be blended with other fibers to create "comfort stretch" and is often blended with denim to create jeans.

SPIDER SILK FIBERS are incredibly strong fibers derived from the genetic manipulation of spiders with other creatures.

SPINNERETS, similar to showerheads, are what liquid polymer is pushed through in order to create manufactured filament (long) fibers.

STAPLE or *basic* colors remain consistent from season to season. Basic colors include black, navy, khaki, and white.

STORY is the written or spoken text of a forecast and can either be narrative or descriptive.

STYLE is a distinctive appearance and combination of unique features that create a look that is acceptable at the time by a majority of a group.

STYLE TRIBES are specialized groups of people that wear distinctive looks to demonstrate their association to the group.

SURVEYS, usually lists of questions, are designed to elicit desired information from consumers.

SUSTAINABLE DEVELOPMENT meets the needs of the present without compromising the needs of future generations.

SUSTAINABLE FABRICS, such as organic cotton, hemp, pineapple, soy, and seaweed, are alternative fibers that have a less harmful environmental impact.

SWATCHES are sample pieces of fabric or materials that are collected from the shows of fabric manufacturers. The fabric firms show their fabrics using swatch cards, types, or head ends to display the available selections or developmental fabrics. Typically, a fabric is available in assorted designs or color ways.

T

TAPESTRIES are beautifully patterned fabrics using floats of yarns to create intricate motifs or designs.

TARGET AUDIENCE is the segment of the population who may adopt new products and ideas at a specific time and is crucial in forecasting the evolution of fashion.

TASTE is the prevailing opinion of what is or is not appropriate for a particular occasion.

TEMPERATURE is a way of describing color. Warm colors such as reds, oranges, and yellows can evoke emotions of excitement or anger, and cool colors such as blues, greens, or purples can be calming and pacifying.

TEMPERATURE SENSITIVE TEXTILES, treated with paraffin, are not only extremely breathable and lightweight but can also regulate body temperature.

TERTIARY COLORS are colors achieved by a mixture of primary and secondary hues.

TEXTILE is a flexible fabric that is woven, knitted, and assembled using other methods of construction and is often composed of layers. Textiles are made from both natural and manufactured films, fibers, or yarns.

TEXTILE STORY is that part of a fashion forecast that is focused on textiles, trims, materials, and findings.

TEXTILES WITH NANOTECHNOLOGY add functionality and value to traditional textiles by creating nanolayers that control the movement of chemicals through the layers of fabric.

THEME is the topic for the forecast with a unifying, dominant idea.

TINT refers to a hue that has white added.

TONE refers to a hue with gray added.

TREND FORECASTERS are the prescient individuals who combine knowledge of fashion, history, consumer research, industry data, and intuition to guide product manufacturers and business professionals into the future.

TREND REPORT, based on observations from runway collections, red carpet events, or street fashion, is an account describing in detail something that already exists or has happened.

TREND SPOTTERS observe change at emerging boutiques, high-end retailers, department stores, or mass market discounters. Around the world, they track the latest stores, designers, brands, trends, and business innovations.

TRENDS are the first signal of change in general direction or movement.

TRENDSETTERS play a critical role in the fashion process. Identifying trendsetting groups while observing their style and taste selections gives the forecaster important clues about upcoming ideas.

TRICKLE-ACROSS THEORY or *horizontal flow theory* of fashion adoption assumes that fashion moves across groups who are in similar social levels.

TRICKLE-DOWN THEORY or *downward flow theory* is the oldest theory of fashion adoption and assumes fashion is dictated by those at the tip of the social pyramid before being copied by the people in the lower social levels.

TRICKLE-UP THEORY or *upward flow theory* is the newest theory of fashion adoption and is the opposite of the trickle-down theory. According to this theory, fashion adoption begins with the young members of society who often are in the lower income groups.

TRIMS such as braid, lace, or novelty stitching are used to create newness.

TWILL WEAVE is a definitive diagonal line that appears on the fabric surface.

TWITTER is a social media Web site also used as a marketing device to spread viral messages about brands, products, and trends.

TYPEFACE or *font* can connect the message of the text with the concept of the theme. A mood can be created by using size (point), font (style of lettering), and effects (such as bold, pictorial, or disorder).

TYPES are used by textile firms to show available material.

U

URBAN LOOK refers to a clothing style popularized by hip-hop and rap musicians from the "streets" that includes colorful oversized garments, low slung pants with underwear visible, huge "bling" jewelry, backward baseball caps, and zany sneakers.

V

VALUE is the lightness or darkness of the color.

VINTAGE DRESSING and retro looks refer to the return of fashion from the past.

VIRAL MARKETING refers to marketing practices that use existing social networks to spread the word through society.

W

WARM COLORS are reds, oranges, and yellows and can evoke emotions of excitement or anger.

WARP KNITS, where the loops appear along the length of the fabric, are made by machine.

WEFT KNITS can be made by hand or machine. These knits are interlooped across the fabric.

WICKING JERSEY is a stretchy performance fabric that includes fibers that have the ability to pull moisture away from the body and leave the skin feeling cool and dry.

WOOL is a protein fiber that comes from the hair of an animal, most often sheep. Wool's positive qualities include warmth, moisture resistance, and elasticlike flexibility, and its negative qualities include scratchiness, tendency to shrink, and susceptibility to damage by moths.

WOVEN FABRICS, created by weaving interlacing yarns at right angles, are the most widely used fabrics.

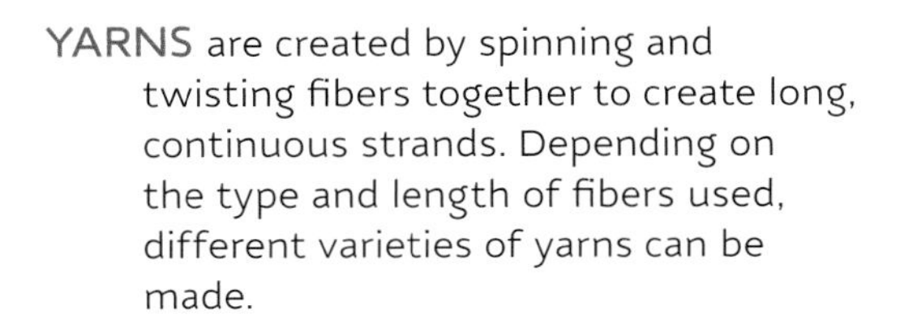

YARNS are created by spinning and twisting fibers together to create long, continuous strands. Depending on the type and length of fibers used, different varieties of yarns can be made.

ZEITGEIST means the "spirit of the times."

Bibliography

CHAPTER 1

Bell, S., and Morse, S. *Measuring Sustainability: Learning by Doing.* Sterling, VA: Earthscan Publications, 2003.

Bolton, A., Chabon, M., and Metropolitan Museum of Art. *Superheroes: Fashion and Fantasy.* New York: Metropolitan Museum of Art; New Haven, CT: Yale University Press, 2008.

Edelkoort, L., and Films for the Humanities. *The Trend Where Fashion Begins.* Video/DVD. Produced by G. Melhos. Princeton, NJ: Films for the Humanities and Sciences, 2002.

Granger, M. *Fashion: The Industry and Its Careers.* New York: Fairchild Publications, 2007.

Jacobs, L., and Skrebneski, L. V. J. *The Art of Haute Couture.*1st ed. New York: Abbeville Press, 1995.

Janson, H. W., and Janson, A.F. *History of Art: A Survey of the Major Visual Arts from the Dawn of History to the Present Day.* 2d ed. Englewood Cliffs, NJ: Prentice-Hall, 1977.

Kerr, H., and Power, K. *Who What Wear.* New York: H. N. Abrams, 2009.

King, L., and McCarthy, D. *Environmental Sociology: From Analysis to Action.* Lanham, MD: Rowman and Littlefield, 2005.

Koda, H., Yohannan, K., and Metropolitan Museum of Art. *The Model as Muse: Embodying Fashion.* New York: Metropolitan Museum of Art; New Haven, CT: Yale University Press, 2009.

McDowell, C. *Galliano.* New York: Rizzoli, 1998.

Milbank, C. R. *Couture, the Great Designers.* 1st ed. New York: Stewart, Tabori, and Chang; distributed in the U.S. by Workman Publishing, 1985.

Perna, R. *Fashion Forecasting: A Mystery or a Method?* New York: Fairchild Publications, 1987.

Poiret, P. G., and Haden, S. *King of Fashion: The Autobiography of Paul Poiret.* Philadelphia: J. B. Lippincott, 1931.

Stall-Meadows, C. *Know Your Fashion Accessories.* New York: Fairchild Publications, 2004.

Stone, E. *The Dynamics of Fashion.* New York: Fairchild Publications, 2008.

CHAPTER 2

Kaplan, T., and Video Edition. *John Galliano: Fabric & Fantasy.* Video/DVD. New York: Video Edition, 2001.

Baudot, F. *A Century of Fashion.* New York: Universe, 1999.

Bell, S., and Morse, S. *Measuring Sustainability: Learning by Doing.* Sterling, VA: Earthscan Publications, 2003.

Berg, R. L. *The Great Depression in Literature for Youth: A Geographical Study of Families and Young Lives.* Lanham, MD: Scarecrow Press, 2004.

Blum, S. *Victorian Fashions and Costumes from Harper's Bazaar, 1867–1898.* New York: Dover Publications, 1974.

Blum, S., and Sears, R. A. C. *Everyday Fashions of the Thirties as Pictured in Sears Catalogs.* New York: Dover Publications, 1986.

Bluttal, S., and Mears, P. *Halston.* London: Phaidon Press, 2001.

Bolton, A., Chabon, M., and Metropolitan Museum of Art. *Superheroes: Fashion and Fantasy.* New York: Metropolitan Museum of Art; New Haven, CT: Yale University Press, 2008.

Burns, L. D., and Bryant, N. O. *The Business of Fashion: Designing, Manufacturing, and Marketing.* New York: Fairchild Publications, 2007.

Cawthorne, N. *Key Moments in Fashion: From Haute Couture to Streetwear, Key Collections, Major Figures and Crucial Moments that Changed the Course of Fashion History from 1890 to the 1990s.* London and New York: Hamlyn; distributed in the U.S. by Sterling Publishing, 1999.

Clancy Steer, D. *Costume Since 1945: Couture, Street Style, and Anti-Fashion.* New York: Drama Publishers, 1996.

Ewing, E., and Mackrell, A. *History of 20th Century Fashion.* New York: Costume & Fashion Press, 2001.

Ferebee, A. *A History of Design from the Victorian Era to the Present; A Survey of the Modern Style in Architecture, Interior Design, Industrial Design, Graphic Design, and Photography.* New York: Van Nostrand Reinhold, 1970.

King, L., and McCarthy, D. *Environmental Sociology: From Analysis to Action.* Lanham, MD: Rowman & Littlefield, 2005.

Koda, H., Yohannan, K., and Metropolitan Museum of Art. *The Model as Muse: Embodying Fashion.* New York: Metropolitan Museum of Art; New Haven, CT: Yale University Press, 2009.

Laver, J., and de la Haye, A. *Costume and Fashion: A Concise History*, rev. ed. New York: Thames and Hudson, 1995.

Lehnert, G. *A History of Fashion in the 20th Century.* Cologne, Germany: Konemann, 2000.

McKelvey, K. *Fashion Source Book.* Oxford, England, and Cambridge, MA: Blackwell Science, 1996.

Olian, J. *Everyday Fashions of the Forties as Pictured in Sears Catalogs.* New York: Dover Publications, 1992.

Perna, R. *Fashion Forecasting: A Mystery or a Method?* New York: Fairchild Publications, 1987.

Poiret, P. G., and Haden, S. *King of Fashion: The Autobiography of Paul Poiret.* Philadelphia: J. B. Lippincott, 1931.

Powe-Temperley, K. *The 60s: Mods and Hippies.* Oxford, England: Heinemann Library, 2001.

Tortora, P. G., and Eubank, K. *Survey of Historic Costume: A History of Western Dress*, 4th ed. New York: Fairchild Publications, 2004.

Troy, N. J. *Couture Culture: A Study in Modern Art and Fashion.* Cambridge, MA: MIT Press, 2003.

Watson, L. *20th Century Fashion: 100 Years of Style by Decade and Designer: In Association with Vogue.* Richmond Hill, Canada: Firefly Books, 2008.

CHAPTER 3

Aburdene, P., and Naisbitt, J. *Megatrends for Women.* 1st ed. New York: Villard Books, 1992.

Brannon, E. L. *Fashion Forecasting: Research, Analysis, and Presentation.* New York: Fairchild Publications, 2005.

Cawthorne, N. *Key Moments in Fashion: From Haute Couture to Streetwear, Key Collections, Major Figures and Crucial Moments that Changed the Course of Fashion History from 1890 to the 1990s.* London and New York: Hamlyn; distributed in the U.S. by Sterling Publishing, 1999.

Entwistle, J. *The Fashioned Body: Fashion, Dress, and Modern Social Theory.* Cambridge, MA: Polity Press; Malden, MA: Blackwell, 2000.

Gladwell, M. *The Tipping Point: How Little Things Can Make a Big Difference.* 1st ed. Boston: Little, Brown, 2000.

Goodman, D. J., and Cohen, M. *Consumer Culture: A Reference Handbook.* Santa Barbara, CA: ABC-CLIO, 2004.

Kaiser, S. B. *The Social Psychology of Clothing: Symbolic Appearances in Context.* 2nd rev ed. New York: Fairchild Publications, 1997.

Marchetti, L., and Quinz, E. *Dysfashional.* Barcelona, Spain: BOM, 2007.

McKelvey, K., and Munslow, J. *Fashion Forecasting.* Ames, IA: Wiley-Blackwell, 2008.

Perna, R. *Fashion Forecasting: A Mystery or a Method?* New York: Fairchild Publications, 1987.

Stone, E. *The Dynamics of Fashion.* New York: Fairchild Publications, 2008.

Vejlgaard, H. *Anatomy of a Trend.* New York: McGraw-Hill, 2008.

CHAPTER 4

Aburdene, P., and Naisbitt, J. *Megatrends for Women.* 1st ed. New York: Villard Books, 1992.

Bell, S., and Morse, S. *Measuring Sustainability: Learning by Doing.* London and Sterling, VA: Earthscan Publications, 2003.

Black, S. *Eco-chic: The Fashion Paradox.* London: Black Dog, 2008.

Brannon, E. L. *Fashion Forecasting: Research, Analysis, and Presentation.* New York: Fairchild Publications, 2005.

Cawthorne, N. *Key Moments in Fashion: From Haute Couture to Streetwear, Key Collections, Major Figures and Crucial Moments that Changed the Course of Fashion History from 1890 to the 1990s.* London and New York: Hamlyn; distributed in the U.S. by Sterling Publishing, 1999.

DeLong, M. R. *The Way We Look: Dress and Aesthetics.* 2nd ed. New York: Fairchild Publications, 1998.

Dorfman, J. *The Lazy Environmentalist: Your Guide to Easy, Stylish, Green Living.* New York: Stewart, Tabori, & Chang, 2007.

Entwistle, J. *The Fashioned Body: Fashion, Dress, and Modern Social Theory.* Cambridge, MA: Polity Press; Malden, MA: Blackwell, 2000.

Gilman, C. P., Hill, M. R., and Deegan, M. J. *The Dress of Women: A Critical Introduction to the Symbolism and Sociology of Clothing.* Westport, CT: Greenwood Press, 2002.

Goodman, D. J., and Cohen, M. *Consumer Culture: A Reference Handbook.* Santa Barbara, CA: ABC-CLIO, 2004.

Hethorn, J., and Ulasewicz, C. *Sustainable Fashion: Why Now?: A Conversation Exploring Issues, Practices, and Possibilities.* New York: Fairchild Books, 2008.

Hoffman, L., and Earth Pledge. *FutureFashion White Papers.* New York: Earth Pledge, 2007.

Kaiser, S. B. *The Social Psychology of Clothing: Symbolic Appearances in Context.* 2nd rev. ed. New York: Fairchild Publications, 1997.

King, L., and McCarthy, D. *Environmental Sociology: From Analysis to Action.* Lanham, MD: Rowman & Littlefield, 2005.

Marchetti, L., and Quinz, E. *Dysfashional.* Barcelona, Spain: BOM, 2007.

May, S., Cheney, G., and Roper, J. *The Debate over Corporate Social Responsibility.* New York: Oxford University Press, 2007.

Maynard, M. *Dress and Globalisation.* New York: Manchester University Press; distributed in the U.S. by Palgrave, 2004.

McKelvey, K., and Munslow, J. *Fashion Forecasting.* Ames, IA: Wiley-Blackwell, 2008.
Poloian, L. G., and Rogers, D. S. *Retailing Principles: A Global Outlook.* New York: Fairchild Publications, 2003.
Seymour, S. *Fashionable Technology: The Intersection of Design, Fashion, Science, and Technology.* Vienna and New York: Springer, 2008.
Stone, E. *The Dynamics of Fashion.* New York: Fairchild Publications, 2008.
Troy, N. J. *Couture Culture: A Study in Modern Art and Fashion.* Cambridge, MA: MIT Press, 2003.
Vejlgaard, H. *Anatomy of a Trend.* New York: McGraw-Hill, 2008.
World Trade Organization. "The World Trade Organization . . . in brief." Last modified July 8, 2011. http://www.wto.org/english/thewto_e/what is_e/inbrief_e/inbr00_e.htm

CHAPTER 5

Diamond, J., and Litt, S. *Retailing in the Twenty-First Century.* New York: Fairchild Publications, 2009.
Gladwell, M. *The Tipping Point: How Little Things Can Make a Big Difference.* 1st ed. Boston: Little, Brown, 2000.
Hines, T., and Bruce, M. *Fashion Marketing: Contemporary Issues.* Boston: Butterworth-Heinemann, 2007.
Kunz, G., and Garner, M. *Going Global: The Textile and Apparel Industry.* New York: Fairchild Publications, 2011.
Poloian, L. G., and Rogers, D. S. *Retailing Principles: A Global Outlook.* New York: Fairchild Publications, 2003.
Stone, E. *The Dynamics of Fashion.* New York: Fairchild Publications, 2008.

CHAPTER 6

Edelkoort, L., and Films for the Humanities. *The Trend Where Fashion Begins.* Video/DVD. Produced by G. Melhos. Princeton, NJ: Films for the Humanities and Sciences, 2002.
McDowell, C. *Galliano.* New York: Rizzoli, 1998.
Vosovic, D. *Fashion Inside Out: Daniel V's Guide to How Style Happens from Inspiration to Runway & Beyond.* New York: Watson-Guptill Publications, 2008.

CHAPTER 7

Brainard, S. *A Design Manual.* Upper Saddle River, NJ: Pearson Prentice Hall, 2006.
DeLong, M. R., Fiore, A. M., and International Textile and Apparel Association. *Aesthetics of Textiles and Clothing: Advancing Multi-Disciplinary Perspectives.* Monument, CO: International Textile and Apparel Association, 1994.
Diane, T., and Cassidy, T. *Colour Forecasting.* Oxford, England: Blackwell, 2004.
Fehrman, K. R., and Fehrman, C. *Color: the Secret Influence.* Upper Saddle River, NJ: Prentice Hall, 2004.
Fukai, A., Cooper-Hewitt Museum, and Kyoto Fukushoku Bunka Kenkyu Zaidan. *Fashion in Colors.* New York: Assouline, 2004.
McKelvey, K., and Munslow, J. *Fashion Forecasting.* Ames, IA: Wiley-Blackwell, 2008.

CHAPTER 8

Colussy, M. K., and Greenberg, S. *Rendering Fashion, Fabric, and Prints with Adobe Photoshop*. Upper Saddle River, NJ: Pearson Prentice Hall, 2004.

Elsasser, V. H. *Textiles: Concepts and Principles*. New York: Fairchild Publications, 2005.

Fletcher, K. *Sustainable Fashion and Textiles: Design Journeys*. Sterling, VA: Earthscan Publications, 2008.

Gaines, J., and Herzog, C. *Fabrications: Costume and the Female Body*. New York: Routledge, 1990.

Johnson, I., Pizzuto, J. J., and Cohen, A. C. *Fabric Science*. New York: Fairchild Publications; Oxford, England: Berg, 2009.

Schor, J., and Taylor, B. S. *Sustainable Planet: Solutions for the Twenty-First Century*. Boston: Beacon Press, 2002.

CHAPTER 9

Aspelund, K. *The Design Process*. New York: Fairchild Publications, 2006.

Brainard, S. *A Design Manual*. Upper Saddle River, NJ: Pearson Prentice Hall, 2006.

Fuad-Luke, A. *ecoDesign: The Sourcebook*. Rev. ed. San Francisco: Chronicle Books, 2004.

Gaines, J., and Herzog, C. *Fabrications: Costume and the Female Body*. New York: Routledge, 1990.

Keiser, S. J., and Garner, M. B. *Beyond Design: The Synergy of Apparel Product Development*. New York: Fairchild Publications, 2003.

Mattus, M. *Beyond Trend: How to Innovate in an Over-Designed World*. Cincinnati, OH: HOW Books, 2008.

McDowell, C. *Galliano*. New York: Rizzoli, 1998.

McQueen, A., Blass, B., Galliano, J., Dolce, D., Gabbana, S., Jacobs, M., Ford, T., Kors, M. L., Lauren, R., and Fashion News World. *The Designers*. Vol. 2. Video/DVD. New York: Fashion News World, 2006.

Norman, D. A. *The Design of Future Things*. New York: Basic Books, 2007.

Perna, R. *Fashion Forecasting: A Mystery or a Method?* New York: Fairchild Publications, 1987.

CHAPTER 10

Aspelund, K. *The Design Process*. New York: Fairchild Publications, 2006.

Brainard, S. *A Design Manual*. Upper Saddle River, NJ: Pearson Prentice Hall, 2006.

Brannon, E. L. *Fashion Forecasting: Research, Analysis, and Presentation*. New York: Fairchild Publications, 2005.

Mattus, M. *Beyond Trend: How to Innovate in an Over-Designed World*. Cincinnati, OH: HOW Books, 2008.

McKelvey, K. *Fashion Source Book*. Cambridge, MA: Blackwell Science, 1996.

McKelvey, K., and Munslow, J. *Fashion Forecasting*. Ames, IA: Wiley-Blackwell, 2008.

Perna, R. *Fashion Forecasting: A Mystery or a Method?* New York: Fairchild Publications, 1987.

Pink, D. H. *A Whole New Mind: Why Right-Brainers Will Rule the Future*. New York: Riverhead Books, 2006.

Art Credits

CHAPTER 1

1.1a Mike Coppola/Getty Images for IMG
1.1b Courtesy of WWD/Davide Maestri
1.1c Courtesy of WWD/Giovanni Giannoni
1.1d Photo by Michael Tran/FilmMagic
1.3 Courtesy of Cotton, Inc.
1.4 © fixer00/Alamy
1.5a Courtesy of WWD/Stephane Feugere
1.5b–c Courtesy of WWD/Steve Eichner
1.5d Courtesy of WWD/Donato Sardella
1.6 Photo by Claude Gassian/Contour by Getty Images
1.7a Courtesy of WWD/Stephane Feugere
1.7b Courtesy of WWD
1.7c Photo by Javier Larrea. Collection: age fotostock.
1.7d Getty Images for De Grisogono
1.7e © Leonard Ortiz/ZUMA Press/Corbis
1.8a–f Courtesy of WWD
1.9a–c Courtesy of WWD/Kyle Ericksen
1.10a–d Courtesy of Fabiana Negron (student)

CHAPTER 2

2.1a *Queen Victoria, 1859* (oil on canvas), Winterhalter, Franz Xaver (1805–73)/The Royal Collection © 2011 Her Majesty Queen Elizabeth II/The Bridgeman Art Library International
2.1b Fashion designs for women from the 1860's (coloured engraving), Worth, Charles Frederick (1825–95)/Victoria & Albert Museum, London, UK/The Bridgeman Art Library International
2.1c The Granger Collection, NYC—All rights reserved.
2.1d Art Resource
2.2a London Stereoscopic Company/Getty Images
2.2b The Granger Collection, NYC—All rights reserved.
2.2c Reception dress: bodice and skirt, 1877–78 (silk), Worth, Charles Frederick (1825–95)/Cincinnati Art Museum, Ohio, USA/Gift of Mrs Murat Halstead Davidson/The Bridgeman Art Library International
2.3a © Brooklyn Museum/Corbis
2.3b Hulton Archive/Getty Images
2.3c © Stocksearch/Alamy
2.3d The Granger Collection, NYC—All rights reserved.
2.3e © Pictorial Press Ltd/Alamy
2.4a ©Mary Evans Picture Library/The Image Works
2.4b Image copyright © The Metropolitan Museum of Art/Art Resource, NY
2.4c Museum of London/PhotoLibrary
2.4d W. G. Phillips/Phillips/Getty Images
2.5a © Lordprice Collection/Alamy
2.5b © Oote Boe/Alamy
2.5c © Leonard de Selva/CORBIS
2.5d © World History Archive/Topfoto/The Image Works
2.5e APA/Getty Images
2.5f–g The Granger Collection, NYC—All rights reserved.
2.6a–d The Granger Collection, NYC—All rights reserved.
2.7a © The Art Archive/Alamy
2.7b ©akg-images/The Image Works
2.7c Photo by Russell Lee/Library of Congress/Getty Images)
2.7d MR ©H. Armstrong Roberts/ClassicStock/The Image Works
2.8a Photo Library/George Marks

2.8b George Hurrell © 1935 Condé Nast Publications
2.8c © Swim Ink/Corbis
2.8d The Granger Collection, NYC—All rights reserved.
2.9a © Press Association/The Image Works
2.9b © Genevieve Naylor/Corbis
2.9c © Ocean/Corbis
2.9d NASA—digital version copyright Science Faction/Getty Images
2.9e © Land of Lost Content/HIP/The Image Works
2.9f The Granger Collection, NYC—All rights reserved.
2.10a The Granger Collection, NYC—All rights reserved.
2.10b Warner Bros/The Kobal Collections/McCarty, Floyd
2.10c CBS Photo Archive/Getty Images
2.10d Sharland/Time Life Pictures/Getty Images
2.10e © Interfoto/Alamy
2.11a © Bettmann/Corbis
2.11b © Montgomery Martin/Alamy
2.11c © Everett Collection Inc/Alamy
2.11d © Archive Image/Alamy
2.11e © Hulton-Deutsch Collection/Corbis
2.12a © Bettmann/Corbis
2.12b © Henry Diltz/Corbis
2.12c © Trinity Mirror/Mirrorpix/Alamy
2.12d © Bettmann/Corbis
2.12e © Henry Diltz/Corbis
2.13a © Michael Norcia/Sygma/Corbis
2.13b © William James Warren/Science Faction/Corbis
2.13c © Bettmann/Corbis
2.13d © Photos 12/Alamy
2.13e © Bettmann/Corbis
2.14a Mary Evans/APL
2.14b © PSL Images/Alamy
2.14c © Douglas Kirkland/Corbis
2.14d © AF archive/Alamy
2.14e Courtesy of WWD/Tim Jenkins
2.15a © J.C. Towers/ClassicStock/Corbis
2.15b Photo by Time Life Pictures/DMI/Time Life Pictures/Getty Images
2.15c Photo by Fox Photos/Hulton Archive/Getty Images
2.15d © Trinity Mirror/Mirrorpix/Alamy
2.16a Picture Bank/Classic Stock
2.16b © Pictorial Press Ltd/Alamy
2.16c © Pictorial Press Ltd/Alamy
2.16d © Bettmann/Corbis
2.17a © moodboard/Corbis
2.17b © dpa/dpa/Corbis
2.17c Photo by Ted Thai/Time Life Pictures/Getty Images
2.17d © Pictorial Press Ltd/Alamy
2.18a Courtesy of Fairchild Archive/Thomas Iannaccone
2.18b © AF archive/Alamy
2.18c © Photofusion Picture Library/Alamy
2.18d © Gregory Davies/Alamy
2.18e Photo by Ron Galella, Ltd./WireImage
2.19a © Jim Sugar/Corbis
2.19b © Darren Kemper/Corbis
2.19c Photo by Chip Somodevilla/Getty Images
2.19d © S K D/Alamy
2.20a Courtesy of WWD/John Aquino
2.20b Courtesy of WWD/Kristen Somody Whalen
2.20c Courtesy of WWD/Giovanni Giannoni

2.20d Courtesy of WWD/Kristin Burns
2.20e Courtesy of WWD/Steve Eichner

CHAPTER 3

3.3 Courtesy of Jackeline Arango (student)
3.4 Courtesy of Ana Escalante (student)
3.5 Courtesy of Brandi Brewton (student)
3.8 Courtesy of WWD
3.9 Courtesy of WWD/Giovanni Giannoni

CHAPTER 4

4.1 Courtesy of Masterfile
4.2a Courtesy of WWD/Jessie Moore
4.2b © Radu Sighetti/Reuters/Corbis
4.2c © Elke Hesser/Monsoon/Photolibrary/Corbis
4.2d Photographer: Vidler. Collection: Mauritius images.
4.3 Courtesy of WWD/Jackson Lowen
4.4 Mark Wilson/Getty Images
4.5 Courtesy of WWD/Steve Eichner
4.6 Courtesy of WWD/Thomas Iannaccone
4.7 Provided by Chelsea Rousso
4.8a © Corbis Bridge/Alamy
4.8b © StockShot/Alamy
4.8c © Carlos Davila/Alamy

CHAPTER 5

5.1 Courtesy of National Retail Federation
5.2 Courtesy of Fashion Group International
5.3 Thomas Barwick/Getty Images
5.4 Photo by Mario Tama/Getty Images
5.5 Courtesy of WWD/Steve Eichner
5.6 Courtesy of TrendTablet.com
5.7 Courtesy of iStockphoto/© Mike Clarke
5.8 © Eric Audras/Onoky/Corbis
5.9 Courtesy of Shaniqua "Paris" Wimbley (student) (parisisfashun.tumblr.com); Courtesy of Christina Penland (student) (christinapenland.tumblr.com); Courtesy of Taissa Forte (student) (trendsguide.tumblr.com); Courtesy of Brittany Koon (student) (onfashionave954.tumblr.com); Courtesy of Katrina Johnson (student) (stayinstyle.tumblr.com)
5.10 Courtesy of WWD/Steve Eichner

CHAPTER 6

6.1a © TAO Images Limited/Alamy (left)
6.1b © Everett Collection Inc/Alamy (right)
6.2 © HBO/Courtesy: Everett
6.3 © Brooks Kraft/Corbis
6.4 Courtesy of WWD/Steve Eichner
6.5a Courtesy of WWD/Kyle Ericksen (middle)
6.5b Courtesy of WWD/Giovanni Giannoni (right)
6.5c Courtesy of WWD/John Aquino (left)
6.6–6.9 Courtesy Erica Mahmood (student)

CHAPTER 7

7.1 Courtesy of Humberto Vidal; Model: Lauren Sparkman; Stylist: Kimberly Parla (student); Makeup Artist: Jenna Marie Streitenfeld
7.2 Courtesy of StyleSight
7.3 Courtesy of Luzmaria Palacios (student)
7.10 WireImage/Getty Images/Alberto E. Rodriguez
7.11 Courtesy of Erica Mahmood (student)

CHAPTER 8

8.1 Courtesy of WWD/Giovanni Giannoni
8.2 © Phil Degginger/Alamy
8.3a © Arco Images GmbH/Alamy (right)
8.3b Meredith Winn Photography/Getty Images (left)
8.4 Miroglio Textiles, Alba Italy

8.5 Courtesy of WWD/John Calabrese
8.6 © Everett Collection Inc/Alamy
8.7 Courtesy of Joel Massiah (student)
8.8 MCT via Getty Images
8.9 Courtesy of WWD
8.10a–b Provided by the Design Library
8.11 Hitoshi Yamada/PictureGroup via AP IMAGES
8.12 Courtesy of Fashion Snoops
8.13 FilmMagic/Dimitrios Kambouris
8.14 Courtesy of Erica Mahmood (student)

CHAPTER 9

9.1 Courtesy of WWD/John Aquino
9.3 Courtesy of WWD/Kyle Ericksen
9.4 Courtesy of WWD/Donato Sardella
9.5 © Samuel Golay/epa/Corbis
9.6 Courtesy of WWD/Paul Cavaco
9.7–9.10 Courtesy of Maggy London
9.11 Courtesy of WWD/Giovanni Giannoni
9.12 Associated Press
9.13 Veer/Blend Images Photography
9.14–9.16 Courtesy Erica Mahmood (student)
9.17a–d Courtesy of WWD/Giovanni Giannoni

CHAPTER 10

10.1a–g Courtesy of Camila Navega (student)
10.2a–f Courtesy of Christina Rondinone (student)
10.3a–d Courtesy of Jaclynn Brennan (student)
10.4a–h Courtesy of Jenna Simon (student)
10.5a–g Courtesy of Lindsay R. Smolinkski (student)
10.6a–g Courtesy of Luzmaria Palacios (student)

APPENDIX

Courtesy of Katherine Galarraga (student)

PART OPENER ART

Part I Courtesy of Stylesight
Part II Courtesy of Fashion Snoops

CHAPTER OPENER ART

1. Getty Images/Mike Coppola
2. Courtesy of WWD/Giovanni Giannoni
3. Courtesy of WWD/Stephane Feugere
4. Courtesy of WWD/Dominique Maitre
5. © Rudy Pospisil, anothernormal.com
6. Courtesy of WWD/Steve Eichner
7. Courtesy of WWD/Giovanni Giannoni
8. Courtesy of WWD/Giovanni Giannoni
9. Courtesy of WWD/George Chinsee
10. Courtesy of WWD/Giovanni Giannoni

Index